THE COMPLETE H

Arch

From the First Civi. .... Present Day

Patrick Nuttgens
with Richard Weston

MITCHELL BEAZLEY

The Complete Handbook of Architecture
by Patrick Nuttgens with Richard Weston

Previously published as
The Mitchell Beazley Pocket Guide to Architecture
by Patrick Nuttgens
Reprinted 1983, 1986
Revised edition 1992

First published in Great Britain in 2006 by Mitchell Beazley,
an imprint of Octopus Publishing Group Ltd,
2–4 Heron Quays, London E14 4JP

Copyright © Octopus Publishing Group Ltd 2006

ISBN 1 84533 187 7

A CIP record for this book is available from the British Library

Set in Baskerville Book

Printed and bound in China by Toppan Printing Company Ltd

Pocket Guide to Architecture:
Executive Editor James Hughes
Executive Art Editor John Grain
Senior Designer Jean Jottrand
Production Katy Sawyer
Illustrators Arthur Baker; Lindsay Blow; Marilyn Bruce; Eugene Fleury;
Chris Forsey; Trevor Hill; Norman Lacey; Uta Schneider-Laurenson;
Andy Macdonald; Gary Marsh; Simon Miller; Coral Mula; Gilly Newman;
Oxford Illustrators Limited; Richard Phipps

Complete Handbook of Architecture:
Commissioning Editor Hannah Barnes-Murphy
Executive Art Editor Christine Keilty
Senior Editor Emily Anderson
Production Gary Hayes
Illustrator John Hewitt

CONTENTS

Introduction 4
Landmarks in architectural history 5

The First Civilizations 7 Mesopotamia and Elam 8 Anatolia 8
Assyria and the new Babylon 9 The Persian and Sassanian empires 10
Ancient Egypt 11 The Old Kingdom 15 The Middle Kingdom 16
The Ptolemaic and Roman periods 19
The Ancient Greeks 20 The Aegean civilizations 25 Athens 26 Sacred sites
of Greece 29 Italy, Sicily and Asia Minor 31
The Romans 32 The Etruscans 34 Rome 35 Italy outside Rome 41
The far-flung colonies 42
South Asia: Hindu, Buddhist and Jain styles 44 India and Pakistan 46
Sri Lanka 50 Nepal, Tibet and Burma 51 Java 51 Cambodia: the Khmer
style 52
China and Japan: Traditional wooden architecture 53 China 53 Japan 58
Pre-Hispanic America: Early civilizations of central and south America 63
From Teotihuacan to the Aztecs 64 The region of the Maya 65 South
America 66
Early Christian and Byzantine styles 67 Rome 70 Ravenna 72 Venice
and Sicily 73 Istanbul, Greece and the Balkans 74 The Middle East and
Armenia 76 Russia 76
Islam: Architecture of the Muslim world 77 The western Middle East 80
Iran 82 Seljuk and Ottoman styles 83 Central Asia 84 India and Pakistan 84
Western north Africa and Spain 86
Romanesque 87 Italy 89 Germany 90 France 92 Britain: Anglo-Saxon
and Norman 93 Scandinavia 95 Castles in the Holy Land 96 Spain and
Portugal 96
Gothic 97 France 103 England 105 Central and eastern Europe 107
The Low Countries 109 Scandinavia 110 Spain and Portugal 110 Italy 111
Italian Renaissance 112 Florence 114 Rome 116 Venice and Vicenza 119
The rest of Italy 121
The spread of the Renaissance 122 France 122 Spain and Portugal 125
The Low countries 126 Central Europe 127 Britain 128 Scandinavia 130
Russia 130
Baroque and Neo-Classicism 131 Rome 133 The rest of Italy 134 France
135 Austria and Czechoslovakia 138 Germany 139 Spain and Portugal 140
Britain 141 Colonial North America 146 Iberian-American Baroque 147
Russia 147
The Nineteenth Century 148 Britain 150 France 152 Germany and
Austria 153 Russia and eastern Europe 154 The Low Countries 154
Italy 155 Denmark 155 The United States and Canada 156
Turn of the Century 159 Britain 161 The United States 162 France and
Italy 163 Spain 164 The Low Countries 164 Germany and Austria 165
Scandinavia and Poland 166
Modern 167 Britain 170 Germany and Austria 172 The Low Countries 173
Finland 174 Sweden and Denmark 174 Italy 175 France and Switzerland 176
Canada 177 The United States 178 Latin America 180 India, Japan and
Australia 181
Post-Modern 183 The United States 184 Britain 185 France 187 Germany,
Austria and The Netherlands 188 Switzerland, Scandinavia, Finland and
Japan 189 Gulf States and S-E Asia and Australia 190
Contemporary Pluralism 192 Spain and Portugal 193 Norway 194
Switzerland 195 Germany 196 The Netherlands and Britain 197
The United States and Japan 198

Glossary 199
Index 202

INTRODUCTION

You cannot fully appreciate a work of architecture without some background knowledge. Social and political developments, availability of materials, advances in learning and technology, changes in fashion and the function of patronage, emulation of foreign cultures—all these factors may help to explain why a building is the way it is. And because the beginnings of great architecture are the tomb and the temple, religion often plays a part too. Therefore, in this traveller's guide to the architecture of the world, I have devoted a fair proportion of space to supplying the background necessary for appreciation.

The book is organized into basic "styles"—the word can be applied only very loosely to some cultures—corresponding to period or region. The divisions are fairly familiar, though modified by me in the light of my own understanding of forces or movements. The story that builds up is broadly chronological, with overlaps. To begin with, each style is analysed with reference to historical and cultural context, main architects, materials, building types, technology and architectural vocabulary. Where appropriate, a style is described by reference to a "key building" which exemplifies its salient features. Illustrations have been carefully chosen, and annotated where appropriate, to facilitate on-the-spot recognition. Perspective views, façades and structural and decorative details will enable different buildings to be compared and contrasted; and plans are included either as a guide for exploring or to explain the organization of spaces and functions within a building.

After the background analysis, accounts of individual buildings are arranged geographically; the user of this guide can therefore read the first part of a chapter to fill in the background, then treat the second part as a guidebook for visiting the sites. There is, after all, no substitute for actually experiencing a building. I intend that, by analysing styles and providing a context for understanding, the book will illuminate even buildings that are not specifically mentioned.

The humbler kind of domestic architecture—often described as vernacular—has had to be omitted for reasons of space, even though it has accounted throughout history for the vast majority of buildings. Landscape and gardens are discussed only where their significance for architecture is inescapable; town planning similarly.

The exigencies of pocket-scale miniaturization make it necessary, even after such drastic limitations have been laid down, to telescope a mass of material and summarize in a few words buildings that deserve an extended account. Even so, I believe no extant work of architecture of major historical significance has been left out. Of course, many of the emphases and nuances are subjective.

Patrick Nuttgens

LANDMARKS

IN ARCHITECTURAL HISTORY

c. **4000** BC First settlement of Babylon.

c. **2650–2600** BC Funeral complex at Saqqara, Egypt: first large-scale structure in stone.

c. **2300–1750** BC Indus Valley civilization, India.

c. **2000** BC Ziggurat at Ur, Mesopotamia. Prehistoric temple at Stonehenge, England.

c. **1500** BC Founding of Hittite capital, Hattushash, Anatolia.

c. **1400** BC Destruction of Knossos, Crete. Beginning of Mycenaean dominance of Aegean.

1085 BC End of New Kingdom of Egypt.

612 BC Fall of Assyrian Nineveh to Medes and Babylonians.

c. **563**–*c.* **483** BC Life of Buddha.

518 BC Palace of Persepolis begun by Darius I of Persia.

c. **509** BC Establishment of Roman Republic.

444–429 BC Age of Pericles in Greece. Parthenon, Athens, begun 447.

323–30 BC Hellenistic period.

237 BC Temple of Horus, Edfu, Egypt.

78 BC Tabularium, Rome: earliest large-scale concrete vault.

31 BC Octavian (Augustus) becomes first Roman Emperor.

c. **120–24** Pantheon, Rome.

c. **300** Diocletian's Palace, Split, Yugoslavia: last great building of Roman Empire.

330 Constantine moves Imperial capital from Rome to Byzantium, renamed Constantinople.

532–7 Santa Sophia, Constantinople: Byzantine.

c. **684** Dome of the Rock, Jerusalem: first great Islamic architecture.

745 Founding of Buddhist temple Tōdai-ji, Nara, Japan.

c. **800** Barabudur temple-mountain, Java.

c. **857** Main hall, Foguang Temple, Wutai Mountain, China: earliest surviving important wooden building.

910 Founding of Cluny Abbey, Burgundy.

c. **1000** Collapse of Maya culture in central America.

1030–60 Speier Cathedral, Germany: earliest large-scale groin vaults in medieval Europe.

1050–1150 High Romanesque period.

c. **1100** Ballcourt, Chichén Itzá, Mexico.

1104 Earliest rib vaults of N Europe, at Durham Cathedral, England.

Early 12th C Angkor Wat temple-mountain, Cambodia.

c. **1140–44** New choir at St Denis, near Paris: first mature Gothic.

1194 Chartres Cathedral begun: start of High Gothic.

c. **1250** Surya Temple, Konarak, India: masterpiece of Orissan architecture.

1337–57 Chancel of Gloucester Cathedral, England: establishment of English Perpendicular.

c. **1345** Doge's Palace, Venice, begun.

1419–44 Foundling Hospital, Florence, by Brunelleschi: earliest Renaissance architecture.

1438–1532 Inca Empire, Peru.

1485 Publication in Italy of *De re aedificatoria*, by Alberti: first architectural treatise of Renaissance.

1499 Bramante moves from Milan to Rome: beginning of High Renaissance.

1501–1732 Persian Safavid dynasty. Royal Mosque, Isfahan, 1612–37.

1520–34 New Sacristy, S. Lorenzo, Florence, by Michelangelo: first Mannerist architecture.

1521 First building by Giulio Romano, in Rome. Destruction of Aztec Tenochtitlán, Mexico, by Spanish conquistadors.

1526–1858 Mughal period in India.

1527 Sack of Rome by Imperial troops.

1546 Lescot commissioned to design Square Court of Louvre, Paris: start of French Classicism.

1549–80 Career of Palladio, most widely influential Italian Renaissance architect.

1550–57 Süleymaniye Mosque, Istanbul, by Sinan.

1558–1603 Reign of Elizabeth I of England.

1568–80 Longleat House, England: first mature Elizabethan mansion.

1568–84 The Gesù, Rome, by Vignola: a major influence on Baroque church design.

1570 Publication of *I quattro libri dell' architettura*, by Palladio: seminal Renaissance text.

1603–25 Reign of James I of England: the Jacobean era.

Early 17th C Katsura Palace, Kyōto, Japan: Zen simplicity.

1616–18 Queen's House, Greenwich, London, by Inigo Jones: introduction of Palladian style to England.

c. **1620–60** Evolution of Baroque style in Rome.

1632–54 Taj Mahal, India: greatest Mughal tomb.

1663–1723 Career of Sir Christopher Wren in England.

1669–1756 Palace of Versailles, France.

c. **1690–1730** Great age of Austrian Baroque.

c. **1710–15** Creation of Rococo style in Paris.

1714–1830 Georgian period in England.

c. **1715–50** Palladian revival in England.

1721–32 Transparente, Toledo Cathedral, Spain: highpoint of Baroque illusionism.

1743–72 Church of Vierzehnheiligen, Bavaria, by Neumann: German Baroque-Rococo.

c. **1750** Emergence of Neo-Classicism.

c. **1750–70** Strawberry Hill, England, by Walpole: beginning of Gothic Revivalism.

1757–80 Ste Geneviève (now Panthéon), Paris, by Soufflot: masterpiece of French Classicism.

c. **1760–1830** Greek Revival in European architecture.

1777–9 Iron Bridge, Coalbrookdale, England: first iron bridge.

1798 Greek Revival brought to USA by Latrobe.

1799 Sedgely, by Latrobe: earliest Gothic Revival house in America.

1800–30 Regency Style in England.

c. **1820–40** Climax of Greek Revival in Europe and USA.

1840–65 Houses of Parliament, London: Victorian Neo-Gothic.

1850–51 Crystal Palace, Great Exhibition, London, by Paxton: first prefabricated building, in glass and iron.

1852–75 French Second Empire. Opéra, Paris, by Garnier, begun 1861.

1859 Red House, Bexley Heath, Kent, by Webb for William Morris: English Domestic Revival.

1873 Tribune Building, New York, by Hunt: one of first buildings with lifts.

1879 First use of reinforced concrete, by Hennebique.

1884 Sagrada Familia church, Barcelona, begun by Gaudí.

1885 Home Insurance Building, Chicago, by Jenney: first skyscraper (10 stories).

1887–9 Eiffel Tower, Paris: celebration of metal as an architectural medium.

c. **1890–1959** Career of Frank Lloyd Wright in USA.

1895 Opening of "Art Nouveau" shop in Paris.

1897 Founding of Vienna Sezession.

1899 Founding of Garden City Association, England.

1899–1904 Carson, Pirie and Scott Store, Chicago, by Sullivan: the Chicago School.

1903 Founding of Wiener Werskstätte in Vienna.

1918–20 Einstein Tower, Potsdam, by Mendelsohn: German Expressionism.

1919 Founding of Bauhaus by Gropius.

1922–76 Career of Alvar Aalto, beginning in Finland.

1923 *Vers une architecture* published by Le Corbusier. His Five Points of a New Architecture exemplified in the Villa Savoie, Poissy, 1929–31.

1924 Schröder House, Utrecht, by Rietveld: De Stijl.

1925–6 Bauhaus building, Dessau, Germany, by Gropius.

1928 Founding of Congrès Internationaux d'Architecture Moderne (CIAM).

1930 Formation of Tecton in Britain.

1932 Term "International Style" first used.

1951 Festival of Britain.

1952 Completion of Lever House, New York: prototype curtain-walled skyscraper on a low podium.

1956–62 TWA Terminus, Kennedy Airport, New York, by Eero Saarinen.

1959–73 Sydney Opera House, Australia, by Utzon.

1960 Establishment of Brasilia, new capital of Brazil.

1967 Expo '67, Montreal: with geodesic dome by Fuller.

1972 Nakagin Capsule Tower, Tokyo, by Kurokawa: Metabolist architecture.

1972–7 Centre Pompidou, Paris, by Piano and Rogers. Hillingdon Civic Centre, London, by Matthew, Johnson-Marshall and Partners.

THE FIRST CIVILIZATIONS

For over 7,000 years from early Neolithic times the hub of the world was an area of the Middle East shaped like an inkblot. From *c.* 7000 BC hunters and food-gatherers formed villages on the hill fringes of Anatolia and the Zagros Mountains, and in the Levant to the w. By the end of the 6th MIL BC, in the lowlands as well as the hills, crops were grown on a large scale. Religion centred on fertility gods and the burial of the dead.

Although Jericho is the oldest town in the world, it was in the plains of s Mesopotamia that the first urban literate culture developed. Irrigation was used to regulate the erratic spring floods of the Tigris and Euphrates rivers, and the canals served also as trade routes, bringing wood, metals, etc.

Mesopotamia was at the crossroads of vast tribal movements. Primacy was assumed in turn by the Sumerians, Amorites, Babylonians, Kassites, Assyrians, Neo-Babylonians, Medes and Persians. City growth spread from Eridu northwards along the Fertile Crescent. City states evolved, among them Babylon, whose long supremacy was interrupted when the region fell prey to waves of Hittites. By the mid 7th C BC power had passed to the Assyrians, who controlled Babylonia, Palestine, Syria and Phoenicia, until their capital Nineveh fell in 612 BC to an alliance of Medes and Neo-Babylonians. The latter were themselves overcome a century later by the Persian, Cyrus the Great, who founded the vast empire of the Achaemenids. This was brought low by Alexander the Great (331 BC). Persian influence revived for a time under the more modest Parthian and Sassanian empires.

Ancient western Asia, *showing principal sites*

The growth of architecture

Anatolia had timber, but in the central Mesopotamian plains the building material was mudbrick. In the 4th MIL the first public buildings appeared: temples of sun-dried brick ornamented with mosaics and murals. Stone was used notably by the Hittites, and by the Assyrians for their palaces. Columns were employed only rarely in the region before the great architecture of the Persians, which drew upon Greek and Egyptian sources.

Mesopotamia and Elam

The earliest architecture developed to accommodate religious, legal, governmental and military systems.

Temples

A temple, erected to a local deity, was usually the nucleus of a civil building complex. The god owned in perpetuity the ground on which his temple stood: successive temples were therefore built on plinths made from the crumbled remains of the old brick, giving rise to the ziggurat (a staged tower with a temple at the summit, reached by stairways). Ziggurats were embodiments of the rain-giving mountains.

The WHITE TEMPLE, URUK (modern Warka), Iraq (4th MIL BC), was a predecessor of the ziggurat. The alternating niches and buttresses were typically Sumerian. Much of the platform (originally white-plastered) and triple stairway survive.

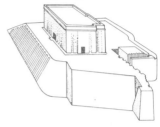

White Temple, Uruk

The ZIGGURAT, UR (modern Muqari'iya), Iraq (c. 2000 BC), shared platform with three other temples.

The ZIGGURAT, CHOGA ZANBIL, Iran (mid 13th C BC), in ancient Elam, is best preserved. Main stairway passed through structure. The oval PRECINCT, KHAFAJE ■ (3rd MIL BC), NE of Baghdad, was a terraced compound containing a temple.

Ziggurat, Ur   **Ziggurat, Choga Zanbil**

Palaces

The PALACE, MARI (now Tell Hariri), Syria (3rd MIL BC), is the best preserved of the early period; arrangement of rooms round a succession of courtyards was typical.

Anatolia

In ancient Anatolia the megaron form was common: a rectangular room with a central hearth and a door set in a deep porch formed by extending the side walls.

Anatolia became the adopted homeland of the Hittites, whose capital at Hattushash was founded c. 1500 BC. Most surviving Hittite architecture dates from 14th and 13th C BC. Massive stone masonry was used. At HATTUSHASH ■ (now Boğazkale, Turkey) the defensive walls, built in stone with upper parts of mudbrick, had a circumference of 4 miles. Fragments of 5 gateways stand today, with parabola-shaped arches formed of monolithic jambs. Three gateways bear monumental reliefs showing lions, sphinxes and a warrior.

Assyria and the new Babylon

In Assyria during the 2nd MIL BC polychrome brickwork
was introduced and high wall slabs carved in low relief.
Temples were sometimes on ziggurats, of up to 7 stories with
a ramp spiralling to the summit. But in the late Assyrian
cities—Nimrud, Nineveh and Khorsabad—the supreme
buildings were palaces, with human-headed winged bull or
lion sculptures guarding the entrances. The architecture of
Babylon, rebuilt by Nebuchadnezzar II in the 6th c BC, was
derived from Mesopotamian and Assyrian styles.

Nimrud and Nineveh
Both cities (founded early 1st
MIL BC) had temples, grand
palaces and fortified walls
with crenellated towers. The
layout of Ashurnasirpal II's
NW PALACE, NIMRUD, with
ziggurat complex, throne
room, administrative block
and residential wing, all
enclosing large public court,
became standard. First wall
slabs carved with scenes of
war occurred at Nimrud.

Nimrud: *relief showing royal hunt*

Khorsabad
Laid out by Sargon II (*c.* 717 BC), KHORSABAD was similar
in plan to Nimrud and Nineveh. The massive defensive
wall of mudbrick and stone, punctuated by double-gated
towers, was interrupted to NW by the citadel. Within this
was PALACE OF SARGON, incorporating three private
temples and small ziggurat, all on a platform.

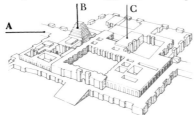

Palace of Sargon, Khorsabad
A *city wall;* **B** *ziggurat;* **C** *throne room*

*Bull sculpture guarding
gate at Khorsabad*

The new Babylon
The rebuilt city contained the
royal palace, the Hanging
Gardens and a ziggurat
(perhaps the Tower of Babel).
A summer palace to N was
linked to inner city by a
grand processional way. This
passed through the famous
ISHTAR GATE, decorated
with blue-glazed bricks
(reconstructed in Berlin
Museum).

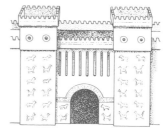

Ishtar Gate, Babylon

The Persian and Sassanian empires

Cyrus the Great's Persian capital at Pasargadae was
spaciously laid out on a plain, whereas the great complex
later built at Persepolis was closely grouped on a rock
terrace. Fine carving in stone is a characteristic of Persian
architecture.

After Alexander's defeat of the Persians, towns such as
Antioch and Seleucia were built by Macedonian and Greek
immigrants. A period of artistic decline was reinvigorated
by the Sassanians, whose capital was Ctesiphon.

The Persians

Begun 518 BC by Darius I, the PALACE OF PERSEPOLIS ✿,
Iran, was built mainly under Xerxes I (reigned 486–465 BC).
Its terrace was approached by a double staircase, leading
to a gatehouse faced with polychrome bricks. To s this led
to the Apadana, a grand audience hall on its own platform
with double-colonnaded porticoes. Adjacent Palace of Darius
was smaller. Xerxes built his own palace and started Hall
of the Hundred Columns (throne room).

The fluted stone columns at Persepolis are distinctive for
capitals incorporating Greek and Egyptian motifs and
animal forms. All monumental staircases and the Apadana
terrace have superb processional reliefs ◆.

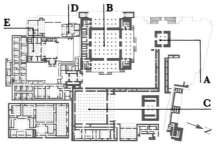

Palace of Persepolis
A *Main gatehouse;* **B** *Apadana;* **C** *Hall of 100
Columns;* **D** *Palace of Darius;* **E** *Palace of Xerxes*

*The Apadana: relief
on staircase showing
Persian dignitaries*

To N of Persepolis at Naqsh-i Rustam is the rock-hewn
TOMB OF DARIUS I, whose columned façade recalls the s front
of Darius' palace; relief over doorway. Nearby is a Fire
Temple, a 5th-c one-celled sandstone tower approached by
an outer staircase.

The Sassanians

The PALACE, CTESIPHON ✿,
near modern Baghdad, is
probably 4th c AD. Still
standing is part of huge open-
fronted audience hall with
elliptical vault of baked brick,
37 m high. Great influence
on modern structural forms.
One of wings survives, with
attached columns and blind
arcades in Roman manner
(but without regular axes).

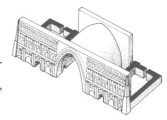

Palace, Ctesiphon: *audience
hall and façade of wings*

ANCIENT EGYPT

The first people of Egypt clustered on the swampy verges
of the Nile, among the palms, reeds and lotus plants later
to feature in architectural decoration. Settlements spread
from the fertile delta southwards along the river's alluvial
strip, where irrigation was introduced to support agriculture.
Two kingdoms of the Nile emerged, unified *c.* 3100 BC under
Menes, first of the Pharaohs, whose capital was Memphis.
The Pharaoh was held to be an incarnation of the God Horus;
after death he became Osiris, king in the underworld.

Science, art and practical skills soon began to prosper.
The annual flood obliterated field boundaries, so accurate
systems of measurement and surveying were devised. The
invention of hieroglyphics, and then of cursive writing on
papyrus, contributed to the growth of a bureaucracy with
an elaborate tax system. Astronomy was practised at
Heliopolis, centre of the cult of the sun-god Re in Dynasty V

The most stable periods of ancient Egyptian history are
the three kingdoms: the Old (Dynasties III–VI, 2686–2181
BC), Middle (XI–XII, 2133–1786 BC) and New (XVIII–XX,
1567–1085 BC). In 525 BC the region was absorbed by the
Persians, who lost it to Alexander the Great *c.* 100 years
later. After his death, under the Ptolemies, an amalgam of
Greek and native culture flourished. Egypt became a
Roman province on the death of Cleopatra.

Architecture under the Pharaohs

During the annual Nile
inundation from July to
October, when peasants were
unable to work on the land,
there was a vast workforce
available for building
projects. For these Egypt had
limestone (e.g., at Tura),
sandstone (of which the finest
temples were built) and
harder stones such as granite
which were floated down on
the flood tides from Aswan.
The Egyptians were the first
to use dressed stone and
invented the column, capital
and cornice. After the main
architectural traditions were
established there was little
deviation from them. In
pyramids and temples—
the chief building types—
interior spaces were mostly
cramped. The accent was on
impressive external forms,
an image of the absolute
power of the Pharaohs.

**The Upper and Lower
Kingdoms of the Nile**

The development of the pyramids

Pyramids, symbolizing the radiant sun, contained in sealed chambers the body of the Pharaoh mummified to preserve it for the soul's return. They derived from low mudbrick rectangular tombs known as mastabas. The four sides usually faced the cardinal points.

The earliest was the STEP PYRAMID OF ZOSER, SAQQARA (3rd MIL BC), built by vizier Imhotep. The first large structure to use dressed stone throughout, it was constructed in several stages over a square mastaba, final form being a 5-stepped pyramid faced with Tura limestone. Beneath, at foot of a shaft from which a maze of tunnels ran, was a tomb of Aswan granite. Access from outside was via underground ramp.

The BENT PYRAMID, DAHSHUR (3rd MIL BC), has a midway change of gradient, probably to reduce weight of upper masonry. Two tomb chambers with corbelled vaults, one reached from N, one from W. Complement of offertory chapel, mortuary temple and valley building (for embalming) found here became a regular feature of pyramids.

The PYRAMID, MAIDUM ◪ (3rd MIL BC) started as a 7-stepped structure. It was enlarged to 8, and later filled out and faced with limestone to become a true pyramid.

The perfectly proportioned PYRAMID OF CHEOPS, GIZA ♧ (3rd MIL BC), containing 4 burial chambers, is the highest ever built (146 m). The King's Chamber has a granite sarcophagus, with 5 tiers of lintels over it separated by empty spaces. The "air shafts" may have been meant as exits for the dead king's soul. Other chambers were never used. The 2.3 m-wide Grand Gallery has inclined corbelled vault (8.5 m high). Limestone facing has eroded, exposing stepped masonry base. Entrance on N side. (See also p 15.)

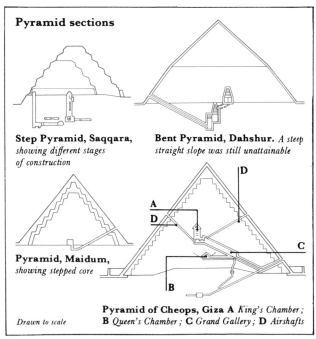

Pyramid sections

Step Pyramid, Saqqara, *showing different stages of construction*

Bent Pyramid, Dahshur. *A steep straight slope was still unattainable*

Pyramid, Maidum, *showing stepped core*

Drawn to scale

Pyramid of Cheops, Giza A *King's Chamber;* **B** *Queen's Chamber;* **C** *Grand Gallery;* **D** *Airshafts*

Mortuary and cult temples

Temples became increasingly important to the Egyptians. The earliest were the Pharaohs' mortuary temples, whose origins were the offertory chapels of pyramids and mastabas. They became similar in design to cult temples, but lacked a processional route round the sanctuary. A cult temple was the dwelling-place of one or more of the gods, where the cult image was clothed and fed. The main type, which evolved in the New Kingdom, is exemplified by the splendidly preserved Ptolemaic TEMPLE OF HORUS, EDFU (237–57 BC).

Temple of Horus, Edfu: *outer face of pylon*

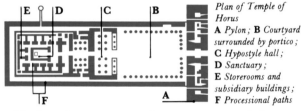

Plan of Temple of Horus
A *Pylon;* **B** *Courtyard surrounded by portico;*
C *Hypostyle hall;*
D *Sanctuary;*
E *Storerooms and subsidiary buildings;*
F *Processional paths*

The basic layout was a sandstone structure enclosing a porticoed courtyard, entered through a tall doorway in a massive two-towered bastion, or pylon. The pylon was battered (i.e., had inclined faces) and was ornamented with painted low-relief carvings, a gorge cornice and roll mouldings. Pennant masts slotted into grooves on the façade, and a pair of obelisks flanked the entrance, symbolizing the sun. Beyond the courtyard was a multi-pillared roofed hall (hypostyle), often followed by smaller halls. Deep inside the building was the sanctuary, surrounded by storerooms.

The temple shared its outer walled enclosure with granaries, priests' houses and other buildings. Approach was via an avenue lined with stone sphinxes.

Mastabas, rock tombs and secular architecture

Mastabas were built by Old Kingdom nobles as private tombs; they were copies of houses. Rock tombs superseded pyramids in the New Kingdom, partly to make burial chambers more theft-proof. Palaces, unlike tombs, were temporary dwellings, therefore built in mudbrick—few remains are left. Elaborate fortresses were built in Middle Kingdom Nubia (e.g., at Buhen).

Columns and capitals

Capitals and shafts copied lotus, papyrus and other plant forms. New Kingdom hypostyle halls formed a papyrus "thicket" of open- and closed-bud columns decorated with carved and painted figures and hieroglyphs.

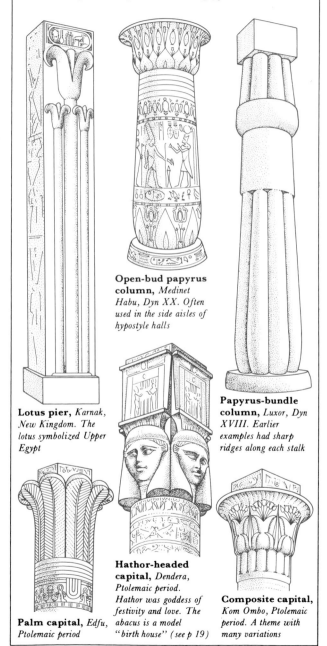

Open-bud papyrus column, *Medinet Habu, Dyn XX. Often used in the side aisles of hypostyle halls*

Lotus pier, *Karnak, New Kingdom. The lotus symbolized Upper Egypt*

Papyrus-bundle column, *Luxor, Dyn XVIII. Earlier examples had sharp ridges along each stalk*

Hathor-headed capital, *Dendera, Ptolemaic period. Hathor was goddess of festivity and love. The abacus is a model "birth house" (see p 19)*

Palm capital, *Edfu, Ptolemaic period*

Composite capital, *Kom Ombo, Ptolemaic period. A theme with many variations*

The Old Kingdom

Imhotep's structures around the main pyramid at Saqqara owed much to forms that were evolved to suit less durable materials, like mud, reeds and timber. The buildings of later dynasties, in contrast, are geometrically severe.

The first buildings in stone

Dominated by its stepped pyramid (see p 12), Imhotep's FUNERARY COMPLEX OF ZOSER, SAQQARA (3rd MIL BC) also has a mortuary temple and an offertory chapel. Sham structures imitating various royal buildings have blind doors, sham beams, alternating projections and recesses, and friezes. The House of the North, an administrative building, has world's first stone capitals: open papyrus buds on engaged columns. Enclosure walls are panelled limestone.

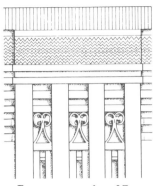

Funerary complex of Zoser, Saqqara: *detail of enclosure wall*

Mastabas

Mastabas had a stairway leading to the tomb chamber. In Dyn IV this was replaced by a vertical shaft, and an offertory chapel was added, which in the next dynasty had pillared halls, courtyards, storehouses, low-relief carvings.

The great pyramids

Pharaohs Cheops, Chephren and Mycerinus had their tombs at GIZA ✪ (*c.* 2600–2500 BC). In each complex was a pyramid with mortuary temple linked by a causeway to a valley building. The PYRAMID OF CHEPHREN still has some limestone facing at top; his valley building, the only one surviving, has a hall which housed 23 royal statues. Rock sculpture of the Sphinx, once painted and gilded, represents him as king and sun-god. (See p 12 for Pyramid of Cheops.)

Near by are over 200 mastabas of Dyns IV and V.

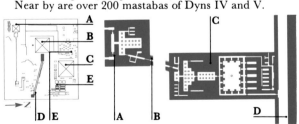

Giza: *plan of ancient site*
A *Pyramid of Mycerinus;*
B *Pyramid of Chephren;*   *Pyramid of Chephren: plan of subsidiary buildings*
C *Pyramid of Cheops;*   **A** *Valley building;* **B** *Causeway;* **C** *Mortuary*
D *Sphinx;* **E** *Mastabas*   *temple;* **D** *Pyramid*

Later pyramids

Pyramids of Dyns V and VI at Abusir and Saqqara are smaller and cruder than at Giza. Attached mortuary temples became more complex, with many storerooms.

The Middle Kingdom

Little survives of Middle Kingdom pyramids, temples and
mastabas. Until Dyn XI geometrical, non-representational
forms (e.g., polygonal columns) seem to have been preferred
to naturalistic decoration. The Pharaoh now began to be
glorified in the company of other gods.

Temples, pavilions and tombs

In the porticoed courtyard of the double-terraced MORTUARY
TEMPLE OF MENTUHOTEP, DEIR EL-BAHRI ▉, Thebes (c. 2050
BC), stood a pyramid; only fragments of platform remain.
Tomb was in the cliff behind. Both terrace faces had a
pillared portico, the upper level reached by a ramp.

The PAVILION OF SESOSTRIS I
(c. 1950 BC) has been
reconstructed in the NW
corner of the precinct at
KARNAK. Pillar reliefs ◆ show
the king making offerings to
the god Amon, depicted with
two goose feathers on his head.
Inside building was originally
a throne where king was
recrowned at his jubilee.

Pavilion of Sesostris I, Karnak

Other buildings of Dyn XII are the TOMB OF SARENPUT II,
ASWAN (c. 1900 BC), and the TOMB CHAPEL OF AMENEMHET,
MEDINET MA'ADI (c. 1900– c. 1800 BC). Latter has papyrus
columns: the vogue for abstract forms was probably by now
coming to an end.

The New Kingdom

The three dynasties of the New Kingdom were the great age
of temple-building. Twenty imposing temples once stood at
Karnak, near Thebes. In this region some of the finest
architecture emerged as the cumulative work of successive
kings. Monumental pylons, and hypostyle halls with massive
columns, told of the Pharaohs' greatness. Rock-cut tombs
instead of pyramids housed the royal dead, with mortuary
temples some distance away.

Deir el-Bahri

The serene and elegant MORTUARY TEMPLE OF QUEEN
HATSHEPSUT, DEIR EL-BAHRI ♦, Thebes (c. 1500 BC), was
inspired by Mentuhotep's temple (see above) at the foot of
the same precipice. It is similarly terraced with ramps
leading up to chief sanctuary hollowed into cliff. On upper
level are mortuary chapel and an altar to Re, as well as
sculptured pillars of Hatshepsut with attributes of Osiris.
Middle level has two shrines and lowest colonnade is flanked
by Osiris pillars.

Mortuary Temple of Queen Hatshepsut, Deir el-Bahri

Karnak

The sacred precinct at KARNAK is built around the GREAT TEMPLE OF AMON (16th–1st C BC), a modest Middle Kingdom shrine enlarged into a magnificent complex of pylons, courts and halls. Hypostyle by Seti I and Ramesses II had a vast roof of stone slabs, supported by 134 papyrus columns. The two rows along the central aisle were higher than the rest. This difference in roof levels accommodated stone grilles, forming clerestory-style windows, which let in subdued light. Inside N hypostyle wall are scenes in raised relief; outside of the wall bears sunken-relief decoration, then gaining popularity. The NE pylon and court are Ptolemaic.

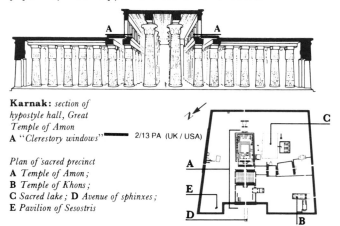

Karnak: *section of hypostyle hall, Great Temple of Amon*
A *"Clerestory windows"* ▬▬ 2/13 PA (UK / USA)

Plan of sacred precinct
A *Temple of Amon;*
B *Temple of Khons;*
C *Sacred lake;* **D** *Avenue of sphinxes;*
E *Pavilion of Sesostris*

To the S of the precinct is Ramesses III's TEMPLE OF KHONS (12th C BC), a cult temple to the son of Amon in the classic New Kingdom format, again with clerestoried hypostyle. Sanctuary housed the divine image and sacred barque, symbolizing boat which ferried the sun-god daily across the heavens.

Luxor

The TEMPLE OF AMON, LUXOR (14th C BC), was built mainly by Amenhotep III. It is more coherent in design than Karnak, although Ramesses II added a court and pylon causing a kink in the axial plan. Amenhotep's clerestoried hypostyle remained unfinished. There were two sanctuaries, one for the seated image, the other for the sacred barque.

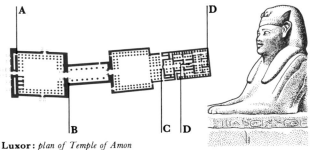

Luxor: *plan of Temple of Amon*
A *Ramesses II's pylon;* **B** *Original pylon gateway;* **C** *Hypostyle hall;* **D** *Sanctuaries*

Statue on avenue of sphinxes, Luxor

The temples of Ramesses II

Ramesses II was an energetic builder of temples in the 13th c BC. His mortuary temple, the RAMESSEUM, THEBES ⚑, is similar in layout to the cult temples. The first of two colonnaded courts contained a colossal royal statue, while the second had a row of pillars showing Osiris as mummified king with crook, flail and double crown. Beyond grand clerestoried hypostyle were two smaller halls. As this was a mortuary temple there was no processional path round sanctuary. Parts of the rough-brick buildings in same enclosure are well preserved: among the best examples of Egyptian civil architecture.

The GREAT TEMPLE, ABU SIMBEL ⚘, is one of two superb rock-cut temples in Nubia. Adapting features of the standard cult temple, it has a corniced façade in the manner of a pylon, with royal statues over 20 m high; and a main hall of 8 Osiris pillars. Storerooms lead off laterally from hall.

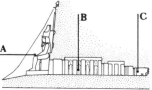

Great Temple, Abu Simbel
Two of the 4 giant statues flanking the entrance

Plan of Great Temple
A *Façade;* **B** *Main hall;* **C** *Sanctuary*

The SMALL TEMPLE, ABU SIMBEL ⚘, is dedicated to the king's wife Nefertari and the goddess Hathor. Battered façade includes large royal statues in niches. Rock-cut hall has 6 Hathor-headed columns.

In the mid-1960s both Abu Simbel temples were lifted to a new site above the old one, to save them from flooding after building of the Aswan Dam.

Other temples

The TEMPLE OF MEDINET HABU (12th c BC), near Thebes, is the mortuary temple of Ramesses III, similar in layout to Ramesseum but better preserved. Outside usual enclosing wall is a fortified outer envelope with stone gate-towers.

The TEMPLE OF SETI I, ABYDOS (*c.* 1300 BC), dedicated to 7 gods, had an unusual plan. At rear of complex are shrines to Osiris and, in front of these, 7 sanctuaries taking up whole width of building; each is preceded by its own aisle through hypostyle. Storerooms etc. are in their own wing. Pylons and courts, now ruined, are by Ramesses II.

The Tombs of the Kings

The VALLEY OF THE KINGS ⚘, w of Thebes, has tombs comprising long descending corridors (some with staircases) ending in a large hall containing sarcophagus. Walls painted with scenes and texts. Best tombs are of Seti I and Ramesses III, IV and IX. To the s are the Tombs of the Queens.

The Ptolemaic and Roman periods

After the end of the New Kingdom the troubled political
climate was an obstacle to building schemes. With the
Ptolemies architecture revived but never recaptured its earlier
vitality. As well as temples, birth houses were built,
representing the birthplace of Horus. Composite capitals
were used, varying in design from column to column. Pylons
were often preceded by monumental gateways in the
enclosing wall. Porticoes characteristically featured a low
stone screen.

The last temples

The irregularly planned TEMPLE OF ISIS, PHILAE (*c.* 280–
c. 50 BC; moved to island of Agilkia), is near the Aswan Dam.
Temple is approached via an avenue flanked by porticoes.
Each of two pylons is carved with a favourite scene: the
Pharaoh about to slaughter a handful of enemies held up
by their hair. A doorway in the first pylon, additional to
main entrance, leads to the birth house. Here are composite
capitals with Hathor-headed abaci. In mid-6th C AD part of
the temple became a Christian church; small Byzantine
crosses were carved on walls. The Kiosk of Trajan, also on
island, is of Roman date.

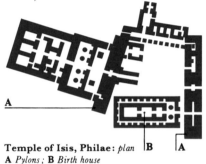

Temple of Isis, Philae: *plan*
A *Pylons;* **B** *Birth house*

*Detail of sunken
relief from pylon
of Temple of Isis*

The TEMPLE OF SEBEK AND HAROERIS, KOM OMBO (*c.* 180 BC–
c. AD 30), had twin sanctuaries, each of which had its own
aisle passing through 5 halls beyond court.

The TEMPLE OF HATHOR, DENDERA (*c.* 110 BC–AD 68), was
begun *c.* 50 years after the Temple of Horus, Edfu (see
p 13), was completed. Enclosing wall and hypostyle with
Hathor-headed columns added in Roman times.
Ceremonies took place in shrines on roof, which still exist.
Pylon and court never completed. Precinct includes a sacred
lake, two birth houses and a small Augustan temple.

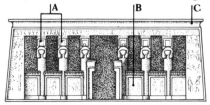

Temple of Hathor, Dendera: *front hall*
A *Hathor-headed columns;* **B** *Stone screen;*
C *Gorge cornice*

*Detail of gorge cornice
from Temple of Hathor*

THE ANCIENT GREEKS

The architecture of ancient Greece was the foundation of many subsequent styles in different parts of the world, as well as offering the most sophisticated and aesthetically perfect body of work in the Western European tradition. The main monuments are therefore crucial to a broad understanding of European architecture.

Greece did not become a single nation until the modern era: with its mountainous mainland and scattered islands it grew up as city states, usually in rivalry.

The first civilization of ancient Greek history was based on Crete (3000–1400 BC) and reached its peak at the palace of Knossos. It was succeeded by a culture located at Mycenae and Tiryns on the mainland, which declined *c.* 1100 BC into a relatively dark age with few remains.

The golden age was the Hellenic period (800–323 BC), which saw the establishment of the city state as the basis of society, the founding of new cities, the emergence of Athens as supreme power after decisive victories against the Persians, and the development of democracy. The zenith was the rule of Pericles (444–429 BC) with its fantastic flowering of philosophy, art, literature, science, mathematics and drama. This cultural blossoming was reflected in architectural achievements, among them the Parthenon.

The prodigious growth of building was favoured by the climate: the clear, dazzling sunshine made for strong shadows and encouraged clean, powerful forms in the landscape. Local limestone and marble provided ideal materials.

In the Hellenistic period (323–30 BC), following the death of Alexander the Great who had unified Greece and extended its domain to the E, the great styles were continued, though with less strength and conviction in an empire gradually taken over by the Romans. Architecture featured mixed Orders (see p 22), wider spans and the occasional use of arches and vaults. Small buildings were often elegant and elaborate, but there was also a liking for monumental structures on a superhuman scale.

Extant Greek architecture consists essentially of public buildings, especially temples and theatres. Few ordinary houses have survived.

The central lands of the Ancient Greeks, *showing principal sites*

Temples

The gods, whose various attributes and activities magnified those of ordinary mortals, were identified with all aspects of Greek life. The architectural expression of their importance, and the dominant building form in the Hellenic age, was the temple—the divine dwelling-place. It was not intended to accommodate a congregation, but together with its external altar was the focus of a space for rituals—a form to be experienced from outside.

From the Mycenaean megaron (chief's hall with porch) developed the rectangular temple surrounded by columns to give it appropriate dignity. This simple concept was elaborated with great sophistication of external, and sometimes internal, design.

The core of the temple was the naos, a chamber housing the divine statue, with main doorway facing E. It stood on a low platform (crepidoma), usually of three steps. In front of the naos was a portico or pronaos. This could be prostyle, i.e., with an open row of columns in front of the doorway; or it could be in antis—with columns (usually two) between the antae (pilasters terminating extended side walls of naos), so that the portico receded into the building instead of projecting from it. Behind naos was sometimes a rear sanctuary (adyton). Desire for symmetry often resulted in an opisthodomos, a rear portico usually without access to main temple. Roof sometimes supported by internal colonnades.

Early temples were of timber and brick, with stone wall-bases. Columns and main walls began to be built entirely in limestone (finished with marble stucco) in 6th c BC. Marble first appeared in Asia Minor. Main roofing material was terracotta tiles.

One of the finest Doric examples is the TEMPLE OF APHAIA, AEGINA (*c.* 490 BC). Stuccoed local limestone was originally embellished with paint. Marks can be seen on pronaos columns where entrance was closed off with high grille.

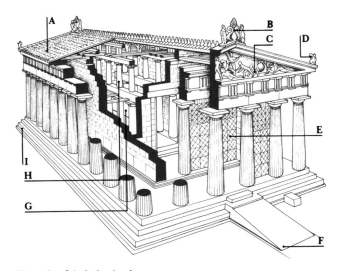

Temple of Aphaia, Aegina
A *Roof tiles;* **B** *Acroterion;* **C** *Pediment;* **D** *Water spout;* **E** *Pronaos entrance;* **F** *Entrance ramp;* **G** *Naos;* **H** *Two-tiered colonnade;* **I** *Crepidoma*

The Classical Orders

Major Greek architecture is trabeated—i.e., made from columns and beams. The column is a module for the whole building: with its capital and base (if any) it corresponds to one of three fundamental styles, known as the Classical Orders.

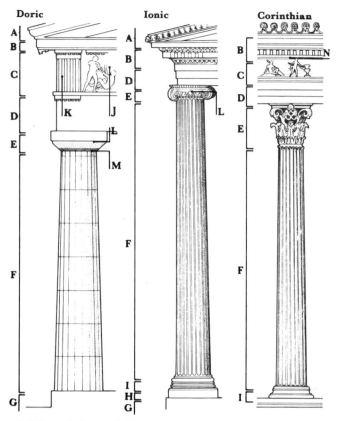

A *Pediment*; B *Cornice*; C *Frieze*; D *Architrave*; E *Capital*; F *Shaft of column*; G *Crepidoma*; H *Plinth*; I *Base*; J *Metope*; K *Triglyph*; L *Abacus*; M *Echinus*; N *Dentils (B, C and D form entablature.)*

The earliest Order was Doric, characterized by powerful-looking columns (usually with 20 sharp-edged flutings) without a base. Column height (incl capital): 4 to 6 × base diameter, increasing to $7\frac{1}{4}$ × in Hellenistic period. Triglyphs and metopes of frieze evolved from timber antecedents.

The Ionic Order, with its volute or scroll capital, originated in Asia Minor in the 6th c BC. Mature columns have 24 flutes separated by fillets. Square plinths appeared in late Hellenic times. The frieze, often sculptured, became universal in late 4th c BC. Column height (incl capital and base): about 9 × lower diameter.

The acanthus-leaved Corinthian capital has entablature indistinguishable from Ionic, almost always with frieze. Popular in Hellenistic period. Column height: usually about 10 × base diameter.

The evolution of temple plans

By experimenting with proportions the temple-builders sought the ideal form. In mainland Doric an elongated plan gradually evolved towards the classic 6 × 13 arrangement of columns in the outer colonnade (pteron). This was popular in the early 5th C BC. Temples in Asia Minor, Italy and Sicily followed a more irregular course.

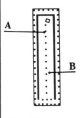

The Heraeum, Samos

(8th C BC). Probably Ionic. Timber colonnade surrounded a long chamber. Internal columns required displacement of statue

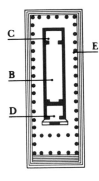

Temple C, Selinus *(c. 570 BC). Elongated form survived later in Sicily. Typical of the island are adyton and double columns before pronaos*

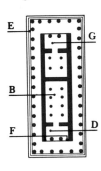

Temple of Apollo, Corinth *(c. 540 BC). Distyle in antis— i.e., with two columns between antae (see p 21)*

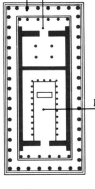

The Parthenon, Athens *(447–432 BC). The pronaos is prostyle. (See p 27)*

A *Central colonnade;*
B *Naos;* **C** *Adyton;*
D *Pronaos;* **E** *Pteron;*
F *Antae;*
G *Opisthodomos;*
H *Flights of steps;*
I *Pilasters;.* **J** *Inner temple*

Drawn to scale

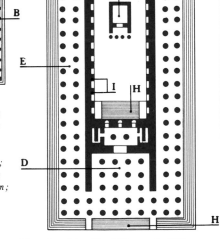

Temple of Apollo, Didyma *(c. 330 BC–AD 41). A dipteral plan (i.e., with double pteron), typical of Asia Minor. (See p 31)*

Temple decoration

Doric pediments often featured mythological scenes in high
relief. Roof tiles were finished off at the eaves by
embellishments known as antefixae, which hid the joints.
All orders used mouldings with many types of profile,
including hawksbeak (typically Doric) and egg-and-dart
(Ionic). Doric decoration was frequently painted. Ionic and
Corinthian made rhythmical use of plant motifs.

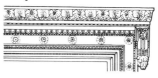

Tholos, Epidauros:
mouldings with antefixa

Erechtheion, Athens:
mouldings on doorway

Sanctuaries, agoras and theatres

The temple stood in a temenos, or sacred precinct, surrounded
by associated buildings. Famous shrines had treasuries near
by, housing offerings from other states and processional
regalia. Another building type was the tholos, a small circular
structure of uncertain purpose.

The secular equivalent of the temenos was the agora, a
meeting-place with buildings for assembly, commerce and
administration. Dignity and form were given to this area
by the placing of stoas (elongated porticoes with shops,
offices and storerooms at rear). Other buildings in or close to
the typical agora were the assembly hall, town hall,
gymnasium, music hall and theatre.

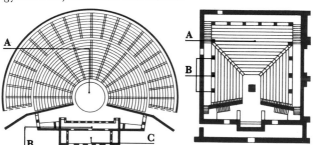

Theatre, Epidauros A *Orchestra;*
B *Proscenium;* **C** *Scene building*

Assembly hall, Priene
A *Stone seating;* **B** *Pillars*

The permanent Greek theatre developed in the 5th c BC
to accommodate the drama derived from the festival of
Dionysos. The spectacle took place in a circular orchestra.
In late Hellenic times this was backed by a scene building
for storing and displaying props, which later came to have
two stories and in front of it a proscenium, the top of which
served as a stage. Stone seating of auditorium was cut into
a hillside. Best example at Epidauros (*c.* 350 BC).

Other building types

The most famous Greek tomb was erected to King Mausolos
(hence the word "mausoleum") at Halicarnassos—one of the
7 wonders of the ancient world. Oblong stadia were built
for athletics. Hippodromes were large stadia for racing.

The Aegean civilizations

The architectural gems of the civilization that sprang up in Crete in the 3rd MIL BC were the three labyrinthine palaces of Knossos, Phaistos and Mallia, dating from *c.* 1900 BC. All three were destroyed *c.* 1700 BC, rebuilt, and destroyed again *c.* 1400 BC.

As the Cretans' fortunes fell, the Mycenaeans' rose. Their palaces, smaller than Cretan ones, were simple fortified residences, whose basic unit was the megaron. Tholos, or beehive, tombs were perhaps the first domed funeral monuments.

The Minoan style

The PALACE OF MINOS, KNOSSOS ♦, chief building on Crete (now partly reconstructed), gave the title Minoan to the Cretan style. Plan was complex, with ingenious disposition of open and closed spaces round central court. Main apartments two-storied. Entrance from N was through columnar gatehouse, the only fortified structure. To S and W were the principal state rooms, to E the royal apartments. Grand staircase ♦ incorporated wooden columns splaying outwards towards top. Lower level of W wing consisted of narrow storerooms.

Palace of Minos, Knossos
A *Throne room;* **B** *Queen's suite;*
C *Staircase;* **D** *Storerooms*

Grand staircase of palace

The Mycenaeans

The coastal citadel, TIRYNS ♦ (*c.* 1300 BC), was defended by massive walls and series of gates. Central feature of palace was large megaron serving as throne room.

The citadel at MYCENAE ♦ (15th–13th C BC) looms menacingly above the Argive Plain. Its best-known feature is the LION GATE ♦ (*c.* 1250 BC); massive stone jambs bear a lintel spanning 3.2 m, above which is a triangular slab carved with pair of lions facing splayed column.

The near-by TREASURY OF ATREUS (*c.* 1325 BC) is a tholos whose corbelled domed stone vault, within the hillside, is approached by an open walled passage.

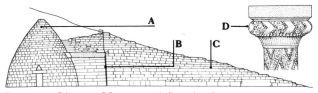

Treasury of Atreus, Mycenae **A** *Domed vault;*
B *Entrance;* **C** *Walled passage;* **D** *Capital of one of columns flanking entrance*

25

Athens

The Acropolis at Athens was the supreme site in the supreme city of ancient Greece. It dominated the whole city and symbolically dwarfed an agora at its base.

The Acropolis ♻

An acropolis, or hilltop temenos, was a crucial element of the city state, the centre of the most important rituals of its public life. Surrounded by a wall and entered through a propylaeum (portico gateway), it contained one or more temples, votive monuments and sometimes treasuries, and a stoa for shelter. One characteristic of such sacred sites was the careful articulation of changing levels, using paved terraces, to unify the buildings and emphasize the most important.

The Athenian ACROPOLIS, on its dramatic limestone outcrop, was the scene of continuous architectural experiment reaching a climax in the Periclean age (mid 5th C BC). The asymmetrical grouping of marble buildings round the giant statue of goddess Athena was designed, by several architects working in harmony, to facilitate movement of processions.

The Propylaea

The subtlety of the Acropolis layout is best illustrated by the steps, ramps and columned spaces of the PROPYLAEA (437–432 BC) with its forecourt and neighbouring buildings. The architect Mnesicles achieved a unique fusion of grandeur and modesty appropriate to the entrance porch of the Acropolis. Outer columns are Doric, while inner ones, in central passage, are slenderer Ionic—a brilliant juxtaposition. The N wing, provided with windows, was a picture gallery.

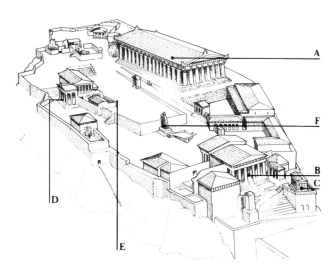

Acropolis, Athens, *at end of Classical era*
A *Parthenon;* **B** *Propylaea;* **C** *Temple of Athena Nike;* **D** *Erechtheion;*
E *Site of Old Temple of Athena;* **F** *Statue of Athena Promachos*

The Parthenon

The jewel of the Acropolis is the PARTHENON (447–432 BC), shrine of Athena, built in Pentelic marble by Ictinus and Callicrates, with Phidias as master sculptor. The basic design is simplicity itself: a Doric temple with a pteron of 8 × 17 columns (10.4 m high) and a prostyle porch duplicated by an opisthodomos (see plan, p 23). The naos contained Phidias' monumental gold and ivory statue of Athena and had an internal colonnade along three sides. Behind it, but accessible only through opisthodomos, was the Parthenon proper, a Hall of the Virgins used as a treasury. Entablature is 3.4 m high. Pediments and metopes had fine painted sculptures (some in Louvre; British Museum; Acropolis Museum, Athens). Ionic-inspired frieze round outer walls of naos, porch and opisthodomos showed Panathenaic procession (part still visible ♦).

Perfection was achieved by refinements of design to correct optical illusions: pteron columns lean inwards, suggesting strength and repose, and would meet if extended upwards about 1½ miles; they are closer together and thicker at corners, and have entasis (i.e., bulge slightly just below middle to prevent their appearing concave); and stylobate is gently domed.

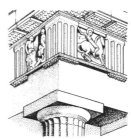

Parthenon: *angle of entablature*

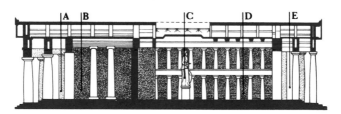

Parthenon: *section*
A *Opisthodomos;* **B** *Parthenon proper;* **C** *Statue;* **D** *Naos;* **E** *Pronaos*

The Temple of Athena Nike

Callicrates' small, exquisite TEMPLE OF ATHENA NIKE (c. 427 BC), perched to the right of the Propylaea, which was planned later but built first, is one of earliest surviving Ionic buildings in Athens. The form is amphiprostyle: a portico at each end but no pteron. Columns are short in proportion to diameter, perhaps to avoid too great a contrast with Propylaea. For first time in Greece architrave had three fasciae.

Temple of Athena Nike,
showing metal lattice

The Erechtheion

Probably by Mnesicles, the ERECHTHEION (421–405 BC) lacks
a main façade and cannot be appreciated from a single
viewpoint. Its irregular planning on two levels was due
to uneven site and need to include shrines to three deities.
Of the three porches, the N one, with delicately ornamented
Ionic columns and richly carved doorway ♦, is the most
beautiful. The s porch is supported by sculptured caryatids.
Frieze of dark grey Eleusian marble was decorated with
white marble sculptures.

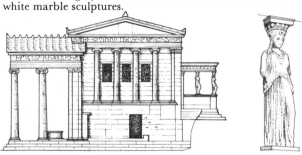

Erechtheion: *view from* w   *Caryatid column,* s *porch*

The Agora

Building in the AGORA at Athens began in early 6th c BC,
with w and s sides, and ended over 10 centuries later. The
agora was the centre of Athenian social, civic and business
life, and also a venue for philosophical debate—scene of
Socrates' dialogues recorded by Plato. Double-aisled STOA
by Attalos II of Pergamon (rebuilt as museum) was a
Hellenistic contribution; two-storied façade has Doric columns
below, Ionic above.

To w is the TEMPLE OF HEPHAESTUS (Theseion; 449–444 BC),
built mainly in marble a few years before Parthenon.
Arrangement of 6 × 13 Doric columns was classic after
c. 500 BC. Metopes on E end and adjacent 4 on sides were
sculptured, as were friezes over pronaos and opisthodomos.
The best-preserved, externally, of all Doric temples.

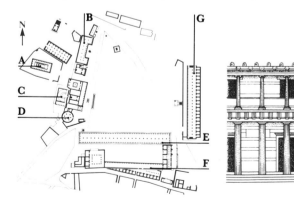

Agora, Athens
A *Temple of Hephaestus;* B *Stoa of Zeus;*
C *Assembly hall;* D *Tholos;* E *Central stoa;*
F *Southern stoa;* G *Stoa of Attalos*

*Stoa of Attalos: detail
of façade showing
superimposed colonnades*

Other buildings in Athens

At the foot of the Acropolis is the THEATRE OF DIONYSOS (founded *c.* 500 BC), prototype of all Greek theatres. Design modifications continued until Roman times. Some of the marble seats of honour (1st C BC) still survive. Seating for about 18,000.

The TEMPLE OF OLYMPIAN ZEUS ◪ (Olympeion; 174 BC–AD 132) was designed by the Roman Cossutius and completed by Hadrian 300 years later. Double pteron had 104 columns (15 remain) with Corinthian capitals.

Monuments

The CHORAGIC MONUMENT OF LYSICRATES (334 BC), one of the most delicate structures in Athens, commemorated a victory in a singing competition. Circular wall has Corinthian columns supporting marble entablature and dome. Height only 10.3 m.

The TOWER OF THE WINDS (*c.* 48 BC), a Hellenistic tower containing a water clock, also had a sundial and weathervane (latter now missing). Much copied in Renaissance Europe. A circular projection on s side housed the water tank.

Tower of the Winds

Sacred sites of Greece

Although the impetus behind the greatest Greek temples came from the cities, the most important religious sanctuaries, including those at Delphi, Olympia and Delos, grew up outside them.

Delphi ♧

DELPHI, perhaps the most ingenious and evocative of all sacred sites, was famous as the seat of the temple and oracle of Apollo, to which all other buildings here subtly related. The most important phase of its history began in 6th C BC.

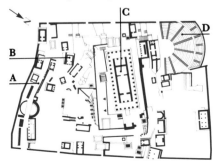

Delphi: *sanctuary of Apollo*
A *Sacred Way;* **B** *Athenian Treasury;*
C *Temple of Apollo;* **D** *Theatre*

Siphnian Treasury:
façade with
caryatid columns

The layout of the sanctuary around the Sacred Way, which zigzags up from s, is seemingly haphazard but in fact carefully contrived to create a succession of views.

The Doric TEMPLE OF APOLLO ■ (366–326 BC) has an elongated plan of 6 × 15 inherited from its 6th-c predecessor. Near by is small ATHENIAN TREASURY (c. 510 BC), first Doric building entirely of marble, with walls bearing hymns and music inscribed to Apollo ✦. The SIPHNIAN TREASURY (c. 525 BC; façade reconstructed in Delphi Museum) was an early mainland example of Ionic, with sculptured pediment— rare for the Order—as well as frieze (see p 29).

To the NW is the acoustically superb THEATRE (early 2nd c BC). Well-preserved stadium nearby. The THOLOS just outside sacred site (c. 400 BC) is partially restored.

Olympia and Epidauros ✿

OLYMPIA, rather more dispersed than Delphi, had two important sanctuaries, to Hera and Zeus. Its stadium was site of Olympic Games.

The TEMPLE OF HERA ■ (c. 600 BC) has the elongated plan (6 × 16) of early Doric. Most of surviving echinus blocks are 5th c (characterized by angled straight sides), but some are · 6th c (gently curved sides).

The TEMPLE OF ZEUS ■ (c. 460 BC) has the mature Doric 6 × 13 plan. Built mostly in stuccoed limestone, with marble sculptures and roof tiles.

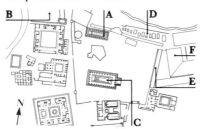

Olympia: *the sacred site*
A *Temple of Hera;* **B** *Gymnasium;* **C** *Temple of Zeus;* **D** *Treasuries;* **E** *Stoa;* **F** *Stadium*

Head of Apollo: detail from w *pediment of Temple of Zeus*

EPIDAUROS boasted the shrine of Asklepios (son of Apollo) as well as a hospital and spa. Most buildings were complete by 200 BC. The THEATRE (c. 350 BC) is the most impressive (see p 24). As at Delphi the acoustics are impeccable.

Other sites

The TEMPLE OF APOLLO, BASSAE (c. 425 BC), unusually faces N. Doric pteron. Naos had interior frieze on Ionic half-columns with novel capitals, and first ever Corinthian column in front of adyton (the base remains). Pediments now missing.

Temple of Apollo, Bassae: *Ionic capital and splayed base*

DELOS was the birthplace of Apollo and Artemis but its most interesting buildings are domestic, e.g., the "MAISON DE LA COLLINE".

TEMPLE OF POSEIDON, SOUNION ✿ (c. 440 BC), intended to be seen from the sea, has unusually slender columns.

Italy, Sicily and Asia Minor

In the E and W colonies, temples tended to be more
individualistic than on the mainland, where purist models
were often followed. An influential, rectilinear style of town
planning emerged in Hellenistic Asia Minor.

Italy and Sicily

S Italy and Sicily have well-preserved Doric temples of the
early 6th and 5th C BC. Both regions, especially Italy, were
characterized by architectural experiment and use of Ionic
features. Italian columns often have exaggerated entasis.

The best Italian site is PAESTUM ♙. The Doric "BASILICA"
(c. 530 BC) is pseudodipteral (i.e., dipteral but with inner
pteron omitted). Cigar-shaped columns have broad capitals
with decoration round neck, inspired by Ionic. Better
preserved is TEMPLE OF POSEIDON (or of Hera; c. 460 BC).
Stairs leading to roof space have partially survived.

In Sicily the large TEMPLE OF OLYMPIAN ZEUS, AGRIGENTO
▣ ♙ (c. 510–409 BC), was pseudodipteral, with a wall joining
the Doric outer columns. Recesses of exterior carried
sculptured figures beneath heavy entablature.

The TEMPLE AT SEGESTA (424–416 BC) was never finished:
columns are unfluted, and bosses for lifting still visible on
stone blocks of platform. Metopes, eccentrically, are wider
than they are tall. Near by is fine late theatre.

Asia Minor

The eastern Aegean was the birthplace of Ionic: the prototype
of the voluted capital first appeared c. 570 BC. The typical
Asiatic column base had a horizontally fluted disc surmounted
by a large convex moulding (torus). The mainland Attic
form, with an upper torus separated from a more substantial
lower one by a concave element (scotia), was not adopted
until 2nd C BC. Friezes introduced in 4th C. From the 560s
temples tended towards the gigantic.

The TEMPLE OF ARTEMIS, EPHESUS ▣ (c. 356 BC) is notable
for its sculpture, especially on the drums of its columns
(fragments in British Museum). The TEMPLE OF APOLLO,
DIDYMA (c. 330 BC–AD 41) had a vast sunken court containing
a miniature temple. Work on outer wall stopped at cornice.

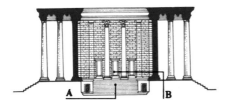

Temple of Apollo, Didyma: *section*
A *Staircase;* **B** *Doorway to pronaos (see plan p 23)*

Temple of Apollo :
Asiatic base

Town planning

The layout introduced in Hellenistic Asia Minor, reputedly
by Hippodamus, was a grid of narrow streets ending in an
outer wall that followed the natural demands of the site.
One of best examples is Miletus, rebuilt from c. 470 BC;
grid has about 400 blocks. Priene, which has remarkably
well-preserved theatre, was planned along similar lines.

THE ROMANS

Tradition has it that Rome was founded in 754 BC by
Romulus, but it was still little more than a group of villages
when in the mid 6th C BC it came under the influence of the
powerful Etruscans, whose territories stretched northwards to
the Po valley, eastwards to the Adriatic and southwards
beyond Pompeii. The first monuments in Rome were built
under Etruscan rule, which ended *c.* 509 BC when Tarquinius
Superbus was expelled to make way for the new Republic.

Rome now began to vanquish her Latin neighbours one
by one and extend her boundaries. By the mid-3rd C BC the
city led a confederacy of Italian states and three centuries
later had made herself mistress of the western world from
the Euphrates to the Atlantic, under rulers like Pompey,
Julius Caesar, Octavian and Trajan.

The Romans, unlike the Greeks, built up their empire by
military aggression rather than by exploring and colonizing.
Neither did they spread their culture by conquest of the mind,
through philosophy, spirituality, poetry or art. They were a
hard-headed, pragmatic people who excelled at making laws,
administering territories, and military and engineering feats.
For its subjects Roman rule meant roads, aqueducts, sewers,
harbours; the dissolution of political and commercial
frontiers; and a supply of commodities from abroad. It
also meant baths to relax in, fora for conducting law and
politics, theatres for drama, circuses for gladiatorial fights,
and temples for a not very demanding religion.

When, after the defeat of Antony at Actium in 31 BC,
Octavian eventually emerged as first Roman emperor, he
accepted the title of Augustus and ushered in the golden
age. He claimed to have found Rome brick and left it
marble. Though in truth he left more concrete than marble,
his reign saw a climax of architectural achievement, in
buildings that were ingenious, elaborate, usually grand in
scale, always masterly.

Roman Empire at its height (*2nd* C AD), *showing principal sites*

Building technology

Roman building technology was the most advanced of its time. Though highly original in many aspects, it appropriated some techniques from the Etruscans, who were probably the first Europeans to make wide use of the true or radiating arch, built up of wedge-shaped blocks known as voussoirs.

Italy, and later the Imperial provinces, offered a far greater variety of building materials than had been available to the Greeks. The Pont du Gard, Nîmes, France, testifies to Roman skill in Etruscan dry-stone techniques (see p 42). More significant, though, was the discovery of how to make concrete from rubble mixed with lime and sand (in particular a volcanic sand called *pozzolana*). This enabled barrel vaults to be constructed using concrete infilling between arched brick ribs. Concrete walls were built using a frame of brickwork.

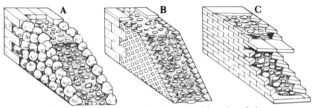

Roman walling techniques, *using concrete with various facings*
A *Rough bricks (Opus incertum)* ; **B** *Diagonally set bricks (Opus reticulatum)* ;
C *Triangular blocks (Opus testaceum)*

Arches, vaults and domes were characteristic architectural elements. Intersecting barrel vaults formed cross, or groin, vaults (e.g., in Baths of Caracalla, Rome: see p 38). The oblique sideways thrust of a large vault was countered by buttresses. Semidome vaulting, fronted by an arch, was often used to cover semicircular recesses (exedrae).

Style and ornament

The Romans continued to build along Etruscan lines until well into the Republic, but then began to assimilate Greek sources. In the distinctive Roman style that emerged prior to the Empire, the aesthetic functionalism of the Greeks gave way to a largely decorative treatment of the Classical Orders. Columns and half-columns were placed along walls that were structurally complete without them. An example is the entablatures of the Theatre of Marcellus, Rome (23–13 BC), which seem to be held up by half-columns but are in fact carried adequately by arches. Conversely, the mundane functions of piers, buttresses and pinnacles were generally disguised.

Half-columns and arches,
Theatre of Marcellus, Rome

Decoration made much use of Corinthian capitals as well as the new Composite Order, an amalgam of Ionic and Corinthian created in the 1st C AD. Rosettes, acanthus motifs and garlanded friezes commonly featured in highly ornamental entablatures. Architraves could be curved forward, or up into arches.

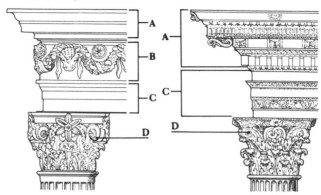

Capitals and entablatures: Corinthian and Composite
(Temple of Vesta, Tivoli ; Temple of Castor and Pollux, Rome)
A *Cornice ;* **B** *Frieze ;* **C** *Architrave ;* **D** *Volutes*

Building types
Roman ingenuity was applied both to existing building types such as temples and theatres and to new ones such as basilicas (legal and commercial centres), public baths (thermae) and ampitheatres. The result was an architecture unprecedented in the variety of functions it served. Roads, aqueducts and bridges—unadorned feats of engineering— are in some ways more impressive than public buildings.

The Etruscans

Etruscan methods of building arches, city walls and drainage channels were taken over by the Romans. It is likely that the atrium type of house (see p 41) was an Etruscan invention, as was the Tuscan Order, an unfluted version of Doric. Rock-cut underground tombs (e.g., near Corneto) are among the few works of architecture surviving.

The TEMPLE OF JUNO SOSPITA, LANUVIUM ▟ (5th C BC) was in the characteristic style, which influenced Roman temples.

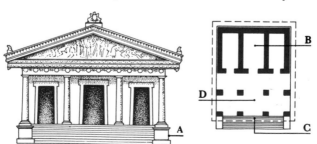

Temple of Juno Sospita, Lanuvium: *Façade and plan*
A *Podium ;* **B** *Triple chamber ;* **C** *Walled flight of steps ;* **D** *Portico*

Rome

The architecture of Imperial Rome reached heights of variety and elaboration never before attained. Although Greek and Greek-trained architects were often employed, their traditional ideas were transformed by engineering skill and by a boldly original vision.

The Imperial fora

The forum, like the Greek agora, was the social and political hub of a city, serving as meeting-place and market. Usually surrounded by colonnades and both sacred and secular buildings.

The first Roman forum, the FORUM ROMANUM, developed in a valley that had been drained by the Etruscans. Political facilities (e.g., the senate house and orators' platforms) were at wider, w end, while religious activities, based on the sacred hearth tended by the Vestal Virgins, took place to E. Shops lined the area. As political functions lost their vitality, architectural embellishment took over.

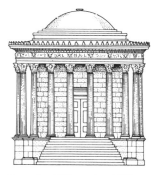

Temple of Vesta *(see p 36)*

This process began with Sulla's TABULARIUM (Record House; 78 BC), the most important building of Republican Rome. Façade of surviving stories has arcades with Doric columns. Caesar added a second forum in 46 BC. Under the Empire many of the more mundane functions were moved out and the emphasis turned to celebration. Additions and modifications were made by Augustus, Tiberius, Vespasian, Nerva and finally Trajan, whose forum contained basilica, temple, two libraries, shops and well-preserved market.

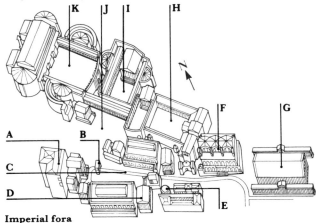

Imperial fora
A *Tabularium;* **B** *Arch of Septimius Severus;* **C** *Forum Romanum;*
D *Temple of Castor and Pollux;* **E** *Temple of Vesta;* **F** *Basilica of Maxentius;* **G** *Temple of Venus and Rome;* **H** *Forum of Vespasian;*
I *Forum of Augustus;* **J** *Forum of Caesar;* **K** *Forum of Trajan*

Temples

Most Roman temples had an external altar and a chamber (cella) housing statuary and treasures. The rectangular type, more common than the circular, stood on an Etruscan-inspired podium with a frontal staircase between side walls. Outer columns of a deep prostyle porch were often continued along sides and rear of cella by attached half-columns—a style known as pseudoperipteral. A temple was often designed to be seen from a forum: the emphasis was on the façade.

Rectangular temples

The Ionic TEMPLE OF FORTUNA VIRILIS (c. 40 BC) has classic pseudoperipteral form. Porch columns are travertine stone, half-columns softer tufa, podium core concrete—a typical economy of materials.

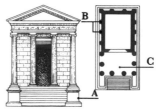

The TEMPLE OF MARS ULTOR (the Avenger; 14–2 BC), in Forum of Augustus, has apse in cella, a feature later to be used in early Christian churches.

Temple of Fortuna Virilis: *façade and plan* **A** *Podium;* **B** *Half-columns;* **C** *Portico*

To SE of Forum Romanum stood the peripteral TEMPLE OF CASTOR AND POLLUX (7 BC–AD 6), of which three Corinthian columns survive with fine entablature ✦ (see p 34). Hadrian's TEMPLE OF VENUS AND ROME ◼ (AD 123–35), also peripteral, had two cellas back to back with contiguous apses (still standing). The pseudoperipteral TEMPLE OF ANTONINUS AND FAUSTINA (AD 141) became a church in 1602.

Circular temples

The TEMPLE OF PORTUNUS (c. 31 BC), near Temple of Fortuna Virilis, is now Church of S Maria del Sole. A circular cella surrounded by 20 marble Corinthian columns stands on platform with steps all round in the Greek mode.

The TEMPLE OF VESTA ◼, site of the sacred hearth, was rebuilt by Septimius Severus AD 205 (see p 35).

The PANTHEON (AD 120–24), now Church of S Maria Rotunda, is the best preserved building of ancient Rome.

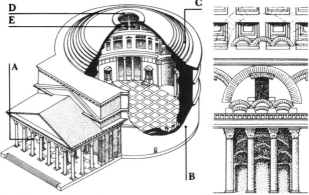

Pantheon: *cut-away view* **A** *Portico;* **B** *Rotunda;* **C** *Stepped dome;* **D** *Oculus;* **E** *Coffered interior*

Detail of Pantheon showing concealed brick arches in walls and dome

The circular part (rotunda) was built mainly by Hadrian, to symbolize the cosmos; the rather ill-fitting portico incorporates a temple completed by Agrippa *c*. 25 BC. Although much of original decoration has gone, the Pantheon's vast scale, geometrical simplicity and well-planned interior are still impressive. The dome, saucer-shaped outside, is a perfect hemisphere inside. It springs from the top of the second tier of a three-tiered wall of faced concrete; support is lent by hidden relieving arches. The coffered ceiling ◆, reducing weight of dome, has foreshortened panels, exaggerating perspective. At crown is an open round hole (oculus) over 8 m in diameter, an effective means of lighting. Opposite rotunda entrance is a semidomed apse and around walls are alternating rectangular and half-round exedrae, originally housing statues of gods. Each has columns and corner pilasters beneath a continuous entablature. Much of second tier ◆ is 18th C; part of original has been restored.

Basilicas

Basilicas (halls of justice and commerce) became the model for early Christian churches. The usual plan was rectangular, comprising a "nave" flanked by lower-roofed aisles, sometimes galleried. Opposite the entrance was usually a semicircular apse for the tribunal. Roofs, generally wooden, sometimes had a vast span. Exteriors were unornamented.

The BASILICA OF MAXENTIUS (or of Constantine; AD 310–13) was unusual in being vaulted, a feature inspired by Imperial thermae. Nave was covered by a three-compartment coffered groin vault, springing from buttress walls that divided each aisle into three barrel-vaulted sections, each surmounted by a clerestory window. Constantine moved the entrance to the long S side and added a second apse to the N.

Basilica of Maxentius: *section and plan*
A *Groin-vaulted "nave"*; **B** *Barrel-vaulted aisles*; **C** *Apses*

Imperial thermae

Thermae, found throughout the Empire, were public baths which served as meeting-places, with facilities for athletics and lectures. They were generally raised on a platform, with heating systems underneath. Main rooms included the calidarium (hot room), tepidarium (warm room) and frigidarium (containing an unheated pool). Other rooms were used for dry sweating, dressing and manicure.

Early thermae such as those at Pompeii were derived from Greek gymnasia and had rooms arranged in series. In Rome, beginning with the Baths of Nero, a more magnificent and complex type developed to cater for an increasing population and symbolize Imperial munificence.

The palatial BATHS OF CARACALLA (AD 211–17), now a skeleton, stood in a park used for sports, round which were grouped halls for lectures and plays. The immense groin-vaulted hall had symmetrical wings either side, but main rooms were along an axis at right angles to these. Plan was devised to avoid congestion: bathers divided into two flows which merged in final sequence. Calidarium was domed, frigidarium open-air. Interior had marble pavements, alabaster and marble columns, and Greek sculptures.

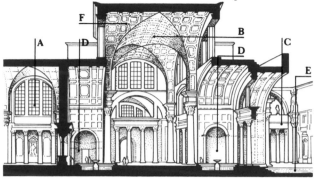

Baths of Caracalla: *section through main rooms, omitting calidarium*
A *Tepidarium;* **B** *Central hall;* **C** *Frigidarium;* **D** *Exedrae with semidomes;*
E *Pool;* **F** *Coffered vaulting*

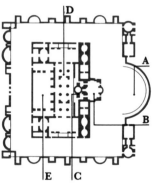

The BATHS OF DIOCLETIAN (AD 302–6) were similar in design to those of Caracalla. Room for over 3,000. Groin vaulting of main hall sprang from granite columns (15 m high) with Composite capitals of white marble. Calidarium was rectangular: more usually it was circular or polygonal; and domed. Outer enclosure wall had both rectangular and semicircular exedrae. Michelangelo converted main hall to a church in 1563, raising floor. Choir added mid 18th c. Plentiful Roman details remain (e.g., mosaics).

Baths of Diocletian: *plan*
A *Theatre;* **B** *Calidarium;*
C *Tepidarium;* **D** *Central hall;*
E *Frigidarium*

Amphitheatres, circuses and theatres

Amphitheatres, found in every important settlement except in the Hellenized eastern provinces, were constructed for the deadly animal and gladiatorial fights which for the Romans passed as entertainment. Oval in plan, with high tiers of seats round an arena, they posed difficult structural problems, solved with great ingenuity. Circuses were an elongated version used for horse and chariot races.

Theatres, less characteristic than amphitheatres, were built on flat ground as well as into hillsides. They differed from the Greek version in being semicircular (instead of covering two-thirds of a circle) and in having a deeper stage, which from the 4th c BC had a high stone façade behind it (scaena frons), joined at the sides to the auditorium. By 2nd c AD this had become elaborately decorated with columns, niches and sometimes broken pediments. Semicircular orchestra was used for additional seating.

The awe-inspiring COLOSSEUM (Flavian Amphitheatre; AD 70–80), elliptical in plan, held 48,000 spectators. The seating tiers rested on converging wedges of masonry with vaulted passageways between them. Outer wall, carried by 80 piers, has 4 arcaded stories, illustrating typically Roman use of Classical Orders as pure decoration. Each level has a continuous entablature. A great number of corridors and stairways, together with encircling double ground-floor passage, made for rapid evacuation. A ring of corbels on the outside of the top storey held anchorage-masts for a huge canvas sunshade. Beneath the arena were dens and rooms for animals and combatants.

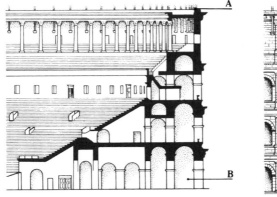

Colosseum: *partial section*
A *Masts for sunshade*; **B** *Double outer passage*

Detail of 4-storied outer wall of Colosseum

The THEATRE OF MARCELLUS (23–13 BC) had three arcaded tiers, lower two still standing (see p. 33).

The CIRCUS OF MAXENTIUS ■ (AD 311) had a large arena divided by a central spinal wall. Stalls from which chariots started still recognizable.

Tombs

Since Roman law prohibited burial within city limits, tombs were generally placed along the main roads out of town. The most magnificent were mausolea, derived from Etruscan tumuli. In 2nd c AD temple-shaped tombs, usually in brick, became more popular.

The MAUSOLEUM OF HADRIAN (*c.* AD 125), greatly tampered with over the centuries and now the Castle of S Angelo, originally had a square podium surmounted by a drum. On the roof was a garden containing a cylindrical tower with a chariot on top. Tomb chamber was at heart of building; reached by a spiralling passage from beneath.

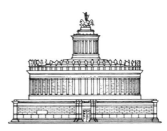

Mausoleum of Hadrian:
Conjectural restoration

Among other examples are the monumental TOMB OF CAECILIA METELLA (*c.* 20 BC), on the Via Appia, featuring frieze of ox-skulls and garlands; crenellations are medieval. The temple-shaped TOMB OF ANNIA REGILLA (*c.* AD 143), near the same road, has excellent brickwork; the podium contains the sepulchre, with mortuary chapel above.

Triumphal arches

Although the earliest triumphal arches date from *c.* 200 BC, surviving examples are Augustan or later. Their function was to commemorate Imperial victories with reliefs, inscriptions and statues. Openings were either single or triple, between piers ornamented with Corinthian or Composite columns or pilasters. After the early 2nd C AD columns were often detached.

The ARCH OF TITUS (AD 81), commemorating the capture of Jerusalem, has attached Composite columns, the first known examples. The inside of the arch has a coffered upper part above relief panels showing on one side the Emperor riding in triumph, on the other the spoils of victory ◆. Above upper tier was a bronze chariot and 4 angle statues.

Arch of Titus   *Column and entablature of arch*

The white marble triple ARCH OF SEPTIMIUS SEVERUS (AD 203), in the Forum Romanum, celebrated victories against the Parthians; detached Composite columns.

The finely proportioned ARCH OF CONSTANTINE (AD 312), also triple, commemorates triumphs over Maxentius.

Triumphal columns

The marble Doric COLUMN OF TRAJAN (AD 113), 40 m high, was built in Trajan's Forum in the reign when the Empire reached its furthest extent. Spiralling low reliefs depict the war with the Dacians in about 2,500 realistic figures. Upper parts could be viewed from libraries to either side. In podium was Trajan's tomb.

The COLUMN OF MARCUS AURELIUS (AD 174) is similar to Trajan's but shorter, with larger, deeper-cut figures.

Column of Trajan: *detail of spiralling relief band*

Italy outside Rome

Rome is best known for its public architecture: private dwellings survive mainly outside the capital, the most interesting being the wealthy town houses of Pompeii and Herculaneum (preserved by volcanic ash and mud after an eruption of AD 79) and the tenement blocks (insulae) of Ostia. Ruins of villas dot the countryside, ranging from luxury retreats to modest farmhouses.

Pompeii, Herculaneum and Ostia

The early type of Pompeiian town house, exemplified by the HOUSE OF THE SURGEON (4th C BC), was grouped round a hall (atrium) whose roof sloped down from four sides to a rectangular opening, beneath which was a rain tank. The 2nd C BC saw the addition of a colonnaded court (peristyle) on the Greek model (e.g., HOUSE OF THE FAUN, 2nd C BC). Layout was more symmetrical than in Hellenistic houses. Peristyle and atrium are usually separated by main living-room (tablinum); but in the HOUSE OF THE VETTII (1st C AD) they are adjacent.

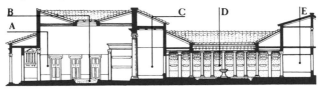

House of the Faun, Pompeii: *section*
A *Atrium;* **B** *Rain tank;* **C** *Tablinum;* **D** *Peristyle;* **E** *Reception room*

Interiors were decorated in a succession of styles, from imitation courses of masonry (HOUSE OF SALLUST, 1st C AD) to painted architectural fantasies. Mosaic floors.

Also at Pompeii: Houses of Pansa, of Diomede, of the Golden Cupids, of the Tragic Poet; basilica; Temple of Apollo; two theatres; amphitheatre; baths. Near by: Villa of the Mysteries.

The plan of HERCULANEUM was based on a Greek-inspired grid. The VILLA OF THE PAPYRI (1st C BC) is typical of Roman gentlemen's country houses: atrium exists only in modified form; large peristyle and peristylar garden. Also at Herculaneum: House of the Mosaic Atrium (1st C AD).

At OSTIA, port of Rome, pressure on space resulted in 4- and 5-storey insulae, with apartments reached by staircases from street between ground-floor shops. Balconies common. Also at Ostia: House of Amor and Psyche; warehouses.

Theatre, Ostia:
carved marble mask   **Insulae, Ostia:** *5-storied apartment block*

Other sites in Italy

HADRIAN'S VILLA, TIVOLI ♧ (c. AD 125–35), was an extravagant and ingenious complex, combining gardens, lakes, copies of Greek sculpture, buildings of many kinds, elegant colonnades. Also at Tivoli: TEMPLE OF VESTA (early 1st C BC), with ox-head frieze (see p 34).

Other sites: Verona (theatre, amphitheatre), Aosta (theatre).

The far-flung colonies

Roman towns in the distant provinces, linked by a vast network of roads, had a forum as in Italy and were often planned on a rectilinear grid like Hellenistic towns but with a greater emphasis on the major axes.

France and Germany

The MAISON CARRÉE, NÎMES (16 BC), is the best preserved Roman temple in the classic Augustan pseudoperipteral style. Corinthian Order; early example of a modillioned cornice ◆. Podium has Greek-style crepidoma. Temple originally stood in colonnaded court.

Maison Carrée, Nîmes

The TEMPLE OF DIANA, NÎMES (c. AD 130) is actually a barrel-vaulted staircase hall which led to some thermae. Nîmes also boasts an amphitheatre and the PONT DU GARD ♧ (c. AD 14), a stunning aqueduct bridge built of large stones using mortar only on upper part.

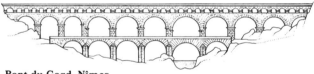

Pont du Gard, Nîmes

Also in France: amphitheatre and theatre, Arles; triumphal arch and theatre (fine scaena frons), Orange.

The PORTA NIGRA, TRIER, Germany (c. AD 300) is a double-arched defensive gateway. Also at Trier: baths; basilica.

Yugoslavia

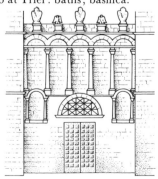

The fortified PALACE OF DIOCLETIAN, SPLIT (c. AD 300), built on the Adriatic coast at a time of Imperial insecurity, was based on the rectilinear plan of a military camp. Imperial apartments were on seaward side, behind temple to Jupiter and octagonal mausoleum with ingeniously constructed dome. Palace has colonnades whose arches spring directly from columns ◆, adumbrating Byzantine construction.

Palace of Diocletian, Split: N *gate*

Britain
The GREAT BATH, BATH (1st C AD), one of three served by a
natural hot spring, was originally open but later covered
by a barrel vault. Doric portico is modern addition.

Other sites: Fishbourne, Sussex (fine 1st-c villa); St Albans,
Hertfordshire (only Roman theatre in UK); Chedworth,
Gloucestershire (villa); Hadrian's Wall, Northumbria (best-
preserved forts at Chesters, Housesteads and Vindolanda).

The eastern Mediterranean
The unusually extensive Roman sacred site at BAALBEK
(ancient Heliopolis), the Lebanon, stands on a raised platform.
The dipteral TEMPLE OF JUPITER (AD 10–249) faced a
colonnaded court, approached via 6-sided forecourt.

Temple of Jupiter, Baalbek:
detail of entablature

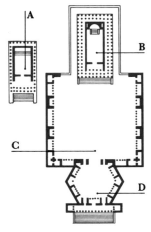

Just to the E is the better-
preserved TEMPLE OF BACCHUS
(2nd C BC); ornate interior
with giant Corinthian half-
columns, each on pedestal
between double tiers of niches.
At inner end of cella a flight
of steps led to sanctuary.

Near by is TEMPLE OF VENUS
(AD 273), baroquely designed
on a complex circular plan.

Baalbek: *the sacred site*
A *Temple of Bacchus;* **B** *Temple of
Jupiter;* **C** *Court;* **D** *Forecourt*

The Roman city of PALMYRA, Syria, has colonnaded
streets; columns have mid-way brackets for statues, a feature
peculiar to the E. The TEMPLE OF BEL (c. AD 1) has triangular
crenellations on entablature (Mesopotamian influence).

At PETRA ♥, Jordan, are over 750 rock-cut tombs.

North Africa
TIMGAD ♥, Algeria (founded
c. AD 100), is a fine example
of Roman town planning;
forum, hill-cut theatre,
library, numerous thermae
and triumphal arch.

The harbour town of LEPCIS
MAGNA, Libya, dating from
the Augustan age, has a
market (9–8 BC) with two
circular halls. A magnificent
second forum was added by
Severus, with basilica at NE
end (c. AD 215).

THEATRE, SABRATAH, Libya
(c. 200 AD), is very fine.

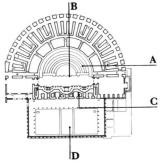

Theatre, Sabratah: *plan*
A *Tiered seating;* **B** *Orchestra;*
C *Scaena frons;* **D** *Colonnaded court*

SOUTH ASIA
HINDU, BUDDHIST AND JAIN STYLES

The scattered regions of s Asia, from Afghanistan to
Indonesia, are historically linked by the permeation from India
of Hinduism and Buddhism, religions whose far-reaching
impact over the centuries is reflected in a proliferation of
beautiful shrines.

The first civilization of India, which emerged in the Indus
valley *c.* 2300 BC, was defeated in the 18th C BC by an
invasion of Aryans from the NW. The Aryans believed in the
Vedic gods, a pantheon of mainly masculine forces worshipped
without resort to images. The fusion of this religion with that
of the native Dravidians, teeming with images and fertility
symbols, gave rise in the centuries immediately before the
Christian era to Hinduism, with its sacred trinity comprising
Vishnu (the preserver), Shiva (the destroyer) and Brahma (soul
and origin of the universe). Preserving the contradictions of
its origins, Hinduism urged release (moksha) from the world
of the senses while attaching great importance to fertility and
eroticism, as embodied in the sculptural embracing couples
(mithunas) that often adorn sacred architecture.

Alongside Hinduism a rigorous caste hierarchy developed,
conferring most power upon the brahmins (hereditary priests).
From the kshatriya (warrior) and vaishya (mercantile) castes
came many patrons and builders of temples, while the shudras
(peasant descendants of the conquered forest peoples) were in
some communities denied entrance to temple enclosures.

Relief showing Vishnu, *from Deogarh*

Buddha sculpture, *from Sarnath*

In 563 BC Siddhartha Gautama was born into the warrior
class. Later to be known as the Buddha ("Enlightened One"),
he inspired a movement which, though accepting some of the
basic concepts of Hinduism, differed from it in concentrating on
ethics as a means of salvation (nirvana) and in opposing the
privileged status of the brahmins. Under the rule of Ashoka
(*c.* 273–232 BC), whose domain included most of India,
Buddhism was introduced into Sri Lanka. Another sect which
rebelled against the caste system was Jainism (from 6th C BC),
which taught a modified version of the transmigration of
souls, with an obsessive emphasis on non-violence.

By the end of the 12th C, well after Indian civilization had
taken root in SE Asia, N India had come under the control of
the Muslims, who had long made periodic raids.

Architectural traditions

Hinduism lacked the congregational aspect of Buddhism and its temples were usually designed accordingly, in "styles" that reflected regional traditions. A Hindu temple was an object of worship in itself and part of the ritual was to walk round it. In keeping with this function its surfaces were generally covered with a jungle-like profusion of reliefs. Deities were often represented with multiple arms, to emphasize their superhuman qualities and enable them to carry numerous symbols. Jain shrines, found only in India, often took decorative elaboration to extremes, but their basic architectural forms are indistinguishable from those of Hinduism.

The focus of the Buddhist ritual, in which circumambulation (pradakshina) also played a major role, was the stupa: a domical mound symbolizing the universe. This derived from burial tumuli and was erected to house relics or commemorate a sacred site. In India small stupas were also placed at the apse end of prayer halls (chaitya halls), which were usually attached to monasteries (viharas).

In SE Asia, where stone-carving reached a pinnacle of achievement, the idea of a religious building as a cosmological diagram, especially of the world-mountain Meru, took deep root and led to vast, multi-peaked temple complexes such as Angkor Wat in Cambodia, in the Khmer style.

Timber, plaster and mud were commonly used for temples but stone, which was used without mortar, was regarded as the most sacred of building materials. Some areas had a tradition of brick architecture.

Types of stupa

The offshoots of the Indian stupa ranged from the bell-shaped dagabas of Sri Lanka to the chambered temple-stupas of Burma, in which the plinth was hollowed out for worship on the analogy of the hill-side cave.

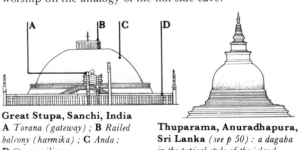

Great Stupa, Sanchi, India
A *Torana (gateway)* ; **B** *Railed balcony (harmika)* ; **C** *Anda* ; **D** *Stone railing*

Thuparama, Anuradhapura, Sri Lanka *(see p 50) : a dagaba in the typical style of the island*

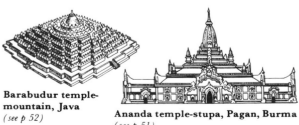

Barabudur temple-mountain, Java
(see p 52)

Ananda temple-stupa, Pagan, Burma
(see p 51)

India and Pakistan

Much of the surviving architecture of India from before the end of the 8th c BC is hewn out of rock and displays dazzling sculptural skill; some details (e.g., carved latticework on façades) were inspired by bamboo and timber prototypes. Free-standing Hindu temples were built in a variety of local styles. Most of those in the N were destroyed by Muslims.

Cave retreats
In the early 3rd c BC cave retreats were created by Ashoka for the Ajivika sect, imitating timber structures exactly. The finest, in the Barabar Hills, are the SUDAMA and LOMAS RISHI caves. The façade of the latter anticipates the horseshoe-shaped windows of chaitya halls.

Lomas Rishi cave: *detail*

Buddhist stupas
The larger, autonomous kind of stupa was surrounded by a processional path and stone railings with 4 decorated gateways (toranas) at cardinal points. The dome (anda) was surmounted by a sacred umbrella emblem.

Sanchi: *detail of N torana*

The finest example is the GREAT STUPA, SANCHI (2nd c BC-1st c AD). Toranas ◆ are carved with scenes from life of Buddha in a manner suggestive of wood-carving. Above solid brick anda, originally stone-faced, is a three-tiered stone umbrella, whose railed enclosure (harmika) derives from an old tradition of fencing off a sacred tree. (See p 45.)

Chaitya halls
Chaitya halls were originally of bamboo and thatch but all surviving examples are rock-cut. An excavated assembly hall, with colonnades forming aisles, housed a stupa in round apse at far end. Roofs were semicircular in section and in the early period (e.g., at BHAJA, 2nd c BC) featured curved stone-cut ribs. Façades ornately carved and pierced by large peaked horseshoe window.

The CHAITYA HALL, KARLI (1st c BC–2nd c AD), has teak ribs set in rock ceiling. Columns have elaborate capitals.

Mithuna couple, Karli

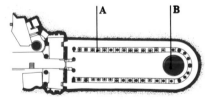

Chaitya hall, Karli: *plan*
A *Colonnade* ; B *Stupa*

Buddhist viharas

The vihara (monastic retreat) was usually a rectangular
courtyard surrounded by verandahs giving access to dormitory
cells. Large complex at NALANDA 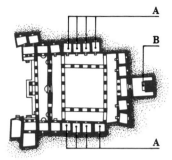, Bengal, last bastion of
Indian Buddhism (flourished 7th–8th c AD). Farther s all
extant viharas are rock-cut.

The caves at AJANTA,
famous for lyrical wall
paintings, are mostly viharas.
At rear of the colonnaded
hall of CAVE 1 is a chamber
containing a Buddha statue.
All interior surfaces were
highly decorated: surviving
fragments depict painted
Bodhisattvas (Buddhas-
before-Enlightenment) as
well as animals and narrative
scenes. Rock-hewn chaitya
halls near by; CAVE 19 (1st c
AD) has ornate façade and
stupa with canopy spire.

Cave 1, Ajanta: *plan*
A *Dormitory cells;* **B** *Buddha statue*

Hindu temples

Some of oldest surviving free-standing Hindu temples were
built at AIHOLE during Gupta era (*c.* AD 320–650) by the
Chalukyan rulers. Most mature temples are in either Northern
style or Southern Dravidian style.

In N Indian temples a
massive spire (shikhara) with
thick, curved walls dominates
small shrine at base. From
10th c lower-roofed assembly
hall (jagamohan) was often
added, while from 11th c a
dancing hall (nat mandir) was
common. The Dravidian
shikhara is often a pyramid of
concentric squares forming a
mandala, a sacred diagram of
cosmos. Dravidian temples of
12th–17th c were a maze of
corridors, courtyards and
pillared halls, with huge
entrance gates (gopurams).

Dravidian style: *mock temple at
Mamallapuram (see p 49)*

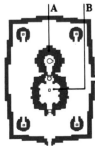

Northern style: *Brahmeshvara Temple, Bhuvaneshvar (elevation and plan)*
A *Shikhara;* **B** *Jagamohan*

The Northern temple style

The climax of the Northern style occurred at Bhuvaneshvar and Konarak in Orissa and Khajuraho in central India. Orissan decoration is elaborate, with stone latticework, and chaitya window hoods framing sculptured figures. Corbelled vaulting; pillars rare.

At BHUVANESHVAR 500 shrines remain from 7,000 grouped around a sacred lake. The PARASHURAMESHVARA TEMPLE (*c.* 750 AD) has the massive beehive-shaped spire, but it was 200 years before typical pyramid-roofed jagamohan occurred. The great LINGARAJA TEMPLE (*c.* 1000) has dancing hall; shikhara incorporates miniature reproductions of itself in massive vertical ribs. Unfinished RAJARANI TEMPLE (*c.* 1000) has unparallelled foliate reliefs ◆; smaller MUKTESHVARA TEMPLE (*c.* 975) a superb gateway.

Brahmeshvara Temple, Bhuvaneshvar: *detail of sanctuary*   **Surya Temple, Konarak:** *carved wheel of sun-god's chariot*

The masterpiece of the Orissan style is the ruin of the unfinished SURYA TEMPLE (Black Pagoda), KONARAK (mid 13th C), conceived as image of sun-god's chariot. Fine musician sculptures on roof of jagamohan, huge carved wheels on plinths, and wealth of erotic carving ◆, possibly reflecting activities of a Tantric cult.

KHAJURAHO has some 20 temples, more compact than those in Orissa and usually raised on high terrace, often with subsidiary shrines at each corner. Interior ambulatories illuminated by means of balconies. Roofs are a complex cluster of spires, representing world-mountain Meru (but with a more vertical emphasis than in Cambodian and Javanese temple-mountains). The KANDARIYA MAHADEO TEMPLE (*c.* 1000), dedicated to Shiva, is the most imposing.

Kandariya Mahadeo Temple, Khajuraho: *side elevation and detail*

Other N Indian Hindu temples include an unusual group at GWALIOR. The TELIKA MANDIR (9th C) has curious roof with interlocking horseshoe arch motifs.

Early Southern temples
The most stunning Indian rock-cut temple is the double-storied KAILASANATH TEMPLE, ELLURA (8th C), dedicated to Shiva. It is sculptured wholly out of rock from above, complete with interior chambers, subsidiary shrines and gopuram. Base has a frieze of carved elephants who carry temple on their backs and symbolize monsoons as well as indomitable strength. Pilastered walls, pyramidal roof and wide overhanging eaves are typically Dravidian. Detached shrine contains image of Shiva's mount, the bull Nandi. Also at Ellura: extensive caves (7th–8th C).

Kailasanath Temple, Ellura

In the 7th C a series of 5 small imitation temples (raths: literally "chariots") was carved out of granite at MAMALLAPURAM, copying various wooden structures, including chaitya halls and a vihara. Fine sculptures on walls. (See p 47.) Near by is the pyramidal SHORE TEMPLE, (early 8th C), the earliest-known structural stone temple in s India.

Mamallapuram: *roof of rath*

The beautiful RAJRAJESHVARA TEMPLE, TANJORE (c. 1000), built in a walled enclosure, has a tall, elegant, pyramid-like shikhara 58 m high, topped, in contrast, by a monolithic dome.

Madura: *detail of pillars*

Later Southern temples
The later Southern style reaches a glorious climax in temple city at MADURA (17th C); a maze of courtyards and corridors, with rows of columns in form of leaping animals. Huge barrel-roofed gopurams carry incredible profusion of sculpture. Similar complex at SHRIRANGAM is laid out N–S instead of E–W.

The central Deccan
Temples of the 11th–14th C in the central Deccan (e.g., KESAVA TEMPLE, SOMNATHPUR) were characterized by a multiplicity of projections, producing a complex star-shaped plan. A greenish-grey local stone was favoured, suited to deep detailed carving. Other examples include a group of 12th-C temples at BELLUR.

Jain temples
After *c.* 1000 Jain temples in
w India developed their own
character, with features such
as assembly halls with
octagonal ceilings supported
on pillars over a square floor
plan. Stone carving was
extravagantly ornate but
aesthetically sterile. Jain
extravagance is typified at
MOUNT ABU in Rajputana. The
DILWARA and TEJPAL
TEMPLES (11th and 13th c) are
both built in white marble.
Domed halls have fancifully
carved columns with leaping
brackets.

Tejpal Temple: *detail of column*

Sri Lanka

Stone and brick architecture on the island dates from the 3rd
c BC, when Buddhism was introduced. The Indian stupa
became the dagaba ("relic womb"): a solid, white-plastered
brick dome rising from a threefold circular base and crowned
by a ringed spire. Many of these dominated ancient capital
Anuradhapura. The new capital Polonnaruwa (founded late
8th c) was richly developed in 12th c.

Anuradhapura: *door guardian*

The earliest architecture
The THUPARAMA DAGABA,
ANURADHAPURA (mid 3rd c
BC), originally conical, was
later rebuilt to inverted-bell
shape (see p 45). Pillars with
typically ornate capitals
supported outer envelope.
   The RUVANVELI DAGABA,
ANURADHAPURA (2nd c BC)
was originally 92 m high;
much restored. Relics were
embedded in small chamber
within the solid dome.

Polonnaruwa
In Great Quadrangle of
lakeside POLONNARUWA ♧ is
the WATA-DA-GE (circular relic
house; 12th c). A podium
carved with lions and dwarfs
carries a round brick shrine
enclosing dagaba. Shrine
achieves fine balance between
plain and decorated surfaces;
once roofed but only pillars
remain. Near by are HATA-
DA-GE, a temple decorated
with great restraint, and the
LATA MANDAPA, notable for its
graceful curling lotus columns.
City abandoned 1290.

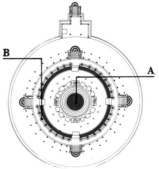

Wata-da-ge, Polonnaruwa: *plan*
A *Dagaba;* **B** *Carved podium*

Nepal, Tibet and Burma

Buddhist styles flourished in Tibet until the 9th c AD but continued in Nepal centuries longer. Some of the finest buildings in Burma are at Pagan, which during its ascendancy boasted some 5,000 sacred structures, mainly Buddhist.

Nepal and Tibet

Stupas in NEPAL had a box-like element with a huge eye painted or inlaid on each side: the all-seeing Buddha. Above was stepped pyramid topped by umbrella finial. Examples are the BODNATH and SWAYAMBHUNATH STUPAS, KATMANDU. The ancient capital BHATGAON is rich in temples.

The most dramatic buildings of TIBET are the monastery complexes which resemble towering hill-top fortresses; walls are sloped, doors and windows narrow towards top. An impressive example is the POTALA "PALACE", LHASA ♣ (17th c).

Bodnath Stupa, Katmandu: *crown of dome*

Golden Gate, Bhatgaon: *carved detail*

Burma

The Burmese stupa—a huge sacred mountain—had a bell-shaped dome with a tall, finely tapering spire. On top of terraced platform was a miniature stupa at each corner. The MINGALAZEDI STUPA, PAGAN (1274) is typical, but more striking is the ANANDA TEMPLE (late 11th c); white brick with gold pinnacles (see p 45). Inside are two narrow concentric corridors, and 4 Buddha statues round the solid central base of the shikhara-like superstructure.

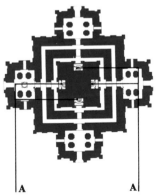

Ananda Temple, Pagan: *plan*
A *Buddha statues*

Java

In Java in the early 8th–10th c, temples drawing upon both s Indian Hindu styles and newly assimilated Buddhist forms, such as the stupa, were built on the central plains. These shrines—the architectural treasures of Indonesia—are all without columns or pillars and sometimes incorporate grotesque masks carved over windows or niches. The most exciting work is the great temple-mountain at Barabudur.

Barabudur

A mound of earth clothed in stone, without mortar, BARABUDUR ♻ (*c*. 800) served as a sacred diagram of the world-mountain and symbolized Buddhist path to Enlightenment. Five square walled terraces rise concentrically, each bearing beautifully carved scenes of life of Buddha ◆. Above are three circular terraces on which stand 72 latticed stone stupas housing Buddhas. Enclosed stupa at apex.

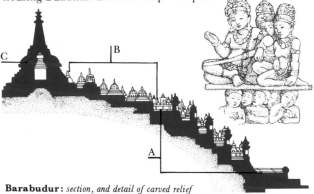

Barabudur: *section, and detail of carved relief*
A *Square terraces;* **B** *Circular terraces;* **C** *Crowning stupa*

Other Javanese shrines

One of island's finest single-celled temples is CHANDI MENDUT (*c*. 800). Other temples: Loro Jongrang, Prambanan (*c*. 900); Chandi Sewa (both ruined).

Cambodia: the Khmer style

The Khmer civilization dominated Cambodia from the 7th to 13th c, the last of which was the classical age of Khmer art. From the 9th c evolved the worship of the god-king, or Deva-Raja, which fostered the temple-cities of Angkor: mountainous terraced pyramids laid out in a network of canals and lakes.

Angkor Wat

ANGKOR WAT (12th c), the world's largest temple, was built as both royal and divine monument and sepulchre. Originally dedicated to Vishnu, later used by Buddhists. Symbol of world-mountain. Superb reliefs. Towers bulge like pine-cones over vast system of galleries. Near by: Angkor Thom.

Angkor Wat: *details of reliefs*

CHINA AND JAPAN
TRADITIONAL WOODEN ARCHITECTURE

Judged solely by existing remains, an architectural history of China would give undue prominence, in the early Buddhist period, to brick and stone pagodas, as little is left from the stronger tradition of building in wood. Some missing pieces of the puzzle are provided by Japanese buildings that copied Chinese styles.

China

Ancient China developed a singular, intensely conservative culture, which at no point sought to enshrine itself in monumental architecture to guarantee its survival. Buildings were mainly wooden and not intended to last, continuity lying instead in the indelible, all-embracing body of beliefs by which architecture was regulated.

The most important of these ideas was Confucianism. A state official in the Zhou dynasty, Confucius (*c.* 551–479 BC) taught the ethical importance of ritual (li) in public and private life. More mystical was Daoism, inspired by Laozi, a contemporary of Confucius, but not crystallized into a religion until the 2nd c AD. It taught that the Dao (way of self-realization) was through patience, simplicity and harmony with nature. Confucianism, with its rigid and hierarchical conception of society, influenced the axial layout of towns, houses, temples and palaces, while Daoism inspired the design of gardens, which were tightly packed with an informal arrangement of pavilions, walkways and lakes.

Brick relief showing the Immortals: *from a garden, Shanghai*

After the opening up of trade routes, Buddhism reached China in the 2nd c BC. Although rock-cut temples were created in the 4th–5th c AD, it was the early decades of the 6th c that witnessed the first great wave of Buddhist temples and pagodas.

Few sacred and no domestic buildings date from before the Ming dynasty (1368–1644), but excavations in the Shang dynasty capitals of Zhengzhou and Anyang in Henan (both 2nd MIL BC) reveal features which we know remained constant. Among these are the raising of buildings on rammed-earth platforms, the placing of entrances in the eaves façade rather than at the gable end, and above all a construction method based on a system of wooden posts and beams, with light, non-supporting walls.

53

Roofs, posts and beams

The most distinctive feature of a Chinese building was its roof. Instead of the rigid triangular frame of roofs in the West, the Chinese roof was supported on a tier system of diminishing beams directing the thrust vertically downwards through the posts. Each main beam carried a pair of short vertical members supporting the beam above as well as the purlins on which the rafters rested. Spans could be widened by increasing the number of tiers: the problem of cluttering the interior with the extra posts required for this was solved by extending the area of support given by each.

Hipped roof

Half-hipped roof

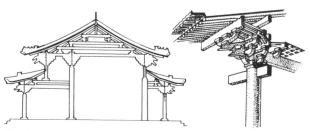

Section of hall, *showing support system*

Bracket cluster

Column bases, *in stone and bronze*

Wide overhanging eaves were carried on multi-tiered bracket clusters (dougong) whose decorative aspects made up for the absence of capitals. From the 8th c eaves were taken out even farther by additional brackets on slanting arms. Rafters were overlaid with battens and then a layer of clay on which tiles were placed. Posts generally stood on stone or brick plinths to protect them from the damp. The flexibility of the beam system allowed roofs to be dramatically angled or curved.

Although roof timbers were meant to be visible, important buildings had decorative ceilings. Another indication of rank was roof form–hipped (noblest style), half-hipped, pyramidal or gabled. In s China roof corners were characteristically upturned.

Ornament
Roof ridges and hips were embellished with acroteria, often
featuring dragon motifs. Bold colours were used, determined by
social rank. In the grandest buildings roofs of yellow or blue
are often offset by red pillars and intricate polychrome
paintwork under the eaves. Imperial buildings had their
coffered ceilings decorated to symbolize the dome of Heaven.
Eaves tiles terminated in decoratively treated roundels.

Decorated eaves, *with name board*

Buddhist architecture
Early Buddhist temples took over from palaces the standard
plan of a rectangular enclosure surrounded by galleries and
containing a series of s-facing buildings arranged axially, with
subsidiary structures to the E and W. To this scheme one or
more pagodas were added. Behind main image-hall was a hall
of meditation with library on upper storey. As well as central
altar furnished with images, the image-hall often housed a
secondary altar dedicated to Guanyin, the Buddhist Goddess of
Mercy.
  The main hall of the FOGUANG TEMPLE, WUTAI MOUNTAIN
(*c.* AD 857), in Shanxi, grandly simple in design though with
richly carved details, exemplifies the style of the Tang
dynasty (AD 618–907). Alternating main and subsidiary
bracket clusters, supporting eaves overhang of 4.25 m, create
a vigorous rhythm over the 7-bay façade.

 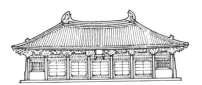

Dule Temple: *Guanyin Hall*   **Foguang Temple:** *main hall*

  The DULE TEMPLE, JIXIAN, in Hebei, has two buildings
dating from the barbarian dynasty of the Liao, who ruled N
China from 907 to 1125. One, the GUANYIN HALL (984), has
two upper stories with a central well to accommodate the
giant icon (15 m high). Gatehouse has fine roof ornamentation.
  Buildings of the Song dynasty (960–1279) were more
intimately scaled than those of the Tang, though often lofty.
Décor became richly polychromatic, with glazed roof and floor
tiles. The LONGXING TEMPLE, ZHENGDINGXIAN, in W Hobei, has
well-preserved examples, including library (11th c) and
pavilion dedicated to the future Buddha (10th c). In keeping

55

with growing preference for elaborate decoration, the CHAPEL OF THE FIRST PATRIARCH, SHAOLIN TEMPLE, MOUNT SONG (1125), in Henan, has carved stone pillars.

Architecture of the Ming period was characterized by a more horizontal emphasis, by shrunken, largely ornamental bracket clusters and by a continued reliance on Song styles. An example is the ZHIHUA TEMPLE, PEKING (c. 1444).

Pagodas

Pagodas were originally attached to Buddhist monasteries and served a votive or reliquary purpose. Shape evolved from reaction of Indian stupa and shikhara upon Chinese multi-storied belvedere (lou). Generally of wood, although brick and stone were also used from 6th c.

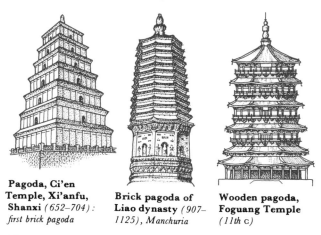

Pagoda, Ci'en Temple, Xi'anfu, Shanxi *(652–704):* *first brick pagoda*

Brick pagoda of Liao dynasty *(907–1125), Manchuria*

Wooden pagoda, Foguang Temple *(11th c)*

The Forbidden City, Peking

The FORBIDDEN CITY, a walled and moated mile-long rectangle, was the Imperial palace of the Ming dynasty after capital moved to Peking c. 1409. Substantial 17th-c reworking did little to alter original appearance and axial, s-facing layout. Entrance through double-roofed, 5-towered WUMEN (Meridian Gate). Within, on a marble platform, is a splendid ensemble of halls: TAIHEDIAN (Hall of Supreme Harmony), ZHONGEDIAN (Hall of Middle Harmony) and BAOHEDIAN (Hall of Protective Harmony), all 17th c. Of 5 marble bridges crossing Golden River, centre one was reserved for Emperor.

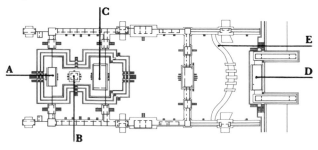

Forbidden City, Peking: *plan*
A *Baohedian;* **B** *Zhongedian;* **C** *Taihedian;* **D** *Wumen;* **E** *Golden River*

Buildings of the Forbidden City show Ming liking for long, low façades. Colour is used to spectacular effect: white marble, red woodwork, polychrome eaves and gently curved roofs in the Imperial yellow. To the N are the more intimately planned Imperial residences.

Bronze lion sculpture

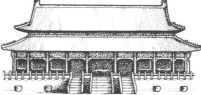

Taihedian, Forbidden City

The Temple of Heaven

To s of Imperial City, Peking, on triple marble platform, stands the circular TEMPLE OF HEAVEN (1420, rebuilt 18th C); triple roof of blue tiles. At near-by ALTAR OF HEAVEN, a mound of three concentric terraces in white marble, the Emperor gave offerings to nature deities revered by Confucian state. Cloud motifs and winged appendages on marble ceremonial gateways.

Temple of Heaven

To E, within the same double-walled park, is the PALACE OF PURIFICATION, an exquisite blue-roofed moated retreat where the Emperor fasted in preparation for ritual.

Bailou

Bailou, derived from Indian toranas, are multiple arches used as ceremonial entrances to temples or tombs, or occasionally spanning a street. There is a fine 5-arched example in white marble with blue tiles at the entrance to the WAY OF THE SPIRITS leading to the Ming tombs NW of Peking.

Bailou, Way of the Spirits, *Ming Tombs, Peking*

Chinese gardens

Gardens (e.g., SUMMER PALACE ✿, NW of Peking) were well furnished with pavilions for contemplation, galleries, bridges, decorative latticework and walls with interestingly shaped doorways and windows.

Japan

Japan's abundant forests combined with the ever-present threat of earthquakes and typhoons to produce a vigorous tradition of wooden architecture. Heavy rains and extreme heat led to low, wide eaves, and for further weather-proofing buildings were raised on open wooden platforms.

Among early native forms, the distinctive thatched shrine evolved by followers of the Shinto religion has survived owing to regular rebuilding. Equally important was the Chinese trabeated style brought over from the early 7th c by Chinese and Korean craftsmen to satisfy the growing demand for Buddhist temples.

During the Asuka (AD 538–645) and Nara (AD 710–84) periods, Chinese culture was an overwhelming influence. Buddhism became the state religion in the mid 8th c when Emperor Shomu commissioned a temple in each province and founded the great Todai-ji (ji means temple) in Nara, a city modelled on the Chinese Tang dynasty capital of Changan.

With the development of a feudal system in Japan the nobility came to rule in the name of the Emperor, now a mere figurehead. After civil wars in the 12th c, power was wrested by the samurai, the warrior class, who were drawn towards Zen Buddhism, an ascetic cult derived from China. The Zen emphasis on austerity in ritual corresponded to a profound respect for natural simplicity embedded in the Japanese character. This found expression in untreated architectural exteriors, in landscape gardening, and in the tea ceremony, from which all social division was banished.

Altar decoration, *Chūson-ji: the peacock became a Buddhist symbol*

The trabeated style

Post-and-beam architecture, at first imitated meticulously from Chinese models, acquired a unique character by virtue of superior woodworking skills, an increasing fondness for asymmetrical layout and a refined airiness of design. Spaces between timber columns were often filled with doors or windows extending from floor almost to ceiling. Decoration was generally restrained.

Decorated eaves, *Hoo-do, Byodō-in*   **Eaves bracket**

Shintō shrines

One of the most venerated types of shrine was a raised hut-like structure with verandah, steep gabled roof with curious round timbers on ridge, and gable-end doorway set to one side of an axial pillar. Best example is the IZUMO SHRINE, SE of Tōkyō, periodically rebuilt since 5th c AD; present structure 18th c. Chinese-style curved roof.

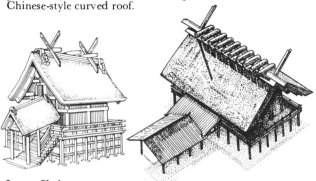

Izumo Shrine,
with typical thatched roof and crossed poles   **Inner Shrine, Ise,** *with entrance in long façade*

The famous INNER SHRINE, ISE, in Mie Prefecture, was dedicated to the sun goddess. Built in untreated white cypress in 5th–6th c style; reconstructed every 20 years.

The ITSUKUSHIMA SHRINE ✛, in Hiroshima Prefecture, integrates sea into arrangement of walkways, platforms, halls. Typical symbolic gate (torii) rises out of water.

Buddhist architecture

The oldest form of Japanese Buddhist monastery was a sacred enclosure in the Chinese style with an image-hall (kondō) and one or more pagodas. From the 9th c the Tendai and Shingon sects built mountain monasteries on a less symmetrical plan. After the emergence in the 10th–11th c of a movement based on the Amida Buddha, many nobles created temples imitating the Amida's Western paradise.

The 7th-c structures of HŌRYU-JI, NARA ✛, are the world's oldest surviving wooden buildings. The layout, with pagoda and hall side by side, abandoned Chinese axial symmetry. Kondō one-storied despite double roof. Gatehouse (chū-mon) is closest to original 7th-c state. Lecture hall (kōdō) 10th c. Elegant 5-storey pagoda houses sacred relic.

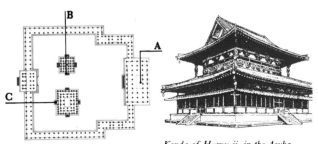

Horyu-ji, Nara
A *Kōdō;* **B** *Pagoda;* **C** *Kondō*

Kondo of Horyu-ji, in the Asuka style. The hall was formerly part of a monastery destroyed in 670

Nara also boasts the vast TŌDAI-JI (founded 745), built to rival Chinese Tang temples. GREAT BUDDHA HALL is world's largest wooden structure, although now only two-thirds of original size. Tiled roof has upswept eaves. Great double s gate, the NANDAIMON, was built late 12th c in forceful s China idiom misleadingly called the "Indian style". Also at Tōdai-ji: HOKKEDŌ CHAPEL (733), with coffered ceiling ◆.

Great Buddha Hall, Todai-ji   **Pagoda, Daigo-ji**

All but one of extant early pagodas are 5-storied. The exception (8th c) is at YAKUSHI-JI, NARA. Pagoda at DAIGO-JI (10th c), Kyoto, based on Tang predecessor.

At TOSHODAI-JI, near Nara, the kondō (late 8th c) is similar in scale and form to main hall at Foguang Temple, China (see p 55). Present roof, steeper than original, follows distinctively Japanese technique of concealing support system between inner and outer skin.

The HOO-DO ♙ (Phoenix Hall) of the BYODO-IN (11th c), Uji, SE of Kyoto, is a representation of Amida Buddha's paradise, named after bird-like plan. Façade, fronting lake, is an elegant miniature of a Chinese Tang palace. Interior is rich in metal- and lacquer-work and mother-of-pearl.

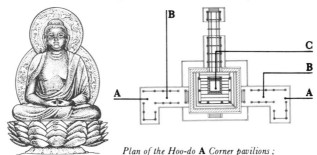

Plan of the Hoo-do **A** *Corner pavilions ;*
B *Connecting galleries ;* **C** *Central pavilion*

Hoo-do, Byodo-in:
Amida Buddha statue

Front elevation of the Hoo-do

Secular architecture

In Kyōto in the 9th C AD an elaborate kind of aristocratic house developed, named the shinden (literally "sleeping palace") style. The shinden, a lakeside building with latticed doors instead of exterior walls, was connected to subsidiary structures by corridors planned in relation to a series of artificial landscapes.

In the Kamakura period (1185–1337) the influential buke ("warrior") style was favoured by the rising samurai class. Main hall divided into rooms by sliding paper-covered partitions (fusuma). Outer walls had paper-covered lattice panels (shōji); floors covered with straw mats (tatami). When the buke style was used by priests, an important feature was the writing room (shoin), with shelves and an alcove (tokonoma). After adoption by wealthy warriors, shoin became larger and gave name to whole style. A simplified version was the informal sukiya (pavilion) style.

The Kinkaku-ji

The famous 14th-C KINKAKU-JI (Temple of the Golden Pavilion), KYŌTO ✪, reconstructed in 1955, owes a debt to the shinden style. However, chapel on uppermost of three stories is influenced by more complex "Chinese style" favoured by Zen Buddhism. Pavilion is set in lake, and seems to float over it gracefully.

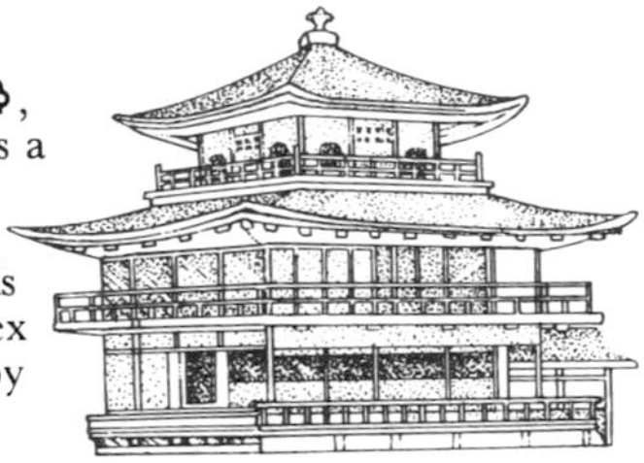

Kinkaku-ji

The Katsura Palace

The most splendid Japanese country house is the KATSURA PALACE, KYŌTO ✪ (early 17th C). Its contrived simplicity reflects the spirit of the tea ceremony. Wood is left plain, sometimes even retaining its bark. Ko-shoin (entrance block) in shoin style; Chū-shoin (middle block) and Shin-goten (rear block) in sukiya style. Sublimely beautiful garden.

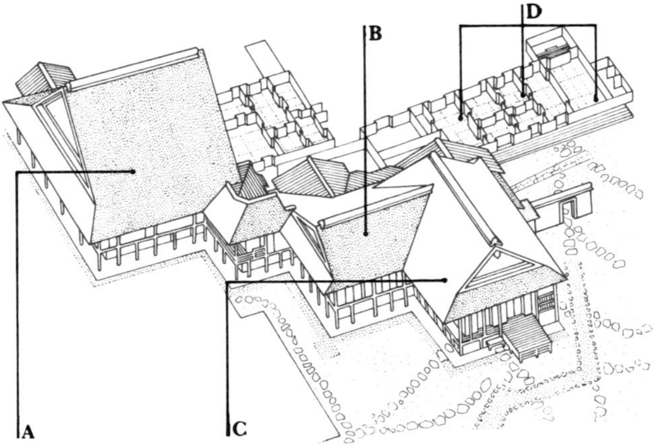

Katsura Palace, Kyōto: *the main buildings*
A *Shin-goten;* **B** *Chū-shoin;* **C** *Ko-shoin;* **D** *Subsidiary rooms*

Teahouses

The tea ceremony, an expression of Zen Buddhism, took place in a thatched teahouse (chaseki) inspired by the farmer's cottage. Ornament was usually limited to flowers or paintings displayed in tokonoma for contemplation. Teahouses were separate buildings from 16th c. The MATSUSHITA-AN TEAHOUSE, KYŌTO, dates from this period, as does the SHŌKIN-TEI, KATSURA.

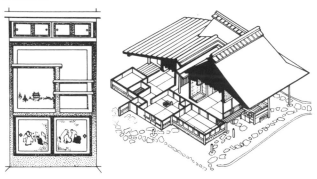

Tearoom, Daitoku-ji, Kyōto: *interior detail*   **Shōkin-tei, Katsura:** *cutaway view*

Castles

The only large stone buildings of Japan are the castles of the late 16th–early 17th c. White brick walls of keep and subsidiary donjons rose in up to 5 stories, each with Chinese-style upturned eaves, above massive plinths of polygonal stone blocks. Interiors, in shoin style, were sometimes palatial. Finest extant stronghold is HIMEJI CASTLE (late 16th c), Hyōgo Prefecture. Main 5-storey keep connected to three smaller keeps by fortified covered corridors. Earliest keep at MARUOKA CASTLE (1576). NIJŌ CASTLE (1603), a fortified palace, was built as Kyōto residence of shogun (generalissimo) Tokugawa Ieyasu.

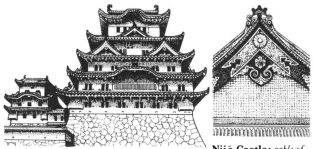

Himeji Castle: *the main keep*   **Nijō Castle:** *gable of waiting-hall*

Nikkō

The Edo period (1603–1868) was an age of architectural opulence, exemplified at its most spectacular by the shrines at NIKKŌ ✿ (1634–6), centred on the TŌSHŌ-GŪ, the mausoleum of Tokugawa Ieyasu. Polychrome and gilded decoration abounds. The famous YŌMEI-MON (middle gate) is encrusted with a plethora of animal carvings.

PRE-HISPANIC AMERICA
EARLY CIVILIZATIONS OF CENTRAL AND SOUTH AMERICA

By 1200 BC the Olmecs had developed a sophisticated culture in the tropical lowlands around the Mexican Gulf. This was the first of a succession of civilizations that flourished in central America until the 16th C. Common to most of these was the building of temple-pyramids (sanctuaries on artificial mounds) for the worship of a pantheon of deities, and a sacred game played with a rubber ball in an I-shaped court.

The most creative of these peoples were the Maya of the Yucatán peninsula and adjacent uplands, who were advanced in mathematics, astronomy and the recording of time. Mayan culture collapsed unaccountably *c.* AD 1000, ushering in the age of the barbaric Aztecs, whose human sacrifices to the sun god are said to have reached an annual total of about 50,000. Like the Toltecs before them, the Aztecs also worshipped Quetzalcoatl, the Plumed Serpent. Their capital Tenochtitlán (founded *c.* 1325) was destroyed in 1521 by the Spanish conquistadors.

The civilization of the Incas emerged in Peru from *c.* AD 1200 and reached its creative climax in the 15th C. In the Cuzco Basin, a fertile pocket punctuating the desolate Andes, they sited the capital of their immense empire, which was linked by roads and bridges across the most difficult terrain.

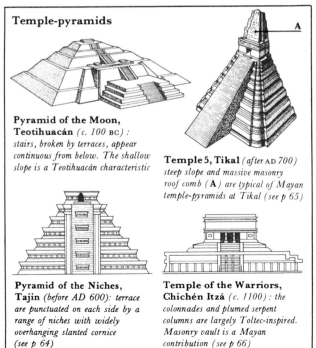

Temple-pyramids

A

Pyramid of the Moon, Teotihuacán *(c. 100 BC)*: *stairs, broken by terraces, appear continuous from below. The shallow slope is a Teotihuacán characteristic*

Temple 5, Tikal *(after AD 700) steep slope and massive masonry roof comb (**A**) are typical of Mayan temple-pyramids at Tikal (see p 65)*

Pyramid of the Niches, Tajin *(before AD 600): terrace are punctuated on each side by a range of niches with widely overhanging slanted cornice (see p 64)*

Temple of the Warriors, Chichén Itzá *(c. 1100)*: *the colonnades and plumed serpent columns are largely Toltec-inspired. Masonry vault is a Mayan contribution (see p 66)*

From Teotihuacán to the Aztecs

The sacred city of Teotihuacán (*c.* 100 BC–AD 750) became larger than Imperial Rome. Toltec architecture features columns and carved eagle, jaguar and plumed serpent motifs. Aztec buildings (few extant) were legendary in magnificence but stylistically unoriginal: their only innovation was the double temple-pyramid.

Early central Mexico

The grandest structures of TEOTIHUACAN are two stone-faced pyramids, dating from time of Christ. The PYRAMID OF THE SUN is a 5-stepped mound about 230 m square and 60 m high, upper platform originally carrying a sanctuary reached by divided stairway on w side. The terraced architecture of Teotihuacan has a distinctive profile: a vertical panel (tablero) slightly overhanging a sloped base (talud). PALACE OF QUETZALPAPÁLOTL (3rd C BC) features fine pillar reliefs ◆.

Teotihuacán: *plumed serpent head*

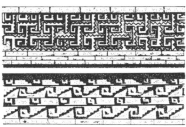

Mitla: *detail of Palace of Columns*

MITLA has palaces with patios, colonnades, large rooms, and white façades superbly decorated with repeated geometrical motifs. The PALACE OF THE COLUMNS (*c.* AD 1000) is well-preserved. The sacred city of MONTE ALBAN ✚ was occupied *c.* 50 BC–AD 1470 by a succession of peoples. Most of remains, which include palaces, temples, an observatory and a ballcourt, date from 8th C AD. PALACE OF "LOS DANZANTES" has Olmec-inspired reliefs on base depicting figures with long earrings.

The most grandiose building of the Toltec capital TULA (founded 9th C) is the 5-storey PYRAMID OF TLAHUIZCALPANTECUTLI (god of the morning star). Upper storey still has 8 columns which supported sanctuary roof: 4 are sculptured warriors with feathered headdresses ◆. To E and W are two examples of typically Toltec hall of columns.

Temple of Tlahuizcalpantecutli, Tula: *warrior column and plan*

XOCHICALCO (7th–10th C) has pyramid to Quetzalcoatl, with meandering plumed serpent carvings on base.

The Totonac capital of TAJIN, Vera Cruz, was subjected to Toltec influence in 10th C. On PYRAMID OF THE NICHES (see p 63) the 365 openings have obvious astrological significance, reflecting pre-Hispanic obsession with time.

Aztec architecture

At TENAYUCA, near Mexico City, is a prototype of the double temple-pyramid (late 15th c). Twin staircase well-preserved. Earlier superimpositions beneath uppermost layer.

Other sites: Pyramid of Huitzilopochtli, Santa Cecilia (only Aztec pyramid retaining sanctuary and roof); Tlatelolco, Mexico City; Calixtlahuaca, near Toluca.

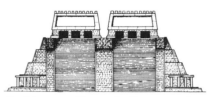

Double pyramid-temple, Tenayuca: *front elevation and plan*

The region of the Maya

Classic Mayan architecture dates from AD 100–900, when temple-pyramids with roof combs were built (see p 63), and low palaces on earth platforms. A common feature was the corbelled vault with steeply sloping sides. Palace façade ornamentation became increasingly abstract and repetitive.

The main sites

City of TIKAL, Guatemala, is a wealth of temples, palaces, ballcourts and plazas, mostly 4th–8th c AD. TEMPLE 1 (*c.* 700) has giant roof comb, double stairway.

At UXMAL, Mexico, is the PALACE OF THE GOVERNOR (*c.* 900). Upper façade has frieze broken by pair of arrow-shaped corbelled arches. Same formal simplicity found in NUNNERY (*c.* 900). Towering PYRAMID OF THE MAGICIAN illustrates Pre-Hispanic practice of placing new buildings over old.

Palace of the Governor, Uxmal

Other Mayan sites: Palenque (Great Palace has 4-storey tower, Temple of the Sun is 7th c); Sayil (3-storey Great Palace); Kabah (Palace of the Masks); Labná (triumphal arch); Copán, Honduras (vast hieroglyphic staircase).

Palace of the Masks, Kabah: *detail of façade*

Triumphal arch, Labná

Chichen Itza

After its occupation by the Toltecs (10th c), CHICHEN ITZA in Yucatán enjoyed a period of architecture in a columnar style derived from Tula. The TEMPLE OF THE WARRIORS has sanctuary combining Toltec columns with Mayan-style vaults. Stairway ends in sculpture of god Chac-Mool. Adjoining COURT OF THE THOUSAND COLUMNS now roofless.

On the temple known as the CASTILLO (*c.* 1200) the serpent motif is featured unsparingly, as throughout city. Breathtaking staircases rise on all 4 sides to sanctuary. Nearby BALLCOURT (*c.* 1100) is 83 m long. Sculptures along walls ♦ show decapitation of losing team-captain. Mound to E has two fine TEMPLES OF THE JAGUARS at different levels.

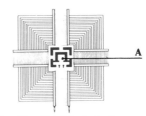

Castillo, Chichén Itzá: *plan*
A *Corbel-vaulted sanctuary*

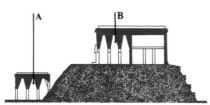

Temple of the Warriors, Chichén Itzá:
section **A** *Colonnaded forecourt;* **B** *Sanctuary*

Ballcourt, Chichén Itzá: *skull relief*

South America

Agriculture in the Andes required terraces bounded by huge stone walls. Influenced by these, Inca builders were concerned not with carved decoration, which is rare, but with masonry construction, often using large polygonal stones.

Pre-Inca sites

At CHAN CHAN ▪ (13th–15th c), N Peru, is a series of 10 great walled complexes, probably palaces of the Kings of Chimor. Some interiors have moulded friezes.

At TIAHUANACO ▪ (*c.* 600 AD), Bolivia, the monolithic GATE OF THE SUN formed part of a vast ceremonial complex.

Inca architecture in Peru

The TEMPLE OF THE SUN, CUZCO (Inca capital 1450–1532), partly survives. Most stunning site is the town of MACHU PICCHU ▪ ✧ (*c.* 1500), saddled high between two mountains.

The fortress for Cuzco was SACSAHUAMÁN (*c.* 1438–*c.* 1500) on hills above: a triple row of zigzagging ramparts whose unbroken N wall is more than a third of a mile long. Some of polygonal stone blocks, fitted without mortar, are over 12 m high. A superb example of Inca engineering skill.

Sacsahuamán: *polygonal masonry*

EARLY CHRISTIAN AND BYZANTINE STYLES

The Roman Emperor Constantine, who made Christianity the state religion in AD 313, gave tangible expression to his faith by commissioning churches: one of these, a huge structure in the Early Christian basilican style, was raised on the site of St Peter's martyrdom in Rome (*c.* 326; later destroyed). Four years later Constantine moved his capital to Byzantium (renamed Constantinople, later Istanbul). In the Dark Ages this former Greek trading-post, a colossus bestriding the gap between East and West, was a bastion for both the Eastern Empire and the Christian Church against the threat of barbarian onslaughts.

The Western Empire was officially recognized as a separate entity on the death of Theodosius in 395. One of his sons, Arcadius, ruled the East from Constantinople, while the other, Honorius, ruled the West, first from Rome but after 402 from Ravenna (later famous for its mosaics).

The Empire was reunited under Justinian (527–65), a great patron of church-building whose finest project was the church of Santa Sophia in Constantinople (532–7). This building was in the new Byzantine style, a fusion of Western Classicism with Eastern attitudes, which developed various regional idioms and reached as far as Russia after the 10th c. Its structural innovations—in particular the superimposition of a dome on a square—were well suited to express the mystical, hierarchical emphasis of the Eastern Orthodox Church, which increasingly preferred intimacy, mystery and silence to the large choirs and congregations of Western Christianity.

After the building of San Vitale, Ravenna, in the mid 6th c, architecture in the West entered a long decline.

6th c Mosaic, *S. Apollinare Nuovo, Ravenna*

Early Christian churches

Some of the earliest Christian buildings in the West were constructed with materials plundered from disused Classical temples: antique columns were surmounted with arcades or entablatures, and floors were paved with old Roman marbles or column slices. Many were round or octagonal, with dome and surrounding ambulatory—a form derived from the Roman mausoleum and used for tombs, baptisteries and martyria (churches on martyrs' graves). The scheme generally used for congregational churches was based on the Roman basilica (community hall; see p 37).

The basilican church was rectangular, with a nave divided by colonnades from two or four side aisles. The aisles were built lower than the nave itself and the upper wall thus exposed (the clerestory) was pierced with windows.

Inside, the eye was led along colonnades (which made the nave appear deceptively long) towards the altar and, behind it, the semidomed apse, often furnished in early churches with tiers of stone or marble seating for the clergy. A horizontal chancel (bema: literally "platform") sometimes divided the apse from the main body of the church. The narthex (anteroom for penitents and novices) was often preceded by a cloistered courtyard (atrium), of which there are few examples extant.

S. Paolo fuori le Mura, Rome: *section and plan* **A** *Apse;* **B** *Bema;* **C** *Nave;* **D** *Aisles;* **E** *Atrium*

Roofs were of timber, with a flat ceiling. The exterior of a church was generally plain, while the interior was embellished with mosaics depicting holy figures on the semidome of the apse, on the arch framing the semidome, and on the walls above the nave arcades.

The Byzantine style

Byzantine architects, seeking the perfect form for a symbolic structure based on the Eastern mystical figure of the circle, tackled the problem of putting a dome over a square (the ancient Romans, in the Pantheon, had already covered a *circular* space with an impressive dome). One answer was to span the corners with quarter-spherical arched or corbelled niches (squinches) to create an octagonal base closer to the circular form. A triumphantly more elegant solution, which became the Byzantine hallmark, was the pendentive: an inverted concave triangle springing from a corner of the square and curving up to meet the other pendentives, the four of them forming at their tops a circular base for the dome, which was of brick, light stone or sometimes pottery.

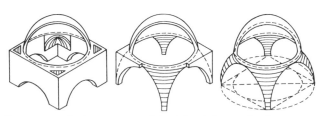

Dome on squinches   **Principle of the pendentive**

A characteristic Byzantine church plan, which came to maturity in the 9th c, was the cross-in-square, which had a dome raised high over the centre on a drum, often with subsidiary domes over the lower-roofed area between the barrel-vaulted arms. Side aisles were generally terminated by apsidal recesses (the prothesis and diaconicon) flanking the main apse —used for storage of sacred vessels, etc.

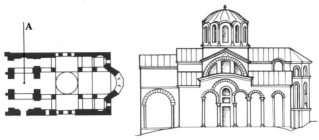

St Theodore, Istanbul, *a typical cross-in-square church: plan and elevation (omitting outer narthex)* **A** *Inner narthex*

Byzantine ornament

Like the Early Christian basilica, the Byzantine church was adorned inside with mosaics. Figures were arranged in a precise hierarchy on dome, drum, pendentives and apse, and the eye was drawn not along nave towards altar but up into dome, where Christ as judge was depicted.

As well as mosaics the interior decorative repertoire included polychrome marble and frescoes. Capitals were often adaptations of the Corinthian Order, or featured intricate incised patterns. Between the abacus and the spandrel of the arch was sometimes an additional slab (dosseret), probably used to give extra height to antique columns. Exterior brickwork was often treated ornamentally, especially in late Byzantine work, with herringbone and chevron designs, niches and blind arches.

Marble wall slab, *St Mark's, Venice (exterior)*

Choir screen panel, *Torcello*

Wind-blown acanthus capital, *St Demetrius, Salonica*

Incised capital with carved dosseret, *S. Vitale, Ravenna*

Incised composite capital *(with volutes), S. Sophia, Istanbul*

Santa Sophia, Istanbul

The church of s. SOPHIA ("The Holy Wisdom"), ISTANBUL (532–7), was the *ne plus ultra* of the Byzantine style. Pendentives, over 18 m high, spring from 4 massive piers to support a shallow dome (33 m diameter), described by a contemporary as seeming "suspended from heaven by a golden chain". To E and W of dome, which is pierced by 40 windows and has part of its thrust absorbed by massive buttresses, are two large semidomes, also supportive. Space covered by each is flanked by semidomed exedrae, and at E end is an apse. Two-storied aisles fill out the plan, which combines basilican and centralized elements, to square. Double narthex. Plain exterior impresses by its size and symmetry, interior is marvellously enlivened by play of light. Walls and piers sheathed in polychrome mosaic. After Turks captured city, building became a mosque: most of original mosaics were plastered over and minarets added.

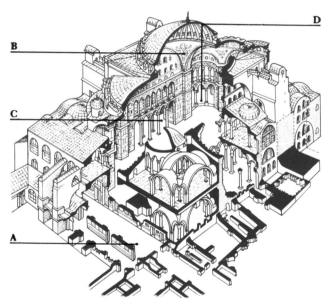

S. Sophia, Istanbul: cutaway view: A *Inner narthex;* **B** *Pendentive;* **C** *Vaulted aisle with gallery;* **D** *Semicircular colonnade*

Rome

Rome still boasts more than a dozen churches dating from the 7th C or before. Many retain their Early Christian character, the least spoiled being the more modest ones built near or outside the walls of the ancient city.

Churches "outside the walls"

s. LORENZO FUORI LE MURA, a galleried basilican church, was originally two buildings dating from 4th and 5th C, joined in 1216 by removal of apses and insertion of columns. Since E part was lower than W, a new floor was put in to avoid having to descend to altar; space beneath became crypt. Mosaic (6th C) on main arch.

Also "outside the walls" is s. AGNESE FUORI LE MURA (rebuilt 625–38 to replace 4th-c church). The apse (stunning 7th-c mosaics ◆) is at w end: deliberate orientation to E was not yet the custom. s. PAOLO FUORI LE MURA is a 19th-c reconstruction of a 4th-c double-aisled basilica.

Other basilican churches

Though now decorated in a Baroque style, s. CLEMENTE, built over an earlier church in 1108 (partial remains in crypt), has many Early Christian features, including antique columns and low marble screen enclosing choir. Mosaic enrichment of apse is 12th-c.

The largest single-aisled basilica is s. MARIA MAGGIORE (432–40), strongly Classical in feeling. Of greater interest is s. SABINA (422–32), on the Aventine Hill, a well-preserved basilica in the Ravenna style. Nave, unusually high and narrow, is lit by large clerestory windows. The 24 Corinthian marble columns are reputedly 2nd-c. Spandrels of colonnades beautifully embellished with inlaid marble designs showing chalices and pattens, symbols of the Eucharist ◆.

S. Sabina: *view along nave towards apse*

Circular buildings

Rome has the largest circular church in existence: s. STEFANO ROTONDO (*c.* 468–83), built on unusual plan of a cross within a circle and probably intended as a martyrium. Arms of cross were side chapels interrupting the outer of two concentric colonnaded ambulatories. Huge central nave is encircled by Ionic columns and lit by 22 clerestory windows.

Only other circular church remaining in city is s. COSTANZA, built *c.* 350 as a mausoleum for Constantine's daughter and converted into church 1256. Barrel-vaulted ambulatory has 4th-c mosaics.

S. Costanza: *plan and view of interior*

Ravenna

Ravenna has the finest glass mosaics in the world on walls and
vaults. Its basilican churches invariably lack a bema and
have an apse wall that is round inside but polygonal outside.
The finely decorated interiors of both basilican and centralized
churches owe much to Greek craftsmen.

Basilican churches

S. APOLLINARE NUOVO (490), by Theodoric the Ostrogoth, has
famous mosaics ◆. High, wide, evenly lit nave. Windows of
10th-c campanile widen with height.

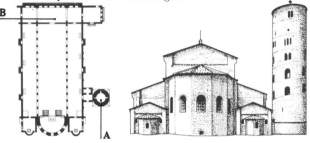

S. Apollinare in Classe:
plan and view from E **A** *Campanile;* **B** *Narthex*

S. APOLLINARE IN CLASSE (begun 532), s of city, has walls of
thin bricks with wide mortar joints in Byzantine fashion,
beautiful 6th–7th c mosaics ◆. One of earliest circular
campanile.

San Vitale

The beauty of the interior of S. VITALE (c. 532–47) lies partly
in its subtle modulation of light and shadow. The inner octagon,
with semicircular colonnaded niches typical of the early
Byzantine centralized plan, opens into a chancel to E
interrupting gallery. Unbuttressed dome made of clay pots
covered with tiled timber roof. Delicately carved capitals with
dosserets. Superb mosaics ◆. The church retains its subtlety
and elegance despite later addition of Baroque decoration.

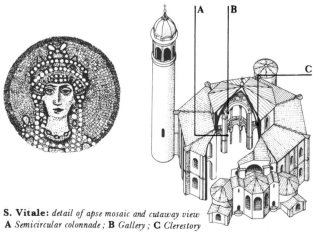

S. Vitale: *detail of apse mosaic and cutaway view*
A *Semicircular colonnade;* **B** *Gallery;* **C** *Clerestory*

Other buildings

Tiny TOMB OF GALLA PLACIDIA (*c.* 425) on cruciform plan, has sarcophagi in three of arms; vivid mosaics. TOMB OF THEODORIC (*c.*.526) has dome carved from solid marble block. ARIAN and ORTHODOX BAPTISTERIES have fine mosaics.

Venice and Sicily

Venice, founded in the 5th c as a refuge from barbarians, eclipsed Ravenna as Italy's prime commercial city, and sought to consolidate its prestige by staging a renaissance of the Byzantine art of Justinian's day.

Sicily's fusion of cultures is shown in churches with combined Saracen and Byzantine features.

Venice

TORCELLO has a fine basilican CATHEDRAL (1008), with carved choir rail ◆ (see p 69) and powerful mosaics.

ST MARK'S, VENICE (1063–85), has cruciform plan, with the narthex continued along the N side of nave; baptistery and funerary chapel to s. Gloomy interior has fine marbles and mosaics ◆ (best are 12th–14th c). Glittering façade is a blend of Renaissance and foreign encrustations.

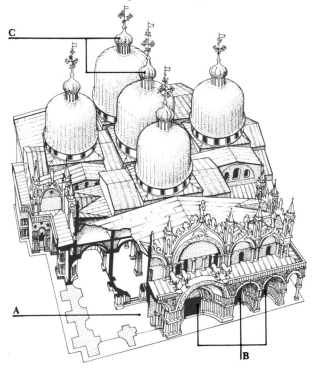

St Mark's, Venice: *cutaway view*
A *Narthex;* **B** *Deeply recessed* w *portals;* **C** *Lanterns over domes*

Sicily

Arabs helped build ST JOHN OF THE HERMITS, PALERMO (early 12th c), which has 5 domes on squinches. Fine mosaics in Palermo at MARTORANA (1143) and PALATINE CHAPEL.

Istanbul, Greece and the Balkans

The outlying Imperial provinces of Greece and the Balkans
produced some exquisite churches, but nothing to rival Santa
Sophia in Istanbul (Constantinople). The cross-in-square
became the classical pattern after *c.* 875. Late churches (13th–
15th c) tended towards taller proportions and ornately
patterned brickwork.

Istanbul

SS SERGIUS AND BACCHUS, ISTANBUL (527–35), slightly ante-dates
S. Sophia, which is related to it in design (see p 70). The
central dome, on small pendentives, has 8 windows.

Other churches: St Irene (begun 532), used for centuries as
an armoury; St Theodore (Kilisse Mosque, *c.* 1100); St
Saviour in the Chora (Kariye Mosque) and St Mary
Pammakaristos, both with fine mosaics.

St Irene: *plan and section*

Salonica

The CHURCH OF THE HOLY APOSTLES, SALONICA (1312–15) is
among finest in all Greece. Five domes are raised on octagonal
drums whose windows are separated by brick columns
carrying arched cornices. Fine brickwork at E end ♦.

Also at Salonica: St Sophia (rebuilt *c.* 700), with possibly
earliest example of a dome surmounted on a low drum pierced
by windows; St George (converted to a church *c.* 400); St
Demetrius (late 5th c).

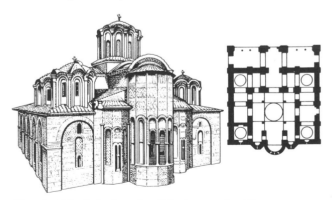

Church of the Holy Apostles, Salonica: E *end and plan*

Yugoslavia

After the creation of an independent Serbian Church in the
early 13th c, an unassertive architectural style emerged in
Raška, the capital, placing a dome over a long, Romanesque-
style nave, usually aisleless. Examples (now in Yugoslavia) at
Dečani, Sopočani and Studenica.

At LAKE OHRID, SW Yugoslavia,
are some attractive churches of
11th–14th C, most on cross-in-
square plan. The fine church
of the monastery of
GRAČANICA (1321) is a good
example of late Byzantine
structural complexity: one
cruciform barrel-vaulted form
is superimposed on another,
the upper, shorter-armed one
having pointed arches which
lead the eye to a high central
dome on a drum. The exterior
combines brick and stone.
Outer narthex was added at a
later date. Near-by
KASTORIA, Greece, has many
small Byzantine churches of
early 11th C, mainly basilican.

Church at Gračanica

Mount Athos

MOUNT ATHOS, or the "Holy Mountain", a 40-mile peninsula
in N Greece, has been an independent monastic community for
over a millenium. The 20 monasteries (15th–18th C) have
central church (generally surrounded by service buildings
and cells) with transepts terminating in apses.

Southern Greece

The KATHOLIKON (c. 1020), larger of two churches at the
monastery of HOSIOS LUKAS (St Luke), PHOCIS, N of Gulf of
Corinth, has a modified cross-in-square plan with dome
covering side aisles in Greek style. The adjacent CHURCH OF
THE THEOTOKOS (c. 1040) has dome rising on 4 single columns
rather than piers—a 9th–11th C development.

Hosios Lukas: *drum of Theotokos*

*Capital and entablature
of Katholikon*

    The church at DAPHNI (c. 1080), near Athens, is a late
example of the use of squinches to create an octagonal base
for dome. The outstanding 11th-C mosaics include a fierce-
looking Christ ◆.

    The attractive "LITTLE METROPOLITAN" CATHEDRAL, ATHENS
(13th C), is probably world's smallest cathedral, reflecting
unimportance of city in late Imperial times. Walls covered with
antique marble reliefs. Also at Athens: St Theodore (c. 1060–
70); Kapnikarea (c. 1060–70).

In the lovely 13th–15th C churches of MISTRA ✿ in the Peloponnese, Western elements (pointed arches, bell towers, fleur-de-lys ornaments) jostle with Byzantine traits. Late 14th-C church of PERIPLETOS has W end hollowed out of rock. The PANTANASSA (1428), a domed basilica, boasts spirited frescoes ◆, while ST THEODORE (*c.* 1296) has exuberant decorative brickwork.

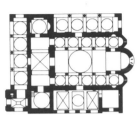 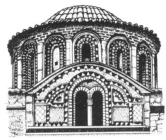

Mistra: *plan of Pantanassa and dome and arm of St Theodore*

The Middle East and Armenia

The early churches of Syria (5th–6th C), mostly basilican, are characterized by an open gallery over the narthex and a single apse built within the E wall. A highpoint of later Christian architecture was the brilliant Armenian style, well illustrated by ruined churches at Ani (now in Turkey). Its greatest exponent was the architect Trdat, who was invited, in the 10th C, to repair the dome of Santa Sophia, Constantinople.

Russia

The earliest Russian churches, influenced by the Constantinople style, sprang up at Kiev at end of the 9th C. By the 11th C Novgorod was a major cultural centre; here, or possibly at Pskov, the Russian onion dome was devised (to cope with heavy snowfall). From the 15th C Byzantine ground-plans were sometimes combined with Renaissance details (see p 130).

Kiev and Novgorod
The CATHEDRAL OF ST SOPHIA, KIEV (1018–37), retains part of its original E wall and Greek mosaics. The present structure is 16th–18th C. It inspired the church of ST SOPHIA, NOVGOROD (1045–52), a cross-in-square with three apses and six domes on drums; onion domes replaced Byzantine ones in the 12th C.

St Sophia, Kiev: *reconstruction, and detail of mosaic*

ISLAM
ARCHITECTURE OF THE MUSLIM WORLD

Islam means "surrender", reflecting the believer's duty to submit to the will of God (Allah) as interpreted in the *Koran* (*Qur'an*), the sacred book of his revelations to the prophet Muhammed (*c.* AD 570–632).

From its source in Arabia, Islam spread rapidly through a combination of religious fervour and military might. Within three centuries the Middle East from Egypt to Mesopotamia was conquered, and the religion had penetrated along the N coast of Africa and into Spain. The main religious centres were Mecca, the prophet's birthplace, and Medina, to which he fled from enemies in 622, first year of the Muslim calendar. Under the Umayyad dynasty (661–750) the chief city of the caliphs (spiritual and political successors to Muhammed) was moved to Damascus. The 7th-c Dome of the Rock, Jerusalem, is the earliest great Muslim building in existence. In this period too the mosque acquired its basic form, to be developed in various ways throughout the Muslim world.

After the 10th c, the power structure of Islam was under the control of a succession of Turkish groups. The Seljuks, prolific builders, ruled from central Anatolia. In 1453 the Ottomans completed their conquest of the Byzantine Empire by taking Constantinople, and by 1600 much of SE Europe, W Asia and N Africa was under their sway. The 16th c saw the creation of the Persian Safavid dynasty (1501–1732), while in India the northern states were unified under the Mughal Emperors (1526–1858), whose Indo-Islamic style reached its climax in the Taj Mahal. The architecture of Moorish Spain (8th–15th c) is notable for its opulent decoration.

Calligraphic tile panel, *Sokollu Mosque, Istanbul*

Mosques

Mosques—meeting places of the Faithful structurally inspired by Muhammed's house at Medina—generally had the following features: a spacious courtyard containing a tank or fountain for ablutions; a decorated niche (mihrab) in a wall oriented to Mecca (qibla); a pulpit (minbar) to the right of the mihrab; a screened enclosure protecting the prayer-leader; and one or more minarets from which the muezzin called believers to prayer 5 times a day.

The 7th–11th c was the age of the great congregational, or Friday, mosques, with courtyards enclosed by flat-roofed porticoes to give protection from the sun, the deep one fronting the qibla wall forming a domed or multi-domed sanctuary. With the 12th c came the emergence (fostered by the Seljuks in Anatolia and Iran and the Ayubbids in Egypt) of the madrasa: a collegiate mosque in which the porticoes were replaced by huge vaulted halls (iwans). Madrasas were sometimes linked with domed mausolea in a single complex. Instead of brick, ashlar masonry was now often used in some areas, sometimes with alternating light and dark courses. In the mid-16th c the Ottomans developed a monumental type of mosque based partly on the Byzantine church of Santa Sophia, Istanbul.

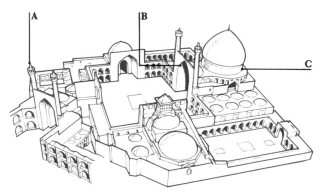

Masjid-i Shah, Isfahan, Iran *(see p 82)* : *a classic madrasa mosque*
A *Portal minaret ;* **B** sw *iwan ;* **C** *Domed sanctuary*

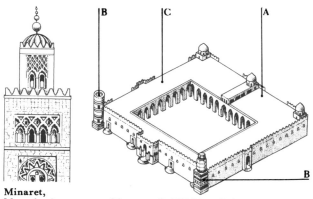

Minaret, Marrakesh, Morocco

Mosque of al-Hakim, Cairo:
A *Sanctuary ;* **B** *Minarets ;* **C** *Flat-roofed portico*

Other building types

A typically Islamic building type is the caravanserai: an inn often lavishly furbished, for traders and pilgrims. It often too the form of a rectangular walled enclosure pierced by a wide portal. Similar in structure is the ribat, a kind of fortified monastery. Hunting-palaces, the speciality of the Umayyad caliphs, were built in a variety of styles. Houses were inward-looking in design and planned to facilitate seclusion of women.

Ornament

Surfaces were often mantled in decoration: brickwork, carved stucco, inlaid marble or lavish polychrome tilework (perfected in Iran and Turkey in the 16th–17th c). Since figurative representation was banned in religious art, decorative energy was channelled into geometric, arabesque and calligraphic motifs. Arches, often horseshoe, trefoil or multiform, sometimes had joggled (i.e., interlocking) voussoirs of alternate colours. A common embellishment was superimposed tiers of complexly articulated arches forming a stalactite (muqarnas) vault.

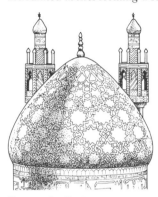

Geometrically decorated dome and minarets, *shrine at Mahan, Iran*

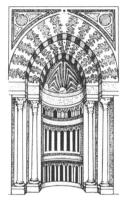

Mihrab with joggled voussoirs, *Cairo*

Interlocking horseshoe arches, *over portal of Great Mosque, Córdoba, Spain*

Muqarnas, *Bu-'Inaniyya Madrasa, Fez, Morocco*

Column base, *Selim Mosque, Edirne, Turkey*

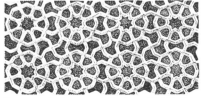

Screen window, *tomb, Fathepur Sikri, India*

The western Middle East

The Umayyads, ambitious builders, drew on the N Syrian stonework tradition as well as on Byzantine styles. The mihrab was perhaps derived from the apse of Syrian Early Christian churches. Most of Baghdad's architecture, influenced by Persian brick and stucco methods, was destroyed by Mongols in the 13th C. Vigorous Islamic architecture of the 9th–14th C may be seen in Cairo, site of a number of iwan type madrasas of the Ayyubid period (1171–1250).

Jerusalem

The DOME OF THE ROCK, JERUSALEM (begun *c.* 684) covers a bare rock representing the summit of Mount Moriah, legendary site of Muhammed's journey to heaven. The structure was influenced by the Graeco-Byzantine rotunda: a gilded timber dome and masonry drum supported on a circular Corinthian colonnade, with an outer lower storey in the form of a double-aisled octagon. High dome was a potent influence on later Islamic architecture. Sumptuous interior is decorated with marble panelling and mosaics. Multipatterned ceramic sheathing of exterior was applied by the Ottomans in 1554, replacing original glass mosaics.

Adjacent to the shrine is the most ancient Jerusalem mosque, the AQSA MOSQUE (715), much rebuilt. Ranges of roofed arcades in front of qibla wall form a sanctuary, crowned by a dome on the axis of the mihrab.

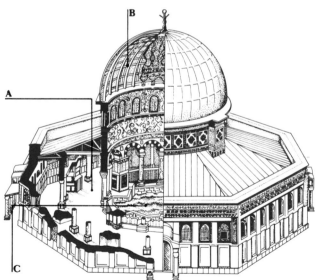

Dome of the Rock, Jerusalem: *cutaway view*
A *Inner ambulatory;* **B** *Concealed timber ribs of dome;* **C** *Rock*

Iraq

At BAGHDAD, the so-called 'ABBASID PALACE (*c.* 1230) is thought to have been a madrasa. Iwan has superb brick ornamentation. Also at Baghdad: Al-Mustansir Mosque (1233).

The GREAT MOSQUE, SAMARRA (847), largest ever built, is famous for its cone-shaped brick minaret with spiralling ramp, in front of walled courtyard.

Syria

The GREAT MOSQUE, DAMASCUS (709–15), the earliest surviving
congregational mosque, was built on site of a Christian church,
in turn built on a Roman sacred enclosure. The original
Hellenistic corner towers became Islam's first minarets. Triple-
arched hall covering mihrab; dome above central aisle. Domed
treasury in courtyard. Fine mosaics, especially in w arcade.

Also at Damascus: Zahiriyya Madrasa (13th c); Ottoman
Mosque of Süleyman (1560), built by Sinan (see p 83);
'Azam palace (1749).

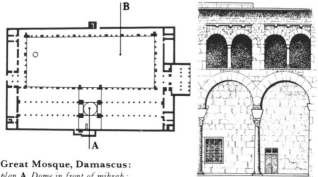

Great Mosque, Damascus:
plan **A** *Dome in front of mihrab;*
B *Central court*

Portico of Great Mosque

Cairo

The IBN TULUN MOSQUE (876–9), influenced by mosque at
Samarra, may have been built by Iraqi craftsmen. Perimeter
wall, with unique ornamental parapet, surrounds on three
sides an outer court (ziyada), which in turn contains central
courtyard (sahn) with domed fountain for ablutions. Mosque
is brick-faced, decorated with stucco motifs. Limestone spiral
minaret.

The MADRASA OF SULTAN HASAN (1356–9) has a cruciform
plan formed by a square courtyard with an iwan on each side.
Founder's domed mausoleum with muqarnas decoration
behind qibla wall.

The MOSQUE AND TOMB OF BARQUQ (1399–1412), in the
necropolis N of Cairo, combines numerous functions in a unified
complex. Near-by COMPLEX OF QAYITBAY (1472–4), of late
Mamluk period, is a finely balanced asymmetrical composition,
with striated masonry and inlaid decorations.

Ibn Tulun Mosque, Cairo:
ablution fountain

Mausoleum of Qayitbay: *detail
of dome*

Iran

Seljuks from central Asia brought a more three-dimensional approach to Iranian architecture, and in the 11th–12th c evolved cylindrical minarets, geometrically patterned brickwork and the 4-iwan madrasa. After the mid-13th c, under the Monguls and Timurids, buildings became more highly coloured and in the Safavid period (mainly 16th–17th c) vast areas were covered with glazed tiles, either in mosaics or individually patterned with several hues.

Isfahan

The Safavid capital of ISFAHAN is dominated by the turquoise-blue domes of its mosques. The MASJID-I SHAH (Royal Mosque; 1612–37), the city's largest building, shows off Safavid tilework at its most exquisite. Entrance portal (with muqarnas) is in the centre of s side of main square, but mosque itself is angled towards Mecca (see p 78).

Masjid-i Shah: *dome*

Friday Mosque: *detail of iwan*

Masjid-i Shah: *minaret*

Friday Mosque: *tile-mosaic*

The chief jewels of the FRIDAY MOSQUE (8th–17th c) are two 11th-c domed chambers, both fronted by deep iwans, at either end of the arcaded court. The so-called "Brown Dome" contains some of Iran's finest Seljuk brickwork ◆.

Also at Isfahan: Mosque of the Shaykh Lutfallah (1617); 'Ali Qapu Palace (early 17th c); Khwaju Bridge (mid 17th c).

Other buildings

The MOSQUE OF GAWHAR SHAD, MASHHAD (1419) is fine example of Timurid tile-mosaic; first mosque to have pair of minarets flanking iwan rather than rising from parapets. Oldest mosque in Iran is TARIK KHANA MOSQUE, DAMGHAN (8th c).

Seljuk and Ottoman styles

The building styles of the Seljuk Turks (12th–13th c) were exploited by their Ottoman successors for half a century, until the Ottomans evolved their own style of mosque, partly inspired by Santa Sophia, Constantinople.

Seljuk Turkey
In Seljuk architecture superb carving is balanced against ashlar masonry. In mosques the domed hall was emphasized.

The INCE MINARE MADRASA (Madrasa of the Slender Minaret), KONYA (c. 1260–65) has a superb iwan portal. Also at Konya: the BÜYÜK KARATAY MADRASA (1251).

Büyük Karatay Madrasa, Konya: *portal*

Ince Minare Madrasa, Konya: *portal*

Other buildings: Shifte Minare Madrasa, Erzurum (1253), with typical Seljuk tomb-tower; caravanserai, Aksaray (1229).

Ottoman Turkey
The Ottoman mosque, austerely geometrical, was grandly and harmoniously designed, with domed interior, pillared forecourt, subsidiary buildings and slender minarets. Tilework reached a peak in the 16th–17th c. Greatest architect was Sinan (c. 1489–1588), whose buildings are well represented at ISTANBUL. His first major work, the SHEHZADE MOSQUE (mid 16th c), is among earliest to have pencil-like minarets. Large central dome abutted by 4 half-domes.

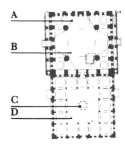 

Shehzade Mosque, Istanbul: *plan and front elevation*
A *Half-dome;* **B** *Main dome;* **C** *Fountain;* **D** *Forecourt*

Sinan's COMPLEX OF SOKOLLU MEHMET PASHA (1572) is cleverly adapted to uneven site (superb tilework, finest over minbar ◆), while his SÜLEYMANIYE COMPLEX (1550–7), rivalling St Sophia, is a vast civic centre with over 500 domes.

Süleymaniye Mosque: *section, and entrance to forecourt*

Final phase of classic Ottoman style is reached in the MOSQUE OF SULTAN AHMET (early 17th C), with 6 minarets. Also at Istanbul: TOPKAPI PALACE with CHINILI KIOSK (1473).

At EDIRNE, the old capital, are the early UCH SHEREFELI MOSQUE (1438–47), and the SELIMIYE COMPLEX, regarded by Sinan as his masterpiece; 4 soaring minarets.

Central Asia

Central Asia's finest Muslim architecture, built in baked brick, is embellished with a wealth of glazed tiles.

Tombs and mosques

The TOMB OF THE SAMANIDS, BUKHARA (10th C), USSR, one of Islam's earliest monumental tombs, has brickwork with basket-weave ornamentation. Finest tilework of the region is at SAMARKAND, especially on the tombs of the SHAH-I ZINDA and GUR EMIR COMPLEXES (14th–15th C). Latter has curious ribbed dome which stands on a high drum. The basic plan of courtyard with minaret at each corner was later adopted in India.

Tomb of the Samanids, Bukhara

India and Pakistan

The earliest mosques of India, built in Delhi and Ajmer at the end of the 12th C, were converted Hindu and Jain temples. The Indo-Islamic style of the 13th C, which continued to use brackets and corbelling in the native mode, was eclipsed under the Mughal Empire (1526–1858), whose architecture progressed from early eclecticism to an emphatically Persian manner. The most enlightened patrons were Akbar (1556–1605), who favoured red sandstone, and his grandson Shah Jihan, whose bulbous-domed monuments in white marble were effectively combined with water gardens.

Delhi

At DELHI stands the first great Indo-Islamic mosque: the
QUWWAT AL-ISLAM MOSQUE (begun *c*. 1197). Its domed gateway
(1305) has non-indigenous squinches and voussoirs, and the
horseshoe arches, with spearhead-shaped undersides, that were
to become typical of Delhi. Adjacent QUTB MINAR minaret
(1199) is very lofty: height of 72·5 m.

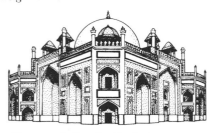

Qutb Minar: *detail*   **Humayun's Tomb:** *upper level*

HUMAYUN'S TOMB ✪ (1565), an early jewel of Mughal Delhi,
marks infiltration of pure styles from Iran and Central Asia.
Symmetrical composition on aracaded podium. Red sandstone
beautifully picked out in white marble inlay. The fortified
TOMB OF GHIYATH AD-DIN TUGHLUQ (1325) has sloping walls that
were later a hallmark of Indo-Islamic building.

Also at Delhi: Friday Mosque (1644–58); Shah Jihan's Red
Fort (1638), with bulbous domes and multifoil arches.

Agra and Fatehpur Sikri

Agra's TAJ MAHAL ✪ (1632–54), greatest Mughal tomb, houses
Shah Jihan and his favourite wife behind delicate marble
screen ◆. Central octagonal chamber on podium with 4
minarets at corners. Façades have huge Persian-style iwans.
White marble exterior decorated with pietra dura (a form of
inlay work). A sublimely beautiful building. Also at Agra:
Tomb of I'timad ad Dawla.

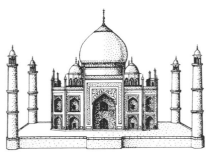

Taj Mahal, Agra: *elevation and plan* **A** *Tombs*

FATEHPUR SIKRI (1569–74) is great sandstone capital built by
Akbar (abandoned 1585). Mughal architecture at most eclectic
in palaces, colonnades and porticoes, asymmetrically planned.

Other sites

The TOMB OF SHIR SHAH SUR, SASARAM (*c*. 1540) uses octagonal
form to perfection. LAHORE, Pakistan, boasts Wazir Khan
Mosque (1634), with superb tile-mosaics; Jihangir's Tomb
(1627); Badshahi Mosque (1673–4).

Western north Africa and Spain

Architecture of the Aghlabid dynasty (800–909), at its best in Tunisia, had powerfully simple forms. Spanish and Moroccan Islamic architecture developed in isolation: the narrow structural vocabulary led to restless virtuosity in decoration. Horseshoe and multifoil arches and exaggerated muqarnas work was widely exploited. Minarets square and sturdy.

Western north Africa

The GREAT MOSQUE, QAIROUAN (9th C), Tunisia, much rebuilt, is structurally the most influential building in N Africa.

At FEZ, Morocco, the QARAWIYYN MOSQUE (rebuilt 12th C) typifies the ornate decoration of the Almoravid period. The town's most monumental mosque is the BU-'INANIYYA MADRASA (1350–5). Also: Kutubiya Mosque, Marrakesh (12th C).

Great Mosque, Qairouan: *minaret*   **Yusuf Madrasa, Marrakesh:** *mihrab*   **Bu-'Inaniyya Madrasa, Fez:** *calligraphic detail*

Spain

The most majestic structure of CÓRDOBA, capital of Umayyad Spain, is the GREAT MOSQUE (began 785), now a cathedral. Sanctuary is supported on a forest of columns.

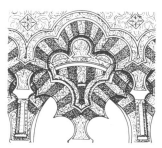

Great Mosque, Córdoba: *arches*   **Alhambra, Granada:** *detail*

The Spanish liking for decorative multiplicity was given full rein at the ALHAMBRA, GRANADA ✧ (1338–90), a vast fortified palace with staggeringly ornate ceramic, stucco and plaster work. Court of the Lions was used for public ceremonials, Court of the Myrtles for sovereign and entourage.

Also in Spain: Aljaferia Palace, Saragossa (11th C); Mosque of Bab Mardum, Toledo (1000); Giralda, Seville (12th C).

ROMANESQUE

The term Romanesque was coined in the 19th c to describe the derivatives of Roman architecture that evolved in w Europe between the collapse of the Roman Empire and the rise of Gothic (*c.* 500–1200), but it is now used to refer principally to the 11th–12th c. The style was a compound of influences, drawing variously upon Roman, Byzantine, Viking, Celtic, Saracenic and other sources. From countless local idioms some common themes emerge: bold experimentation, coherent planning (with special attention to the E end of churches) and the structural principle of round arches dictating strong, heavy forms.

Romanesque was propagated by the monastic, pilgrimage and Crusading movements against a background of feudalism and political instability. Much of the wealth needed to create it came from the monasteries. Of these the most important was Cluny in Burgundy (founded 910), where a succession of imposing churches was created. The Crusaders built robust castles during campaigns against the Turks in Palestine. Highlights of High Romanesque (1050–1150) include the English Norman style and the spacious French abbey churches built along the pilgrimage routes to Santiago de Compostela in Spain.

One of the forerunners of Romanesque was the Carolingian style (late 8th–10th c), generated by Charlemagne's renaissance of Constantinian Christianity.

Last Judgement sculpture: *tympanum, Ste Foy, Conques, France*

Romanesque churches: the structural forms

The monumental effect of Romanesque church exteriors was heightened by towers—often a large one over the crossing (where the transept intercepted the main body of the church) and twin towers flanking the façade. A detached bell-tower (campanile) was common in Italy. German churches often had at their w end a towered apse (westwork) containing an upper-storey chapel.

Aisles were easily vaulted, but constructing a semicircular tunnel vault or intersecting groin vault over a wide nave posed structural problems. Wooden roofs therefore persisted, but fire-proofing, aesthetic and acoustic considerations led in some regions to experiments with masonry vaults. To give necessary support for these, walls became thicker and vaulted galleries were often placed over aisles. In nave arcades groups of columns commonly alternated with massive piers to produce a satisfying visual rhythm. Shafts applied to piers sometimes continued up the walls to form transverse arches across the vaults, creating a clear division into bays. In 1104, in Durham Cathedral, England, groin vaulting was for the first time constructed using exposed diagonal ribs, anticipating Gothic.

Ornament

Ornament was deployed to emphasize underlying structure. Blind arcades, sometimes of intersecting arches, animated exteriors. Carved ornament was in some regions naturalistic, though largely geometrical in Norman work. Where plainness was preferred, the transition between the column and the square seating of the arch was effected by a convex shape below the abacus, sometimes scalloped. In Italy and s France, however, capitals were delicately ornamented. Over a church doorway a semicircular carved panel (tympanum) was often carved with a didactic scene, such as the Last Judgement.

Capitals: *Winchester (scallop); Toulouse; Canterbury (in crypt)*

Pier, *Moissac Abbey*   **Tower arcade,** *Cluny*   **Arcade,** *Monreale, Sicily*

Church planning

Romanesque church plans evolved in response to monasticism. More priests celebrating daily Mass meant that more altars were required, so after *c.* 980 aisles of cruciform churches were sometimes extended past the transept and terminated by chapels either side of the central apse. The high altar was later moved closer to E end, and a separate altar for laity was placed to w end of screened choir reserved for clergy. To allow pilgrims to view sacred relics behind high altar without interference to services, the great pilgrimage churches (*c.* 1050–1100) evolved the chevet: i.e., chapels radiating from a semicircular ambulatory round the apse.

In Benedictine and Cistercian monasteries monks entered church not by main w door but through door from cloisters, which were linked to living quarters and were usually s of nave. To E of cloisters was the chapter house, the monastic assembly room. Other buildings included refectory, kitchens, sacristy, infirmary, abbot's lodgings.

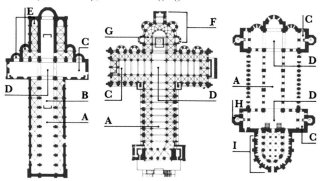

Church and cathedral plans: *St Albans, England ; St James, Santiago, Spain ; St Michael's, Hildesheim, Germany*
A *Nave;* **B** *Choir;* **C** *Transept;* **D** *Crossing;* **E** *Staggered apses;* **F** *Chevet;*
G *Ambulatory;* **H** *Staircase turret;* **I** *Westwork*

Italy

Although Romanesque originated in N Italy in the late 9th c, it was not until the 12th c that the style enjoyed its heyday there. Experiments with ribbed vaults took place in Lombardy, where churches had severe, screen-like, gabled façades. Columns of entrance porches, as in central Italy, often rested on the backs of sculptured crouching beasts.

In Tuscany church architecture was structurally conservative, and favoured the timber-roofed basilica, often using antique columns. Lavish marble exteriors incorporated tiers of arcading, even high on the gables.

In Sicily successive influences—Byzantine, Islamic, Norman—gave rise to a fascinating mixture of styles.

North Italy

S. AMBROGIO, MILAN (begun *c.* 1080), has probably Lombardy's first rib vaulting and only surviving atrium. Beneath wheel window of w front, S. ZENO MAGGIORE, VERONA (begun *c.* 1123), has porch with columns on stone lions (like that of VERONA CATHEDRAL). Wooden roof (14th c). Shallow pilasters (Lombard strips) on façade linked at top by small corbelled arches in typical Lombard style. Brick and marble campanile.

Verona Cathedral: *porch*

S. MICHELE, PAVIA (begun *c.* 1117), is cruciform, with ribbed vaults, clustered piers, deep internal buttresses. Severe façade. Also in N Italy: SS Maria and Donato, Murano.

Tuscany, Apulia and Sicily

The basilican church of S. MINIATO, FLORENCE (*c.* 1013–90), combines Early Christian, Byzantine and Romanesque features. White and green marble panels inside and out.

S. Miniato, Florence   **Cathedral, Pisa**

The celebrated composition at PISA is homogeneous in style. Superb CATHEDRAL (1063–1118) has tiers of delicate ornamental arches (dwarf galleries) on façade. Red striations on white marble exterior. The CAMPANILE (Leaning Tower; begun 1174) is a cylindrical version of Cathedral's w front. Circular BAPTISTERY (1153–1265) has Gothic additions.

The prototype of Romanesque in Apulia is S. NICOLO, BARI (begun *c.* 1085). Arcade screens bema from nave. Excellent masonry. Refined decorative details in Classical tradition.

The Norman CEFALU CATHEDRAL, SICILY (*c.* 1131–1240), has Byzantine mosaics and Saracenic motifs. MONREALE CATHEDRAL (begun 1174) has fine cloisters ◆.

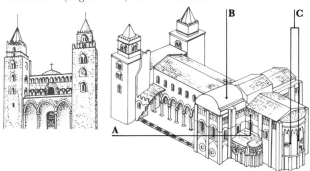

Cefalù Cathedral: *façade and cutaway view*
A *Interlaced blind arcading;* **B** *Barrel-vaulted s transept;* **C** *Lombard strips*

Germany

Double-apsed churches in the German Romanesque style often had slightly projecting transepts with crossing towers and staircase turrets. Regional features included square towers with gables and lozenge-sided roofs in the Rhineland, and trefoil E apses around Cologne. Exteriors, influenced by Lombardy, had dwarf galleries under eaves, blind arcading and pilaster strips. Ornament was used sparingly.

Carolingian architecture

The ABBEY GATE-HOUSE, LORSCH (*c.* 800), fuses local styles with Roman revivalism. Engaged columns with Composite capitals. In the ROYAL CHAPEL, AACHEN (dedicated 805), Charlemagne's builders applied Roman construction techniques to a design derived from San Vitale, Ravenna. It is more sombre and weightier than its Byzantine prototype.

Gate-house, Lorsch

Romanesque churches

WORMS CATHEDRAL (*c.* 1110–81), with its crossing towers, staircase turrets, double transepts and chancels, Lombardic exterior and plain interior, is typical of the region. Heavy piers support nave arcades. As was usual in German Romanesque, each main bay equals two bays of the aisles.

SPEIER CATHEDRAL (1030–60) has probably the earliest medieval large-scale groin vaults in Europe. Fine crypt ◆.

The abbey of MARIA LAACH (1093–1156) has three E apses and cloistered atrium. Nave and aisle bays same width. The CHURCH OF THE APOSTLES, COLOGNE (begun *c.* 1190), has typical E end, with apsidal transepts flanking choir.

Other cathedrals: Mainz and Trier.

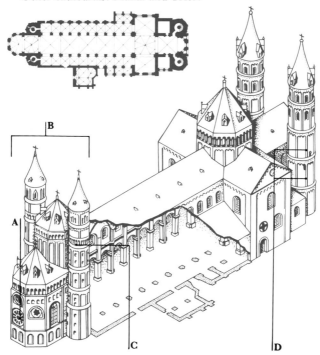

Worms Cathedral: *plan and cutaway view* **A** *Semi-Gothic apse;* **B** *Westwork;* **C** *Italianate dwarf galleries;* **D** *Lombard strips*

France

In France, whose richest period of Romanesque building was 1080–1150, political disunity encouraged the growth of a wide variety of sub-styles. Burgundy's monasteries produced churches with pointed arcades, a triforium (narrow arcaded passage above nave arcade) instead of a gallery, and an open or closed vestibule (narthex). Other local features included lavishly sculptured façades in Aquitaine and Poitou, Classical Roman influences in Provence, and a greater experimentalism in N France, where rib vaults (and early stained glass) were developed.

Normandy

The church of ST ETIENNE, part of the Abbaye-aux-Hommes, CAEN (begun *c.* 1068), has a simple w façade with two high towers, which later acquired delicate Gothic spires. Interior elevation, formed by nave arcade, gallery and clerestory, looks forward to Gothic. Sexpartite vaulting. Also at Caen: church of the Abbaye-aux-Dames (La Trinité; 12th c).

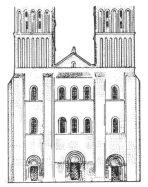 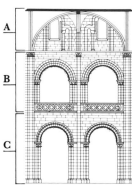

St Etienne, Caen: *lower façade and elevation of nave bays*
A *Clerestory;* **B** *Gallery;* **C** *Nave arcade*

Auvergne and the south-west

The chevet churches of Auvergne have barrel-vaulted naves and no clerestory. NOTRE-DAME-DU-PORT, CLERMONT-FERRAND (12th c), features a "lantern transept" formed by heightening bays flanking crossing and inserting windows.

ANGOULÊME CATHEDRAL (*c.* 1105–28), in Aquitaine, is typical of a group of domed, aisleless churches in the SW.

Angoulême Cathedral: *façade, and detail of tympanum*

ST FRONT, PERIGUEUX (mid 12th c), also domed, bears a resemblance in plan to St Mark's, Venice; narrow aisles.

ST SAVIN-SUR-GARTEMPE (early 12th c) is one of a series of Poitou hall churches, with narrow aisles as tall as nave; fine frescoes. NOTRE-DAME-LA-GRANDE, POITIERS (1130–45), has a profusion of sculpture on w front. Further s is ST PIERRE, MOISSAC (12th c), with superb cloister ✦ and porch. The most visited of the pilgrimage churches is ST SERNIN, TOULOUSE (1077–1117), with chevet and fine carvings in ambulatory; restored 19th c. STE FOY, CONQUES, is also of interest.

Burgundy and the south-east
The beautiful Cluniac abbey church of STE MADELEINE, VÉZELAY (early 12th c), has a high groin-vaulted nave divided into bays by striated columns and transverse arches. Magnificent inner w portal with tympanum ✦.

Ste Madeleine, Vézelay: *nave*   **Autun Cathedral:** *capital*

AUTUN CATHEDRAL (*c.* 1120–32) has fine carved capitals and impressive w porch. ST PHILIBERT, TOURNUS (begun *c.* 950), is notable for unusual barrel vaults in nave. In the SE: St Trophîme, Arles; St Gilles-du-Gard.

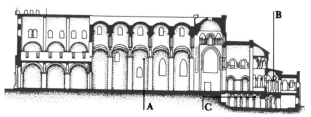

St Philibert, Tournus: *section*
A *Barrel-vaulted nave;* **B** *Ambulatory of chevet;* **C** *Crypt*

Britain: Anglo-Saxon and Norman

Extant Anglo-Saxon churches are mostly in a primitive style, often with pilaster strips attached to exteriors. After 1066 Norman invaders built in a vigorous variant of Romanesque characterized by geometrical ornament. The chevron was a common motif. The great cruciform cathedrals, with long choirs and naves, often had a tri-apsidal E end. Timber roofs remained popular. Most large churches had a central tower over the crossing, sometimes with a pair of towers flanking the façade. The Cistercians built remote abbeys that eschewed ornamentation.

Anglo-Saxon churches

The largest surviving Anglo-Saxon church is BRIXWORTH, Northamptonshire (*c.* 670): an apsed basilica with powerful-looking nave arcades. ST LAURENCE, BRADFORD-ON-AVON, Wiltshire (10th C), has ashlar-faced walls with blind arcading. Other survivals: Sompting, Sussex, with pyramid-roofed tower; Earls Barton, Northamptonshire (10th-C tower with pilasters and triangular strips).

St Laurence, Bradford-on-Avon: *view showing porch*

Durham Cathedral

A Romanesque masterpiece, DURHAM CATHEDRAL ♧ (1093–*c.* 1130) was the earliest European building to use ribbed vaults on a large scale, anticipating Gothic. Half-barrel vaults over gallery are, in effect, flying buttresses. Geometrically carved piers with chevrons and diapers (i.e., small repeated patterns); dog-tooth moulding and cushion capitals.

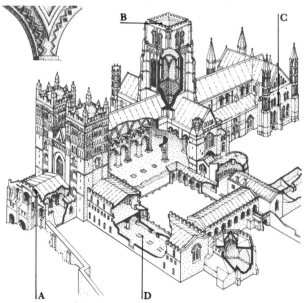

Durham Cathedral: *detail of chevron moulding and cutaway view*
A *Galilee Porch;* **B** *Gothic crossing-tower (1465–90);* **C** *Chapel of the Nine Altars (13th C);* **D** *Cloisters*

Other Norman churches

Most medieval English cathedrals have some Romanesque features. NORWICH (begun 1096) has intact crossing tower, CANTERBURY (begun *c.* 1070) a superb crypt, and SOUTHWELL MINSTER a timber-roofed nave. Cistercian abbeys: FOUNTAINS ▨ ♧ and RIEVAULX ▨ ♧ (both 12th-C foundations with substantial Gothic additions).

Castles

After the Conquest the Normans built castles comprising a
moat-encircled steep mound (motte) adjoined by a larger
enclosure (bailey). By 12th c wooden palisade crowning
motte was replaced by either a round shell keep (e.g.,
Carisbrooke, Isle of Wight) or a rectangular keep, of which
largest and earliest example is the WHITE TOWER, TOWER OF
LONDON (begun 1078). Other keeps: Dover; Hedingham.

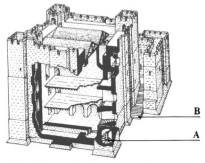

Keep, Dover Castle: *cutaway view*
A *Spiral staircase;* **B** *Entrance stairs*

Motte and bailey plan
A *Motte;* **B** *Bailey*

Scandinavia

Only from the mid 11th c did Romanesque appear in
Scandinavia. LUND CATHEDRAL, SWEDEN (begun 1103), is built
on a Rhenish scheme (after Speier), with Lombardic
decoration.

During the later 12th c numerous brick churches were
constructed in Denmark (mostly in Zealand), including
Ringsted, Sorø, Vitskøl and Kalundborg. ROSKILDE
CATHEDRAL (begun *c.* 1175) has ambulatories on the French
pattern, as well as transitional Gothic features.

In NORWAY, where the timber tradition was especially
persistent, stone churches were built in significant numbers
only after *c.* 1100. A 12th-c building type was the wooden
stave church, with vigorously carved exterior.

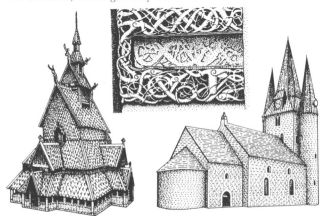

Borgund Church *and* **Urnes Church** *(detail)*, *both in Norway;*
Husaby Church, Skaraborg, *Sweden*

95

Castles in the Holy Land

The Crusaders' Hospitaller castles built in the Crusading principalities (1150–1250) are characterized by a concentric layout, boldly projecting round or horseshoe entrances and well-placed loopholes. The KRAK DES CHEVALIERS ♧, Syria (13th C), is one of the most magnificent of all fortifications.

Spain and Portugal

With s Spain under Muslim occupation until the 13th C, only in the N and in Portugal did Romanesque flourish. French influences were carried by pilgrims en route to Santiago.

Spain

Spanish Romanesque first appeared in Catalonia. The abbey church of S. MARIA, RIPOLL, retains from period only 12th-C sculptured w portal. Duoro region of w Spain is characterized by ribbed domical lantern towers (cimborios), e.g., at ZAMORA and SALAMANCA cathedrals. S. DOMINGO DE SILOS (11th C), a remote monastery, has splendid sculpture in cloisters. Corner piers carved with scenes of Christ and Apostles.

S. Domingo de Silos: *detail of cloister*

The cathedral of ST JAMES, SANTIAGO DE COMPOSTELA (1078–c. 1211), has a severe and little-altered interior; outside masked by 17th- and 18th-C flamboyance. Spain's first chevet, with 5 chapels. Superb Pórtico de la Gloria ✦ (1188). Octagonal lantern.

Salamanca Cathedral: *lantern*

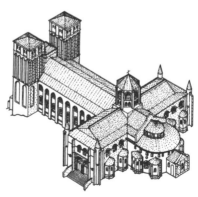

St James, Santiago: *reconstruction*

Portugal

The ALCOBAÇA is the finest Cistercian abbey in the peninsula; church has aisles as high as nave. Other churches: Braga and Coimbra cathedrals, influenced by Santiago but without ambulatories; Templars' church at Tomar.

GOTHIC

Gothic architecture was so dubbed by Italian artists of the Renaissance, who considered it so barbaric that it might have been created by the Goths, the 5th-c ravagers of Rome. The father of the style was Abbot Suger, whose innovatory new choir (1140–44) for the abbey church of St Denis reflected the rise of France as a political and cultural force and inaugurated a glorious outburst of French cathedral-building that lasted until *c.* 1300.

The basic elements of Gothic—the pointed arch, rib vault and flying buttress—were not original in themselves. What was new was their combination in a structural and aesthetic system that delighted in a dynamic unity created out of interdependent parts. Buttresses and flying buttresses, for example, contributed to the visual impact of a cathedral exterior, as well as allowing the side walls to become virtually panels holding up little more than themselves. Windows could therefore be enlarged to form vast membranes of stained glass, enlightening the faithful by pictorial representations of the scriptures and exhilarating them with glorious panoplies of hanging light.

Stained glass was a manifestation of the belief that a cathedral could be an image of the truth communicating a vision of heaven. Hence also the soaring spires pointing strivingly and devotedly to God. In its deployment of a complex structural logic in the service of faith, the cathedral had affinities with medieval scholasticism.

Stained glass: *St Denis and Freiburg*

By *c.* 1250 Gothic had displaced local Romanesque styles in most regions of w Europe, its growth expressing the dominance of the Church. Houses clustered round a church or cathedral like liegemen kneeling at the feet of their lord. Monasteries continued to spatter the countryside, although the contemplative Benedictines and Cistercians were now rivalled by Dominicans and Franciscans who went out to the people to preach. Town halls, guild halls, university buildings, castles and even bridges came to take on the ornamental features of Gothic, and in the Low Countries and Italy, where civilization was urban and mercantile rather than feudal, the greatest Gothic architecture was secular.

The technology of rib vaults

The purpose of rib vaults (i.e., groin vaults with diagonal arches over each bay like the ribs of an umbrella) was partly aesthetic. However, there were great structural advantages. Whereas a tunnel or groin vault required a wooden scaffolding (centring) along its whole length during construction, Gothic builders used centring only to put up the ribs, which were afterwards given a light filling.

The main defect of the semicircular rib vaults occasionally used in Late Romanesque was that where an oblong bay was to be vaulted the diagonal, transverse and wall ribs required clumsy adjustments, by means of stilted or depressed arches, to give them equal height. In Gothic this difficulty was overcome by ribs in the form of pointed arches, whose height could be kept constant whatever the span.

Oblong bays thus created bunched the piers closer together, which reduced the load on each and quickened the rhythm towards the altar—a directional emphasis offset by an upward drive along unbroken shafts from the piers to the vault.

Chartres Cathedral: the High Gothic style

The CATHEDRAL OF NOTRE DAME, CHARTRES, France, rebuilt from 1194 after a fire destroyed all but the w front (c. 1150) and the crypt (early 11th c) of an earlier church on the site, is the first example of the style known as High Gothic.

Chartres Cathedral: *cutaway view and detail of Royal Portal*
A *16th-c N spire;* **B** *Triple s porch;* **C** *Flying buttresses;* **D** *Chevet*

The earliest Gothic cathedrals had a three-storey interior elevation: nave arcade, gallery, clerestory. At Noyon and Laon a narrow arcaded wall-passage (triforium) was introduced between gallery and clerestory. Chartres now took step of suppressing gallery, replacing square sexpartite rib vault covering two bays by oblong rib vault over one bay, and continuing wall shafts down to bases of piers. These devices intensified the eastward and upward drive and set the pattern for High Gothic.

Out of 9 towers planned at Chartres only two were built. That to s crowned by 12th-c spire (first in France); N spire (c. 1507) more ornate. Supreme stained glass: 176 windows of 12th and 13th c survive, most famous being La Belle Verrière ✦ in s ambulatory of chevet, and Jesse Tree window ✦. At w end is triple Royal Portal, with some of world's most memorable sculpture, including Christ in majesty ✦ over central door. Stern elongated figures. Flying buttresses in three tiers, lower two connected by "spokes".

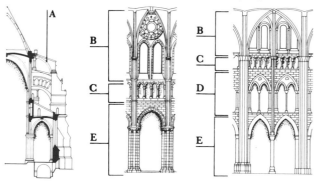

Chartres: *half-section and nave bay*   **Noyon:** *nave bay*
A *Flying buttress;* **B** *Clerestory;* **C** *Triforium;* **D** *Gallery;* **E** *Nave arcade*

Cathedral plans

French cathedral plans are relatively compact. English plans are longer and narrower, with subsidiary buildings, a central tower and longer, sometimes doubled, transepts. In Germany, Italy and Spain the nave was widened into one vast hall.

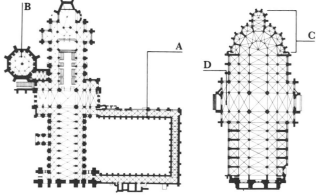

Cathedral plans: *Wells and Amiens*
A *Cloister;* **B** *Chapter house;* **C** *Chevet;* **D** *Short transept*

Vaulting types

Rib vaults evolved, particularly in England and Germany, towards a greater decorative complexity. Secondary ribs (tiercerons) were added, leading from the springers (from which the main ribs issued) to the transverse ridge rib. To create a greater emphasis on the crown of the vault they came to be supplemented by tertiary ribs (liernes), which did not touch the springers. Liernes could be multiplied to form net vaults or arranged in star patterns to form stellar vaults. Curvilinear ribs developed in Spain and Germany.

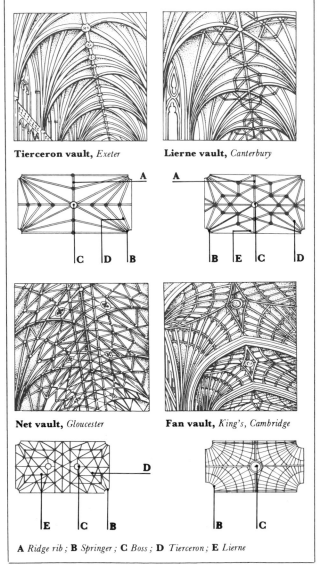

Tierceron vault, *Exeter*

Lierne vault, *Canterbury*

Net vault, *Gloucester*

Fan vault, *King's, Cambridge*

A *Ridge rib;* **B** *Springer;* **C** *Boss;* **D** *Tierceron;* **E** *Lierne*

Timber roofs

Timber roofs, one of the glories of English Gothic, followed a process of elaboration which culminated in the hammer-beam roof, taking its name from horizontal elements which lessened the span and helped to reduce lateral pressure. The most impressive example is at Westminster Hall, London. Fine timber roofs in many English parish churches.

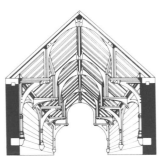

Hammer-beam roof

Window tracery

Gothic windows developed from plate tracery, with circles "punched" through stone above pointed openings (lancets). Openings later foliated or cusped. Intersecting ribs formed decorative bar tracery, invented in France.

Plate tracery,
12th–early 13th c

Geometrical,
13th c

Intersecting,
13th–14th c

Reticulated,
early–mid 14th c

Curvilinear,
14th–15th c

Flamboyant,
15th c *(France)*

English Perpendicular,
late 14th–15th c

**Mature English
Perpendicular,** *15th* c

Ornament

Gables, capitals, pinnacles and finials were elaborately carved, generally with vegetable forms. Portal sculpture featured elongated figures. The Spanish Plateresque and Portuguese Manueline styles were fantastically ornate.

Leaf capital, *Southwell*

Carved corbel, *Lincoln*

Tower, *Florence*

Gable, *St Stephen's, Vienna*

Manueline window surround, *Tomar, Portugal (see p 110)*

Secular architecture

Castles developed independently of the transition from Romanesque to Gothic in other building types. The finest examples of the period are English castles built in, or on the borders of, Wales (1220–1326) and the Hospitaller castles of the Crusading principalities. Gate-houses, with loopholes covering all approaches, superseded keeps. In the late Gothic age civic pride gave rise to superb municipal buildings.

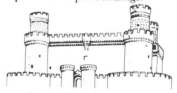

Castle, *Manzanares el Real, Spain*

Town hall, *Louvain, Belgium*

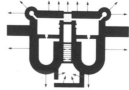

Gate-house, *Beaumaris, Wales, showing firing-lines from loopholes*

France

The interior scheme introduced at Chartres Cathedral—nave arcade, triforium, clerestory (see p 99)—became the norm for High Gothic and prepared the way for spectacular structural developments. A tendency towards higher and higher naves, with slender supports and vast walls of stained glass, reached a peak at Beauvais. Bar tracery, which first appeared at Rheims (early 13th c), evolved into the Flamboyant style of the 15th c, distinguished by a passion for the ogee, or s-shaped curve.

Early Gothic

Of the abbey church of ST DENIS (rebuilt after *c.* 1137), near Paris, only the light, airy choir and much restored w front, with one tower, remain from 12th c. LAON (1160–1225) was the first complete Gothic cathedral. Like NOYON (1145–1228; see p 99) it has both triforium and gallery. The 5 towers, out of 7 planned, have remarkable sculpture, including carved oxen ◆. First gargoyles. Square E end in English style.

NOTRE DAME, PARIS (1163–*c.* 1250), is the last early cathedral with gallery above arcade. Harmonious w front has 3 recessed portals beneath wheel window.

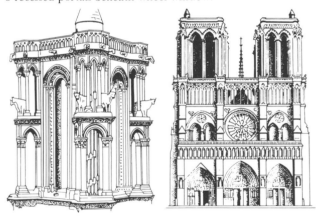

Laon Cathedral: *tower*   **Notre Dame, Paris:** w *front*

High Gothic and Flamboyant

The cathedral of BOURGES (1195–1275) has unique 5-level elevation: outer, lower aisle has its own triforium. w façade has 5 portals instead of usual 3. Fine 13th-c glass.

Bourges Cathedral: *section and view of* E *end*

The cathedral at RHEIMS (begun 1211) was used for royal coronations. Sculptured w front has nearly 500 carved figures, including Angel of Rheims ◆, and stained glass windows instead of tympana over doorways. Complex and elegant flying buttresses. Twin towers never received spires. Interior restrained in decoration.

Rheims Cathedral: w *front and sculpture on portal*

The largest French cathedral is AMIENS (1220–88), which deepened and perfected the tripartite elevation established at Chartres. Chevet of 7 chapels. Over 5,000 sculptured figures on façade. Superb carved woodwork in choir stalls ◆.

Amiens Cathedral: *detail of* w *front*   **Strasbourg Cathedral:** *Portal of St Lawrence*

The w rose window of STRASBOURG (begun 1230) is linked to portal below by openwork gable with tall finials. Elaborate N doorway. Interior has unique 13th-c Angels' Pillar ◆.

At BEAUVAIS (begun 1247) the choir sweeps up to a dramatic 48 m—the loftiest vault in Europe. Projected nave never built. LA SAINTE CHAPELLE, PARIS (1243–8), has 13th-c stained glass magnificently displayed in 85 major panels.

In the s of France, the fortress-church of ALBI (1282–1390) shows Catalan influence. Interior is a wide vaulted hall.

The Flamboyant style is well represented by the churches of ST OUEN (1318–1515) and ST MACLOU (1432–1500) at ROUEN and by NOTRE DAME, ALENÇON (late 15th c).

Secular architecture

Typical fortified towns are CARCASSONNE and AIGUES MORTES (both 13th c), behind defensive curtain walls. Both public and private buildings made use of Flamboyant decoration. The PALAIS DE JUSTICE, ROUEN (1493–1508), has spiky carvings, steep roof, fine octagonal tower. Lavish carving inside and out also occurs at HOUSE OF JACQUES COEUR, BOURGES (1442–53); 7 stairway turrets. The HÔTEL DIEU, BEAUNE (c. 1443), has roof of polychrome tiles.

Hôtel Dieu, Beaune: *gable*

England

The earliest mature type of English Gothic — Early English — appears from c. 1180 and is characterized by simplicity and airiness of design, as found at Salisbury Cathedral. In the Decorated period (c. 1250–1370) ornament became more luxuriant. The Perpendicular style (c. 1300–1540), so called because of its panelled windows, favoured complex lierne and fan vaulting (see pp 100 and 101).

Salisbury Cathedral

Begun the same year as Amiens, SALISBURY (1220–1380) is classic Early English. The cathedral has double transepts, an octagonal chapter house and a Decorated square crossing tower topped by a smooth, cool spire — the highest in England (123 m). Impressive early Decorated cloisters.

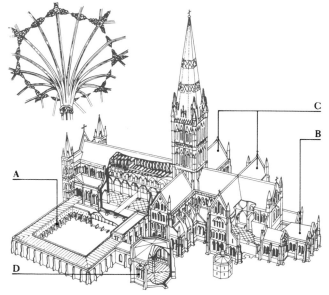

Salisbury Cathedral: *column of chapter house and cutaway view*
A *Cloisters;* **B** *Lady Chapel;* **C** *Double transepts;* **D** *Chapter house*

Other cathedrals

The E end of CANTERBURY (begun *c*. 1070) illustrates beginnings of English Gothic. Basically French, though with English double transepts. Perpendicular nave with lierne vaults, cloister with heraldic bosses. Fine 12th–13th-c glass. Romanesque crypt.

WELLS (*c*. 1180–1485) marks the start of Early English but the magnificent W screen façade is uncharacteristically bejewelled with sculpture. Unique scissor-arches (1338) built as bracing-struts under crossing. Gravely beautiful N porch.

LINCOLN (rebuilt 1192–1320) is sometimes considered the finest cathedral in the country. Tierceron vaults of nave resemble palm leaves. Screen façade has pleasing rhythmic pattern. Angel Choir ◆ (1256–80) has luxuriant carving in stone and wood.

Wells Cathedral: W *front*   **Lincoln Cathedral:** *Angel Choir*

YORK MINSTER is the largest of England's medieval cathedrals. Imitation vaulting in wood set a precedent. Wealth of 14th-c stained glass. Enormous E window has 15th-c glass. N front has "Five Sisters" lancet windows (13th c).

EXETER (largely 1275–1369), a good example of Decorated, has superb tierceron vault (see p 100). Lavishly moulded corbels and bosses. BRISTOL (choir begun 13th c) has aisles as tall as nave, like German hall-churches; lierne vaults. At ELY a stone octagonal lantern was erected 1322–42 after Norman crossing fell down; lead-clad wooden lantern with beautiful wooden vault ◆. Separate rectangular Lady Chapel has riot of angles and curves. The S transept at GLOUCESTER (begun 1329) is finest example of early Perpendicular. E end of nave has largest Perpendicular stained-glass window. Earliest fan vaults in cloisters ◆.

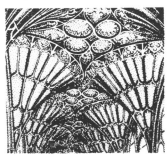

Gloucester Cathedral: *cloister vault*

Ely Cathedral: *lantern*

Westminster Abbey

With its flying buttresses, chevet and soaring vault,
WESTMINSTER ABBEY is more French than English. E arm,
transept and 5 bays of nave built 1245–69. Nave continued
westwards 1375–1506 in Perpendicular style. Henry VIII
chapel behind England's only complete chevet has fan vault
with dropping pendants. Superb hammer-beam roof ✦ on
WESTMINSTER HALL (1399).

Parish churches

Many parish churches were built or added to in the
Perpendicular period, although earlier phases are also well
represented. Best examples are in East Anglia, the Cotswolds
and Somerset. Glorious towers, carved wooden screens.

Church towers: *Leigh-on-Mendip, Oxford, Patrington, Boston*

Secular buildings and chapels

England is unrivalled in the number and variety of its
medieval secular buildings—manor houses, alms houses,
hospitals, colleges, guild halls, tithe barns, etc. An emphasis
on concentric symmetry in military architecture may be seen
at HARLECH and BEAUMARIS castles in Wales (see p 102).

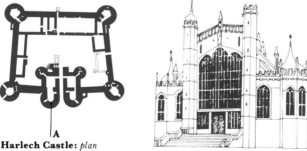

Harlech Castle: *plan*
A *Gate-house*

St George's Chapel, Windsor

Among Perpendicular chapels ST GEORGE'S, WINDSOR
(begun 1481), and KING'S COLLEGE CHAPEL, CAMBRIDGE (1446–
1515), are most famous. Latter known for fan vaults ✦.

Central and eastern Europe

Little Gothic architecture was built in the Germanic regions
before the end of the second quarter of the 13th c. A
characteristic German Gothic building-type was the hall-
church—*Hallenkirche*—with aisles the same height as the nave.
Openwork spires and flying ribs on vaults were typical.

Germany and Austria

COLOGNE CATHEDRAL (begun 1248), the largest Gothic church in N Europe, owes much to Amiens, but lacks its refinement. The vault, at 46 m, is almost as high as at Beauvais, and spiny twin towers rise to 152 m. Piers of nave arcades bear figure sculptures under canopies. FREIBURG CATHEDRAL (*c.* 1250–1360) has fantastic filigree spire on octagonal W tower. Net-vaulted choir has ribs springing from piers without intervention of capitals.

A typical hall-church, ST ELIZABETH, MARBURG (*c.* 1257–83), has French-inspired rib vaults and bar tracery, but the trefoil E end derives from Cologne. Exterior walkways pierce buttresses.

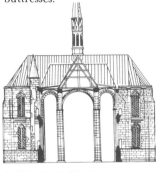 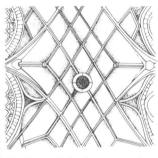

St Elizabeth, Marburg: *section*

Freiburg Cathedral: *net vault, choir*

Really a parish church built by the guilds, ULM MINSTER (1377–1492) has an openwork spire on an extremely tall tower (total height 161 m). At ST LAWRENCE, NUREMBURG, an enclosed Romanesque nave opens into a hall-like choir (begun 1439) with stellar vaulting.

The CHURCH OF THE HOLY CROSS, SCHWÄBISCH-GEMUND (begun *c.* 1350), belongs to the golden age of hall-churches. Built by Heinrich Parler, an influential stone-mason. Tall, Germanic lancet windows symmetrically arranged on façade.

In Austria, ST STEPHEN'S, VIENNA, is a modified Romanesque church (rebuilt 1300–1450) retaining original W front. Tower added over S portal 1368–1433. Steeply pitched roof has patterned polychrome tiles.

Church of the Holy Cross, Schwäbisch-Gemund

St Stephen's, Vienna: *cutaway view showing interior and roof construction*

Germany has Gothic town halls at Cologne, Münster, Regensburg, Lübeck and elsewhere.

Town Hall, Münster: *upper part*   **Town Hall, Brunswick**

Prague
Based on a French plan, PRAGUE CATHEDRAL (1344–96), in
the capital of Charles IV's Holy Roman Empire, was begun
by Matthias of Arras and continued by Peter Parler (d. 1399).
The ambivalence between structural and decorative features,
and interior and exterior, is characteristic of late Gothic.
Flowing window tracery (famous window in s transept ◆),
complex rib vaults.
　　Also at Prague is VLADISLAV HALL (begun *c.* 1487), with
fantastic interplay of petal-shaped ribs on vault.

The Low Countries

In Belgium and the Netherlands the increased grandeur of
secular rather than religious building reflects the rise of
commerce as the new patron of the arts.

Belgium
The cathedral of TOURNAI (1066–1340), with 5 towers, shows
strong French influence. Gothic choir and chevet added to
Romanesque nave. Plan of ANTWERP CATHEDRAL (1352–
1411), in mature Flemish style, is remarkably wide: nave is
flanked by triple aisles, though transepts are aisleless.
　　The CLOTH HALL, YPRES (1202–1304; reconstructed 20th c),
has superb unbroken façade, steep roof, pinnacled tower. The
CLOTH HALL, BRUGES, features preposterously tall tower with
lantern. Impressive town hall at LOUVAIN (1448–63; see p 102).

Town Halls, Louvain *and* **Brussels; Cloth Hall, Ypres:** *details*

The Netherlands
UTRECHT CATHEDRAL (begun 1254), on French pattern, was a
major Dutch prototype. ST JAN, 'S-HERTOGENBOSCH (1370–
1559), is richly decorated.

Scandinavia

The most important Norwegian Gothic cathedrals— STAVANGER (begun *c.* 1130) and TRONDHEIM (begun *c.* 1185)— betray English influences. Largest Scandinavian cathedral is UPPSALA, Sweden (begun *c.* 1270), with French chevet. Late Gothic churches owe much to N Germany.

Spain and Portugal

Spanish Gothic cathedrals are characteristically wide in plan. Moorish influences are apparent in the S, French in the N and in Catalonia, where hall-churches with side-chapels replacing aisles were built. The encrusted style of late Gothic decoration (from late 15th C) is known as Plateresque (from *platería*, meaning silverwork). The corresponding phase of fantastic ornament in Portugal is Manueline (1495–1521).

Spain

Spain's first Gothic cathedral is BURGOS (begun 1221), on French cruciform plan. Central tower is Plateresque (16th C). Openwork spires by Hans of Cologne. Octagonal side chapel has fine late detail. Also French-inspired: TOLEDO (1227– 1493) and LEÓN (1255–1303).

Toledo Cathedral: *section*

Burgos Cathedral: *lantern vault*

Aisleless nave of GERONA CATHEDRAL (begun 1312) is Europe's widest vaulted room (22 m), while SEVILLE (begun *c.* 1402) is largest medieval cathedral; bell tower of latter was once minaret. Plateresque exemplified on W fronts of SALAMANCA and S. PABLO, VALLODOLID.

Salamanca Cathedral: *portal*

Palma Cathedral, *Majorca*

Portugal

Manueline is epitomized at BATALHA MONASTERY (begun 1387) and the CONVENT OF CHRIST, TOMAR (1160–*c.* 1515), where W window of chapter house features a profusion of carved ropes and other nautical motifs (see p 102).

Italy

Italian Gothic churches were often brick-built and faced with marble, which lent itself to flat polychrome patterning, and frescoes were developed in place of stained glass. Friars' hall-churches were common. Milan Cathedral is the only building close to the mainstream of French Gothic. Italy took the lead in secular building in the late 13th c.

Religious architecture

Bands of dark and light marble on both the interior and exterior of SIENA CATHEDRAL (*c*. 1226–1380) make it very striking. Unusual hexagonal crossing surmounted by dome and lantern. Magnificent façade by Giovanni Pisano.

Siena Cathedral: *angle of* W *front, and upper façade*

FLORENCE CATHEDRAL (begun 1296), with green and white marble facing, occupied many architects during long period of building. Giotto designed free-standing campanile (1334). Renaissance dome (see p 115).

ORVIETO CATHEDRAL (1290–
1330) has basilican-like
interior. Striped marble, as at
Siena.

Begun two years after St
Francis' death, S. FRANCESCO,
ASSISI (1228–53), is imposingly
sited on two levels on a hill
top. Aisleless interiors have
famous frescoes ◆.

Also: S. Maria della Spina,
Pisa (1323).

S. Francesco, Assisi: *vault*

Secular architecture

The PALAZZO PUBBLICO, SIENA
(1288–1309), is in stone and
brick, with chimney-like bell-
tower. Lower arcade is
typically Sienese.

The DOGE'S PALACE, VENICE
♣ (14th c), is among world's
most beautiful buildings.
Three-level façade, which
perfectly integrates structure,
material and decoration, has
been likened to an altar
frontal in rich brocade. Also
at Venice: Ca d'Oro (1424–36).

Doge's Palace, Venice: *detail*

ITALIAN RENAISSANCE

The Renaissance, the flowering of the arts that began in
14th-C Florence, was associated with a growing secularism
and a renewed interest in Classical Roman civilization.
Patronized by merchant-aristocrat families such as the
Medici, Strozzi and Rucellai, a new kind of architect
emerged who was no longer a craftsman but a creative and
versatile artist in pursuit of aesthetic truth. Filippo
Brunelleschi (1377–1446), whose Foundling Hospital and
cathedral dome at Florence are the inaugural buildings of the
Renaissance, was a goldsmith, while Michelangelo (1475–
1564) considered himself primarily a sculptor.

Foundling Hospital, Florence *(Brunelleschi) : loggia*

The respect accorded to such men was part of a new
humanist view of the universe. Portraits of merchant patrons
showed them among the saints in heaven. Architects found
ideal proportions in the human body and applied them to
buildings that emulated the dignity and the decorative and
structural details of ancient Roman architecture. The seminal
text was Vitruvius's *De Architectura* (1st C BC), which codified
the Classical Orders, and was a source for architects and
theorists such as Leon Battista Alberti (1404–72), who
defined perfect harmony in a building as a balance from
which nothing could be added or subtracted without
destroying the whole.

High Renaissance and Mannerism

In 1499 Donato Bramante (1444–1514) moved from Milan to
Rome, where he initiated the High Renaissance phase of
architecture, characterized by harmony, simplicity and
repose. After *c.* 1520 Michelangelo, and later Giulio Romano,
designed buildings full of tension and virtuosity, in which the
clarity of the High Renaissance ideal was subverted by a
rebelliously theatrical sophistication. This tendency was
known as Mannerism, precipitated by a period of political
instability culminating in the sack of Rome (1527) by
Imperial troops. The finest architect of the later 16th C was
Andrea Palladio (1508–80), whose villas in the region of
Vicenza, as well as his treatise *I quattro libri dell'architettura*
(1570), were highly influential in England and America in
the 18th C.

Palace façades

Architects applied great ingenuity to creating harmonious designs for the outer and the courtyard façades of palaces. Walls were rusticated (i.e., the stones were cut in massive, often rough-textured blocks, with deep joints). Alberti pioneered the addition of pilasters in tiers following hierarchy of the Classical Orders demonstrated by Colosseum (see pp 22, 34, 39). Giant Orders (i.e., pilasters or columns to height of two stories) were much used by Michelangelo. Venetian façades were characteristically airy, with traceried windows.

Palazzo Strozzi, Florence: *rusticated façade*

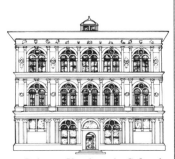

Palazzo Vidoni-Caffarelli, Rome: *detail*

Palazzo Ducale, Urbino: *courtyard*

Palazzo Vendramin-Calergi, Venice: *canal-side façade*

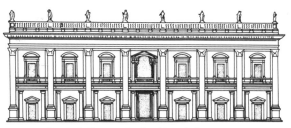

Palazzo, Capitol, Rome, *showing Giant Order*

The layout of palaces

The typical palace, influenced by Roman insulae (apartment blocks; see p 41), was built round a central court with a loggia on each side. Shops or warehouses were on the ground floor, main rooms on the first floor (piano nobile), and servants' quarters on the top floor (attic storey).

Villas and churches

A major secular building type was the villa, situated either in the country (and often attached to a farm) or in the suburbs. Palladio's symmetrically designed villas generally had colonnaded porticoes imitating Roman temple fronts.

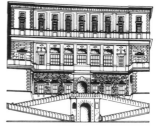

Villa Malcontenta, *near Mestre* *(Palladio)*

Villa Farnese, Caprarola *(Vignola)*

In churches Alberti and others followed the Latin cross plan, refining it by adding chapels along the side walls, sometimes as a substitute for aisles. The façade of Alberti's S. Maria Novella, Florence (1458), with its large scrolls, set a fashion. The Roman triumphal arch was also influential. Experiments were made with plans based on squares and circles, and there was a fascination with domes and Classical circular temples. Vignola's church of the Gesù, Rome (1568), had a scheme, designed for preaching, that was copied all over Europe.

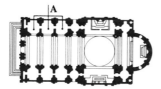

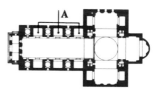

Church plans: *The Gesù, Rome; S. Andrea, Mantua. Both have side chapels* (**A**)

Church façades by Alberti: *S. Maria Novella, Florence; S. Andrea, Mantua (lower part, based on Roman triumphal arch)*

Florence

The Florence of Cosimo de' Medici and his grandson Lorenzo was Italy's major city. Its fortress-like palaces later influenced street frontages in London and elsewhere.

Brunelleschi

Brunelleschi probably discovered the laws of perspective. In the DOME OF FLORENCE CATHEDRAL (begun 1420) he solved the structural problem posed by the existing wide drum with a double-shelled dome, ribbed in the Gothic manner and pointed to minimize outward thrust. Heavy lantern served as counterweight.

The loggia of the OSPEDALE DEGLI INNOCENTI (Foundling Hospital; 1419–24) has an airy delicacy indebted to earlier Tuscan architecture. (See p 112.)

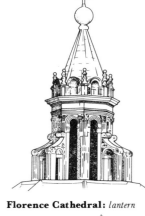

Florence Cathedral: *lantern*

S. Lorenzo: *view across nave*

Pazzi Chapel

S. LORENZO (begun 1419) is notable for the precision of its proportions; New Sacristy (begun 1520), housing Medici tombs, is by Michelangelo—an early example of Mannerism.

Other buildings: Pazzi Chapel (begun 1429), a copy-book for the Renaissance; S. Spirito (1434–82).

Alberti

Alberti was the first architectural theorist of the Renaissance.

His earliest building was the PALAZZO RUCELLAI (1446–51); superb façade has rusticated masonry, pilasters imitating Classical Orders, and graceful double windows on upper stories.

The influential façade added by Alberti to S. MARIA NOVELLA (see opposite) harmonizes successfully with the medieval building. Begun 1458. Superb decoration in green and white marble. Proportions based on exact mathematical calculations.

Palazzo Rucellai: *façade detail*

Palaces of the Quattrocento

The PALAZZO MEDICI-RICCARDI (begun 1444) was the first Florentine Renaissance palace. Rustication graduates from heavy and rugged on ground floor to smoother stonework above, making palace seem taller. Inner courtyard has graceful arcade. The PALAZZO GONDI (begun *c.* 1490) has unusually rounded rustication on the ground floor. The PALAZZO STROZZI (begun *c.* 1490) has massive cornice projecting over 2.1 m (see p 113).

Palazzo Medici-Riccardi: *court*

Palazzo Gondi: *façade detail*

Mannerism in Florence

Michelangelo's BIBLIOTECA LAURENZIANA (begun 1524) had to fit into long wing raised above entrance level. Vestibule, containing three-pronged staircase by Vasari and Amannati, is uncomfortably tall. Interior details (e.g., huge paired consoles) show Mannerist perversity.

Also in Florence: Palazzo Pitti garden front (Amannati; begun *c.* 1558); Palazzo degli Uffizi (Vasari; 1560–74); SS Trinità façade (1593–4).

Biblioteca Laurenziana: *vestibule staircase and door to library*

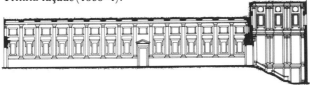

Section of Biblioteca Laurenziana

Rome

From the early 16th c Rome became again the cultural centre of Europe. The architectural geniuses of the age were Bramante, Michelangelo and Raphael. Palaces tended towards the gigantic. In church design the need to house large congregations led to a longitudinal plan with a centralized E end. Vignola, architect of the widely influential Gesù church, also introduced oval forms (further developed in Baroque).

The late Quattrocento

The subtly proportioned PALAZZO DELLA CANCELLERIA (1486–96) shows influence of Alberti. Unfinished courtyard of PALAZZO VENEZIA (begun *c.* 1470) has arches on solid piers with engaged half-columns as in the Colosseum.

Palaces and villas

The unfinished VILLA MADAMA (Raphael and Antonio da Sangallo the Younger; begun *c.* 1516) was planned with circular courtyard and rooms containing apses in manner of ancient baths. Loggia inspired by Nero's house.

Peruzzi's PALAZZO MASSIMI (begun *c.* 1535) betrays elements of Mannerist feeling: e.g., attic windows have curious surrounds like picture-frames. Curved façade.

The PALAZZO FARNESE (Sangallo the Younger; begun 1534) set a fashion for monumentality; top floor by Michelangelo.

Also: Villa Farnesina (Peruzzi; 1509–11).

Palazzo Massimi

Palazzo Farnese: *central window*

Bramante in Rome

Bramante's first work in Rome was the cloister of S. MARIA DELLA PACE, completed 1504: a two-storied loggia with columns between upper-floor piers giving extra support to entablature. Façade of church by Pietro da Cortona (17th C)

In the cloister of S. PIETRO IN MONTORIO, supposed site of St Peter's martyrdom, Bramante built the TEMPIETTO (1502), a domed circular monument, partly inspired by the pagan Temple of Vesta, which perfectly fulfils Alberti's rules of harmony. Frieze has metopes and triglyphs in Classical manner. A peristyle of antique Tuscan granite columns encircles a taller inner cylinder forming the cella.

Tempietto

S. Maria della Pace: *cloister*

St Peter's

Bramante began St Peter's in 1506, but its character—Giant Orders encircling the exterior, 4 massive piers inside, pointed dome (1585–90)—owes more to Michelangelo, who worked (1547–64) to a subtle modification of Bramante's Greek-cross plan. In early 17th c Carlo Maderna lengthened nave and added present façade and portico. Bernini began Baroque piazza 1656 (see p 133).

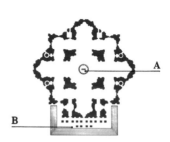

A *High altar;* **B** *Portico (never built: space occupied instead by Maderna's extension)*

St Peter's: *dome*

Michelangelo's plan of St Peter's

The Capitol

The CAPITOL, centre of Roman government, was replanned from 1546 by Michelangelo. Three palaces enclosing central space show his masterly use of Giant Orders, with smaller columns giving index of scale. Scheme later altered by della Porta, who made it more expansive in feeling.

Vignola

Giacomo Vignola (1507–73) was Rome's leading architect in generation after Michelangelo. His church of the GESÙ (begun 1568) was designed in accord with the Counter-Reformation emphasis on preaching (see p 114). Light pours in from drum of dome over crossing. Barrel-vaulted side-chapels.

Also by Vignola: Villa Giulia (1550–55), now Museum of Etruscan Antiquities; S. Andrea in Via Flaminia (1550–54), first church to have an oval dome.

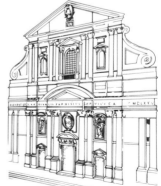

Villa Giulia: *detail of Nymphaeum by Amannati*

Gesù: *façade by della Porta— a modification of Vignola's design*

Venice and Vicenza

Early Renaissance buildings in Venice continued to make use of Venetian Gothic features. In palace architecture the medieval Doge's Palace was a strong influence. Canal-side palace façades had marble facing, balconies and closely grouped windows.

Venice before Palladio

Sansovino's LIBRARY OF ST MARK's (begun 1537) has a long, graceful façade arcaded on two stories; richly decorated frieze pierced by attic windows. Same architect's PALAZZO CORNER DELLA CA' GRANDE (begun 1537) brings to the standard Venetian palace a number of innovations from outside the Republic, including rusticated ground floor and triple-arched entrance.

Also: The Mint (Sansovino; begun 1537); S. Maria dei Miracoli (Lombardi; 1481–9).

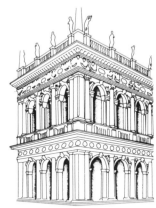

Library of St Mark's, Venice: *angle*

Palladio

Palladio, though restlessly inventive, created symmetrical buildings with a decidedly un-Mannerist sense of repose.

At VENICE the REDENTORE (Church of the Redeemer; begun 1577) has three pediments on temple-front façade. Choir screened by semicircular colonnade.

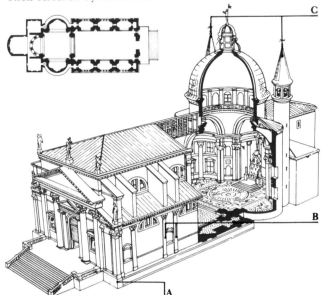

Redentore, Venice: *plan and cutaway view*
A *Podium ;* **B** *Giant pilasters ;* **C** *Bell-towers*

The chaste, white, domed church of s. GIORGIO MAGGIORE (begun 1566) also has façade based on interlocking temple fronts. The plan has apsed transepts, and monks' choir to E; latter separated from congregation by screen of columns.

S. Georgio Maggiore: *façade and section*

Palladio's first work was at VICENZA: the addition of a two-storey loggia to medieval BASILICA (begun 1546). Each bay has an arch supported on twinned columns flanked by flat-headed openings—the so-called "Palladian window".

The famous VILLA CAPRA (or Rotonda; begun *c.* 1550), just outside Vicenza, has a perfectly symmetrical plan: central room is a circular hall crowned by a low dome, and each façade has a flight of steps leading to a temple-like portico. Inspired Lord Burlington's villa, Chiswick, London.

Palladio's earliest Vicenza palace is the typically symmetrical PALAZZO PORTO (1552). His elegant PALAZZO CHIERICATI (begun *c.* 1550), now a museum, has façade opened up into vast loggias. In his last work, the TEATRO OLIMPICO (begun 1580), also in Vicenza, false perspectives of built-in set are one source of long tradition of illusionism in European architecture.

Also by Palladio: Villa Barbaro, Maser (1560–8); Villa Malconenta (1560), near Mestre (see p 114).

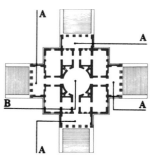

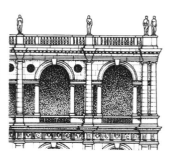

Villa Capra, Vicenza: *plan*
A *Porticoes ;* **B** *Domed central hall*

Basilica, Vicenza: *detail showing Palladian windows*

Villa Barbaro: *façade*

The rest of Italy

From Florence Renaissance architecture spread to other towns in N and central Italy. The southern part of the country was scarcely affected until the Baroque age.

Milan

In the 1470s Bramante began to remodel the Early Christian church of s. MARIA PRESSO S. SATIRO. Because of restricted site, E end is made to seem spacious by an illusion of perspective. Also by Bramante are E end (1490s) added to Gothic s. MARIA DELLE GRAZIE and three cloisters (1490s) added to s. AMBROGIO and adjacent monastery. By Michelozzo: Portinari Chapel, centrally planned.

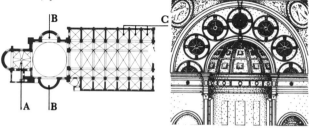

S. Maria delle Grazie, Milan: *plan and view of choir*
A *Choir;* **B** *Apsidal transepts;* **C** *Side chapels*

Other regions

The PALAZZO DUCALE, URBINO ♣ (mainly 1460s), the most beautiful and dramatically sited of all Renaissance palaces, was built by Luciano Laurana for Duke Frederigo of Urbino, a Renaissance "universal man". Gracefully arcaded courtyard (1480; see p 113). Façade incomplete.

The VILLA FARNESE, CAPRAROLA (begun early 1520s), near Viterbo, has pentagon plan with inner courtyard. Vignola took over building 1559. (See p 114.) COLLEONE CHAPEL, BERGAMO (Amadeo; 1470s), shows triumph of decorative tradition of N Italy.

At MANTUA, GIULIO ROMANO'S HOUSE (1546), by Romano, is Mannerist in triangulated string course over doorway and curious framing of windows. The church of s. ANDREA, MANTUA (Alberti; begun 1470), has triumphal arch façade.

Giulio Romano's house: *window detail*

Palazzo del Tè: *garden front*

Also at Mantua is the PALAZZO DEL TÈ (Giulio Romano; 1526–*c.* 1534), a Mannerist single-storied pleasure house.

Other buildings: Tempio Malatestiano, Rimini (Alberti; 1446); Villa Medici, Poggio a Caiano.

THE SPREAD OF
THE RENAISSANCE

The influx of Italian Renaissance building styles into N Europe
and Spain was belated and uneven, and at first took the form
of small features such as tombs, and later of superficial
decoration on Gothic structures. Among the first to accept
the new ideas were the French, who penetrated N Italy in
1494 and 1499 and set up a court at Milan.

France

The uneasy alliance between native Gothic masons and
imported Italian architects in the early 16th c is seen in the
Loire valley châteaux, in bizarre combinations of
Renaissance ornament with steep roofs, dormer windows and
prickly skylines. The "Fontainebleau style", a mixture of
painting, high-relief stucco and strapwork (stucco shaped like
curled leather), became a European fashion. Pierre Lescot
(*c.* 1500–78) and Philibert Delorme (*c.* 1510–70) laid the
foundations of French Classicism.

The school of the Loire

The CHÂTEAU DE CHAMBORD (begun 1519) was a palatial
hunting-lodge for François I. Massive round towers and
fantastic turreted skyline are medieval, but main block, or
donjon, is Italianate in plan, with 4 identical apartments
symmetrically disposed. Superb double spiral staircase ◆.
Exterior has Renaissance niches, columns, pilasters, etc.

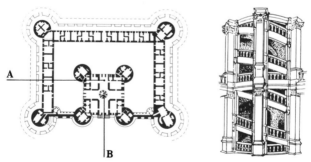

Château de Chambord: *plan and spiral staircase*
A *Main block ;* **B** *Staircase*

Château de Chambord seen from s

The CHÂTEAU DE CHENONCEAUX ♧ (1515–23) is built on piles over R. Cher; bridge by Delorme (1555–9). The compact CHÂTEAU D'AZAY-LE-RIDEAU ♧ (1518–27) shows Italian influence in flat, unobtrusive pilasters. CHÂTEAU DE BLOIS (begun 13th c) has hybrid wing (1515–25) built by François I. His octagonal tower in façade contains spiral staircase ◆, with panels of arabesque decoration on Corinthian piers.

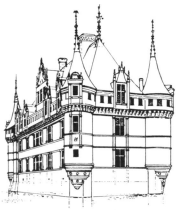

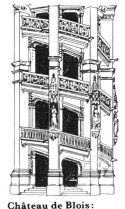

Château de Blois:
staircase

Château d'Azay-le-Rideau

Fontainebleau

The great palace at FONTAINEBLEAU, Ile de France (begun 1528) was transformed from a hunting lodge by Gilles le Breton for François I. Gate of Cour d'Ovale (the Porte Dorée) has three superimposed slightly flattened arches. Each flanking tower has line of vertically linked windows, a traditionally French feature. To w of court is Le Breton's Gallery of François I ◆ (1530s). In the decoration here Mannerism made its French début; first ever strapwork. The Cour du Cheval Blanc has walls of plastered rubble with brick detailing—an influential treatment. Gallery of Henri II by Delorme. Belle Cheminée wing 1568.

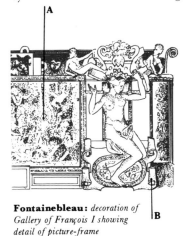

Fontainebleau: *decoration of Gallery of François I showing detail of picture-frame*
A *Painting;* **B** *Strapwork*

Porte Dorée, Fontainebleau

The Square Court of the Louvre

François I moved his capital from the Loire valley to Paris and commissioned Lescot to rebuild the old château of the LOUVRE. Under Henri IV he completed the w wing (1559), whose inner façade, where horizontals and verticals are perfectly balanced, shows a confident and original use of columns, pilasters, entablatures and other Italianate features. Ground floor arches frame segmental-headed windows, thereafter frequent in French architecture.

Court of the Louvre: *façade and detail*

After Henri IV's death Lescot added half the s wing, and from 1624 Lemercier extended w wing northwards, repeating Lescot's elevation. Claude Perrault added controversial E front (begun 1668); the podium-like ground floor supports a colonnade of coupled Corinthian columns.

Philibert Delorme

Little remains of the CHÂTEAU D'ANET (*c.* 1547–52), w of Paris, built by Delorme for Diane de Poitiers. The Mannerist entrance gate, which incorporated bronze relief of Diana by Cellini, is based on Roman triumphal arch; top of complex superstructure has clock with a stag which strikes the hours with its hoof. Chapel exterior is also Mannerist. Its plan, a Greek cross combined with a circle, was ahead of its time. Château frontispiece (i.e., projecting entrance bay) reconstructed in grounds of École des Beaux-Arts, Paris.

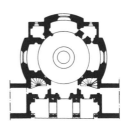

Château d'Anet: *detail of frontispiece and plan of chapel*

Salomon de Brosse

Salomon de Brosse (1571–1626) became architect to the Crown in 1608. PALAIS DU LUXEMBOURG, PARIS (begun 1615; enlarged 19th c), exemplifies his feeling for mass. Follows traditional plan of main block with wings and screen wall enclosing courtyard.

Spain and Portugal

Stimulated by wealth from America, and in Spain by the need to build in regions conquered from the Moors, architecture of a lavish kind flourished in the peninsula in the 16th c. Renaissance details infiltrated into the native Plateresque style of ornament (see p 125). By the 1520s a more truly Classical manner had emerged. The greatest architect of the period was Juan de Herrera (1530–97), whose majestic, cold style was favoured by Philip II.

Spain

The façade of the UNIVERSITY OF SALAMANCA (begun c. 1515) is a Plateresque masterpiece, with Italianate, heraldic and other motifs.

The vast ESCORIAL ♧, NW of Madrid, was built for Philip II to house a palace, college and monastery. Begun by Juan Bautista de Toledo, completed by Herrera after 1572. Based on Temple of Solomon. Austere, symmetrically planned. Church dominates. Location of choir over vaulted vestibule of w end is typically Spanish.

University of Salamanca: *Plateresque portal*

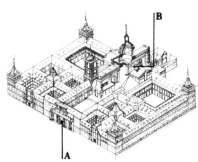

Escorial: *cutaway* **A** *Grand entrance;* **B** *Church*

Palace of Charles V, Granada: *detail*

The unfinished PALACE OF CHARLES V, GRANADA (Manchuca; begun 1526), is suffused with spirit of High Renaissance. Circular central courtyard with colonnades. GRANADA CATHEDRAL (begun 1528) is austere, though by Diego de Siloé, a master of Plateresque. Also by de Siloé: Golden Staircase, Burgos Cathedral.

VALLADOLID CATHEDRAL (Herrera; begun 1580) was conceived on a gigantic scale but completed 1730–3 less ambitiously; influential in Spain and Spanish America. Fine double cloister in TAVERA HOSPITAL, TOLEDO (1542–79).

Portugal

The purest example of the Renaissance style in Portugal is the CLOISTER OF THE CONVENT OF CHRIST, TOMAR (Diego de Torralva; begun 1555), which features Palladian window.

The Low Countries

Belgian Renaissance architecture remained loyal to medieval structural forms. In the mid 16th c Cornelis Floris and Vredeman de Vries widely promoted a blend of Classical ornament and strapwork as used at Fontainebleau, which was applied especially to curvilinear and stepped gables.

After *c.* 1580 Holland took the lead in architecture. A phase of Palladianism after *c.* 1625 was led by Jacob van Campen and Pieter Post. The late 17th c was French-influenced.

Belgium

The TOWN HALL, ANTWERP (Floris; 1561–5) is first N European building by a non-Italian in the true Renaissance spirit. CHANCELLERY, BRUGES (1535), has pseudo-Doric Orders on façade. The GRAND' PLACE, BRUSSELS, built after 1695 siege, is last public square surrounded by guild houses.

Grand'Place, Brussels: *guildhouses*

Town Hall, Antwerp: *centrepiece*

Amsterdam

Henrik de Keyser's ZUIDERKERK (begun 1603) was first church specifically suited to Protestant needs. Similar in structure but more accomplished is his WESTERKERK (1620), with airy aisled interior for preaching. Elegant tower.

Philips Vingboons built about 40 houses (1637–69), abandoning fanciful gables for more Classical forms.

The TOWN HALL (van Campen; begun 1648), now the Royal Palace, has a Palladian dignity and structural clarity.

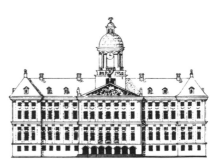

Westerkerk, Amsterdam

Town Hall, Amsterdam

The rest of the Netherlands

At LEIDEN, Lieven de Key's TOWN HALL (1595) has busily decorated gabled centrepiece, with strapwork and obelisks. The CLOTH HALL (1639–40) exemplifies Dutch Palladianism, as does the smaller MAURITSHUIS, THE HAGUE (van Campen; c. 1633), the façade of which has a Giant Order of pilasters.

At HAARLEM the MEAT HALL (de Key; 1602–3) mixes brick and stone in Dutch manner. Also: van Campen's New Church (1645).

Town Hall, Leiden: *bottom of façade*　　**Mauritshuis, The Hague**

Central Europe

Hungary was the first country to assimilate Renaissance influences. In Germany Classicism occurred only sporadically before 1550. Wendel Dietterlin's treatise on the Orders (1593) created a fashion for profuse ornamentation.

West Germany

The barrel-vaulted Antiquarium in the RESIDENZ, MUNICH (1569), has "grotesque" style of ornament recalling Raphael. Also at Munich, the Jesuit church of ST MICHAEL (1583–9) shows influence of Gesù, Rome. Wide barrel-vaulted nave has 4 barrel-vaulted chapels on either side. Italianate interior.

AUGSBURG TOWN HALL (Elias Holl; 1614–20) features an upper central section imitating façade of 16th-c Roman church. FUGGER FUNERAL CHAPEL (1518), ST ANNE'S, AUGSBURG, was first Italian Renaissance architecture in Germany.

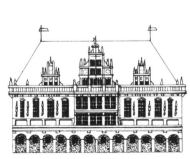 

Town Hall, Bremen　　　　**St Michael's, Munich**

TOWN HALL, BREMEN (early 15th c, additions 1609–14) has steep roof and gables contrasting with Italianate arcade.

At HEIDELBERG CASTLE the derelict Ottoheinrichsbau (1556–9) has superimposed pilasters and half-columns.

127

Britain

Henry VIII's Reformation in the 1530s broke off emergent Italian influences. Under Elizabeth I (reigned 1558–1603) Renaissance architecture was absorbed through Flanders and France. The new secular style combined large mullioned windows (i.e., with vertical subdivisions as in Perpendicular Gothic) with strapwork and symmetrical façades. In the Jacobean era (1603–25) brick replaced stone in aristocratic houses, which commonly had stepped or curved gables. In the 1620s Inigo Jones (1573–1652) began a Classical reaction against Jacobean decorative exuberance.

Tudor architecture

The first great Elizabethan mansion was LONGLEAT HOUSE, Wiltshire (1572–80), symmetrical and restrained in plan and elevation. Large windows characteristically Elizabethan, in contrast to smaller windows of Jacobean style. Classical pilasters on façade are a rumour of the Renaissance.

Longleat House

HAMPTON COURT PALACE, SW LONDON (begun 1514), was built for Wolsey and enlarged by Henry VIII, whose master-carpenter built hammer-beam roof of Great Hall ♦. Original parts in red brick. s and E wings by Wren.

In WOLLATON HALL, Nottinghamshire (1580–88), architect Robert Smythson took basic central courtyard plan and filled in space with towering Great Hall, surmounted by angle-turreted great chamber. Exterior has pilasters and strapwork.

Wollaton Hall: *façade and plan*
A *Hall;* **B** *Screens passage;* **C** *Gallery (above);* **D** *Kitchen*

The massive BURGHLEY HOUSE, Northamptonshire (begun 1556), adds gatehouse and angle towers to Longleat plan. Strapwork, heraldic beasts and obelisks on courtyard tower show Flemish Mannerist influence. In same county KIRBY HALL (1570–3) has first English use of giant Order. HARDWICK HALL, Derbyshire (1590–6), has variant of traditional H-shaped plan with hall between residential and service blocks: here, hall is at right angles to front door instead of parallel.

LITTLE MORETON HALL, CHESHIRE, is superb mid-16th-c half-timbered house surrounded by moat, with projecting long gallery added 1580. Carved corner posts and black and white patterned surfaces are typical of Tudor Midlands.

Also: Condover Hall, Shropshire (*c.* 1598); Montacute House, Somerset (1580–99).

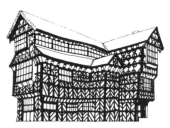

Little Moreton Hall

Jacobean mansions

BLICKLING HALL, NORFOLK (*c.* 1620), in brick with stone facings, has rectangular plan incorporating two internal courts separated by hall. Four corner towers containing staircases. Ornate plaster ceiling in Long Gallery ♦.

Blickling Hall: *façade and chimney-piece*

HATFIELD HOUSE, Hertfordshire (1607–12), follows a not quite symmetrical half-H plan. Brick dressed with stone. Plain N front. s front has Italianate loggia, three-storey centrepiece. Fine interior wooden staircase ♦.

Other buildings: Audley End, Essex (1603–16); Bramshill House, Hampshire (1605–12).

Inigo Jones and his followers

Inigo Jones's knowledge of Roman antiquities and admiration for Palladio's work were unique in England at the time.

His first important commission was the QUEEN'S HOUSE, GREENWICH, London (1616–18 and 1629–35), the first English villa in an Italian style. Originally two blocks connected by a bridge straddling the London–Dover road. Upper-floor loggia set off by rusticated basement. Interior of N block dominated by superbly proportioned cubic hall.

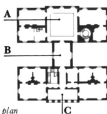

Queen's House, Greenwich: *view from* E *and plan*
A *Hall;* B *Bridge;* C *Loggia*

129

Jones worked with his pupil John Webb on WILTON HOUSE, Wiltshire, where he designed the sumptuously ornamented Double-cube Room ♦. Deeply coved ceiling.

The BANQUETING HOUSE, WHITEHALL, LONDON (1619–22), is a robust, English version of a Palladian palace. Interior is superb double-cube room, with painted ceiling by Rubens ♦.

Webb added a porch to THE VYNE, HAMPSHIRE (1654), the first of a series of temple porticos embellishing English

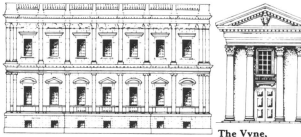

Banqueting House, Whitehall

The Vyne, Hampshire: *portico*

country houses. The KING CHARLES BLOCK, GREENWICH HOSPITAL is his, as is ELTHAM LODGE, Kent (1664).

Scandinavia

The impact of the Renaissance in Denmark is shown by castles at KRONBORG (*c.* 1574–85) and FREDERIKSBORG (*c.* 1602–20), worked on by Dutch architects. In the late 17th c Sweden created majestic buildings such as the castle at DROTTNINGHOLM. In Norway and Finland the timber tradition persisted.

Russia

Italian architects worked in MOSCOW in the late 15th–early 16th c. Novi's ST MICHAEL THE ARCHANGEL, THE KREMLIN (1505–9), has Venetian shell-like gables. The "FACETED PALACE" (1487–91) is even more Italianate. The brilliantly polychrome ST BASIL'S (1555–60), in Red Square, moulded the style of Russian architecture for 100 years. Its pyramidal central tower is indebted to church at KOLOMENSKOE (1532).

St Michael the Archangel, Moscow

St Basil's, Moscow

BAROQUE AND
NEO-CLASSICISM

The Baroque style evolved in Rome *c.* 1620–60 as an expression of the Catholic resurgence that followed the Counter-Reformation. Its theatrical and emotional qualities made it powerful as political propaganda, but its purest achievements are churches in Rome, Austria and s Germany.

The word "baroque" originally meant misshapen, with reference to pearls, but its derogatory tone is scarcely applicable to the irresistible vitality of this architecture. The square and the circle were abandoned for shapes that swirled and moved—undulating façades and plans based on ovals—and dramatic effects were obtained by orchestrating façades in a rhythm towards a central towering mass. Ornament became sensuous and highly elaborate, with a penchant for marble, gilt and bronze. Boundaries between art forms dissolved and materials were transmuted for illusionist effects. Thus, sculpture was coloured, and was used structurally, or to disguise structure; false perspectives were painted on walls; and wood was carved or painted to look like draped fabric.

In S. Maria della Vittorio, Rome, the *Ecstasy of St Theresa*, sculptured by Gianlorenzo Bernini (1598–1680), who with Francesco Borromini and Pietro da Cortona created the Baroque, has heavenly rays fashioned from gilt metal. Light itself was often manipulated as part of an effect which drew the onlooker into a complex involvement. Above all, decoration and architecture were unified.

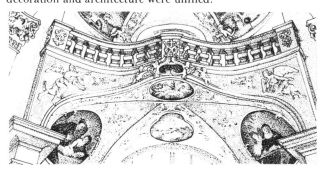

Church interior, Banz, Austria: *gallery and painted vault*

The last phase of the Baroque, from *c.* 1700 until the coming of Neo-Classicism, was the Rococo, especially fashionable in France and s Germany. Invented to suit Parisian tastes, it was characterized by elegant, light-hearted décor, with a fondness for pastel colours, and by an abandonment of Baroque structural bravado.

Neo-Classicism
Baroque was inimical to the Protestantism of N Europe. An alternative theme was Classicism, a refinement of the various national Renaissance styles, ranging from Palladianism in Britain (and N America) to the less definable idioms of François Mansart and Louis Le Vau in France.

After *c.* 1750 *Neo*-Classicism emerged—a return, in the name of reason, simplicity and grandeur, to the antique, which the new science of archaeology was investigating. Rationalists such as Claude-Nicolas Ledoux and Étienne-Louis Boullée went further and advocated (but were seldom able to build) an architecture based largely on geometry.

In the early 19th c Neo-Classical idealism was modified by an awareness of the value of the antique as propaganda, and as a means of evoking the past in the spirit of Romanticism. The Romantic movement was heralded in England by the 18th-c taste for the Picturesque, manifested in whimsical treatments of Neo-Gothic, rustic and exotic themes.

Architectural themes

Neo-Classicism: *Brandenburg Gate, Berlin (detail)*

Baroque church interior, *with spiralling columns: St John Nepomuk, Munich*

The grand palace with formal garden: *Versailles*

Baroque church façade: *Borromini's S. Agnese, Rome*

Sculptural column: *Belvedere, Vienna*

Rome

Carlo Maderna prefaced Rome's 17th-c Baroque style with his façade for S. Susanna (1597), but it was the genius Bernini who epitomized the era. His dramatic naturalistic sculptures started a new European fashion, and his grand, lavish architecture won him such fame that Louis XIV invited him to Paris to enlarge the Louvre. Borromini, though daringly original, produced work generally smaller in scale and in simpler materials like brick and stucco.

Bernini, Borromini and their contemporaries

Baroque preoccupation with staircases shows in the masterly SCALA REGIA (Royal Staircase; 1663–6), where Bernini fitted main entrance to Vatican in awkwardly converging space. Ingeniously constructed tunnel-vaulted colonnade.

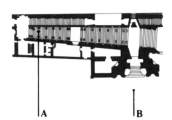

A **B**

Scala Regia: *plan and detail of doorway*
A *Narrowing staircase;* **B** *Narthex of St Peter's*

Bernini's famous double colonnade of the PIAZZA AND COLONNADE OF ST PETER'S (1656–67) dynamically symbolizes Pope's arms extended to the faithful. Inside the colossal bronze BALDACCHINO (canopy) spirals over high altar.

S. ANDREA AL QUIRINALE (1658–78), considered by Bernini to be his masterpiece, has oval plan, with altar and entrance porch on short axis. Emotional sculpture and painting.

S. Andrea al Quirinale: *cutaway view*

S. Susanna: *façade*

Maderna's S. SUSANNA (1597–1603) is similar to the Gesù in façade, but details are in higher relief and proportions more dynamic. His greatest work was nave and w façade (1602–26) added to ST PETER'S; towers never built. (See also p 118.)

Borromini's S. CARLO ALLE QUATRO FONTANE (begun 1633) has complex plan. Undulating walls resolve back to oval at dome level. Dynamic façade. Also by Borromini: S. Agnese (1653–5); S. Ivo della Sapienza (1642–60).

Pietro da Cortona (1596–1669), primarily a painter, created typically dynamic Baroque façade for s. MARIA DELLA PACE (1656–7), bunching together columns and pilasters. s. MARIA IN VIA LATA (1660) shows his later graver style.

The less adventurous Carlo Fontana (1634–1714) helped to create the Classicizing academicism of later European Baroque. For Bernini he worked on s. MARIA DEI MIRACOLI (completed 1679).

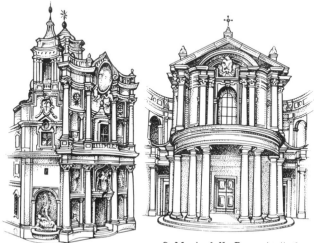

S. Carlo alle Quatro Fontane

S. Maria della Pace: *detail of façade*

The rest of Italy

In Naples a rich Baroque style using coloured marbles was developed by such as Cosimo Fanzago (1591–1678) and Ferdinando Sanfelice (1675–1750). In Turin Guarino Guarini (1624–83) took spatial complexity to fantastic extremes.

Turin and Venice

Guarini's s. LORENZO, TURIN (begun 1668) is indebted to Borromini's plans, but is more intricate in the mathematics of its concave and convex curves.
Interlaced strap-like ribs of amazing dome are inspired by mosque at Córdoba.

S. Lorenzo, Turin: *view into dome*   **Basilica di Superga, Turin**

The dome of Guarini's CHAPEL OF SS SINDONE, TURIN (1667–90), is made of superimposed arched ribs. His PALAZZO CARIGNANO (begun 1678) has concave-convex rhythm of Borromini's churches.

The BASILICA DI SUPERGA (Filippo Juvarra; 1716–27) is dramatically sited on a hill above Turin. Dome, with coupled columns and heavy ribs, derives from St Peter's. Porch is severely Classical. (See p 134, bottom.) Also by Juvarra: Palazzina di Stupinigi (1729–33), a grandiose hunting-lodge.

Only Baroque building to break Palladian stranglehold on Venice was S. MARIA DELLA SALUTE (Baldassare Longhena; 1631–82), at entrance to Grand Canal. A wave of crested pediments laps halfway up walls, while above them huge scrolled buttresses carry thrust of dome.

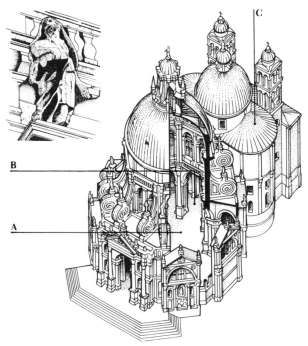

S. Maria della Salute: *cutaway view and exterior detail*
A *Inner octagon;* **B** *Octagonal aisle;* **C** *Chancel, with* N *and* S *apses*

Southern Italy and Sicily
The PALAZZO CASERTA (Luigi Vanvitelli; 1751–74), near Naples, built for Charles III, has monumental staircase ◆

In Sicily, S. GIORGIO, RAGUSA (Gagliardi; 1744–66), has triple-tiered façade held together by swirling volutes.

France
In the first half of the 17th C a Classical style was created in France by François Mansart (1598–1666) and Louis Le Vau (1612–70), whose work echoed the dramatic grandeur of the Italian Baroque. The Rococo never developed to more than an elegant style of interior decoration in France. Neo-Classicism was practised notably by Jacques Germain Soufflot.

François Mansart

Mansart, who gave his name to the "mansard roof" (flattish upper part with steeply pitched sides), first made his mark with the unfinished ORLÉANS WING (1635–8) of the CHÂTEAU DE BLOIS. Curved ground-floor colonnades hint at Baroque.

The MAISONS-LAFITTE (1642–8), near Paris, are a restrained masterpiece. Oval rooms in wings; interior decoration survives. The church of VAL-DE-GRACE, PARIS (begun 1642), has large scrolls on façade. Commissioned by Anne of Austria to celebrate birth of future Louis XIV.

Maisons-Lafitte   **Val-de-Grâce, Paris**

Hardouin-Mansart

Le Vau's successor was Jules Hardouin-Mansart (1646–1708), great-nephew of François Mansart. His tendencies towards the Baroque climaxed in CHURCH OF THE INVALIDES, PARIS (1679–91). From inside, an opening in the inner dome reveals a richly painted outer dome, lit by hidden windows —a typical Baroque effect. Oval chancel.

Also by Hardouin-Mansart: planning of Place Vendôme, Paris (begun 1698); Grand Trianon, Versailles (1687).

Church of the Invalides, Paris

Le Vau

Le Vau's mansion of VAUX-LE-VICOMTE (begun 1657) has a lavish interior with central oval salon capped by dome and lantern. Formal gardens by André Le Nôtre (1613–1700), who later planned famous gardens at Versailles.

Vaux-le-Vicomte: *interior detail and general view*

The Palace of Versailles

Le Vau began Louis XIV's much-copied palace in 1669. Hardouin-Mansart in the late 1670s added wings trebling length of façade, and also added GALERIE DES GLACES ✦, most magnificent of French rooms. The palace staterooms are planned on one axis with aligned doors which, when open, give long vistas. This arrangement (*enfilade*) became a feature of Baroque palaces after *c.* 1650. PETIT TRIANON ✦ (1763), by Jacques-Ange Gabriel, is a beautifully proportioned pavilion; Romantic Classicism.

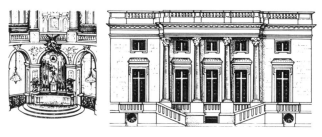

Versailles: *detail of chapel, and Petit Trianon*

Neo-Classicism

The masterpiece of French Neo-Classicism is the PANTHÉON, PARIS (Soufflot; 1757–80), with daringly thin piers.

By Claude-Nicolas Ledoux. Also in Paris: Barriere de La Villette, Place de Stalingrad (Ledoux; 1780s); Madeleine (Vignon; 1806–42).

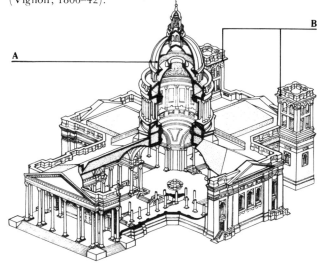

Panthéon, Paris: *cutaway view (restored)*
A *Dome with triple-shell construction;* **B** *Towers (never built)*

The Rococo

An early exponent of Rococo was Pierre Lepaultre (*c.* 1648–1716), whose style may be seen in the chapel at VERSAILLES and the choir of NOTRE DAME, PARIS. Also in Paris: the Oval Salon of the Hôtel de Soubise (Germain Boffrand; 1738–40).

Austria and Czechoslovakia

Austrian Baroque, which flourished 1690–1730, is epitomized by the churches and palaces of Johann Bernhard Fischer von Erlach (1656–1723; a pupil of Carlo Fontana) and of Lukas von Hildebrandt. The Danube valley has lavish monasteries by Jakob Prandtauer. In Prague, second capital of the Holy Roman Empire, the Dientzenhofers excelled.

Monasteries in Austria

The Benedictine monastery of MELK ♣ (Jakob Prandtauer; 1702–14) is set on a bluff over the Danube. Domed church with two multi-pinnacled frontal towers stands behind two monastery buildings which bend inwards and are joined by a Palladian arch flanked by low curving wings. Stunning composition.

The monastery of ST FLORIAN, near Linz, was rebuilt by Prandtauer from 1711. Superb open staircase on façade follows a design by Carlo Antonio Carlone.

Monastery of Melk · **St Florian:** *detail of façade*

Salzburg and Vienna

Fischer von Erlach, Court Architect from 1704, demonstrates his debt to Borromini in three Salzburg churches built from 1694: the KOLLEGIENKIRCHE, DREIFALTIGEITSKIRCHE and URSULINENKIRCHE. His eclectic KARLSKIRCHE, VIENNA (1716–37), combines oval dome with a Palladian portico and two replicas of Trajan's Column, Rome. Twin towers project from curving recesses in façade, as in Borromini's S. Agnese, Rome. Also by F. von Erlach: Imperial Library, Vienna (begun 1723, year of his death, and completed by his son).

THE BELVEDERE, VIENNA (Hildebrandt; 1720–4), a lakeside summer palace, is youthful and lighthearted.

Karlskirche, Vienna · **Belvedere, Vienna:** *detail*

Prague

The TROJA PALACE, PRAGUE
(1679–96), has restrained
exterior with raised central
block decorated on garden
front by ornate staircase.

Finest Baroque church in
city is ST NIKOLAUS ON THE
KLEINSEITE (Dietzenhofers;
1703–11). Interior has
complex interlocking vaults
and curved balconies.

Troja Palace

Germany

After Germany's recovery from the Thirty Years' War, the
Asam brothers' Bavarian churches (1730s) ushered in an age
of great Rococo architects: Johann Michael Fischer (1691–
1766), Dominikus Zimmermann (1685–1766) and above all,
in Franconia, Balthasar Neumann (1687–1753).

Berlin and Dresden

THE BRANDENBURG GATE, BERLIN (1789–93), is Neo-Classical;
a triumphal arch on Doric columns with temples either side.
Exemplifies antiquarian trend of later 18th c. (See p 132.)

THE ZWINGER, DRESDEN (M. D. Pöppelmann; 1711–22), is a
fantastic Rococo summer palace, with decorated pavilions.

Bavaria

Early creations of the Asam
brothers include churches at
ROHR (1718–25) and
WELTENBURG (1717–21), but
their best-known work is the
tiny ST JOHN NEPOMUK,
MUNICH (1732–46); interior
has swirling balconies and
twisted pillars. Cornice
supports emotional Trinity.

Outside Munich is the
NYMPHENBURG PALACE (1717–
23). Of its four Rococo
pavilions, the AMALIENBURG
PALACE (1734), is notable for
its French elegance.

The ABBEY CHURCH,
OTTOBEUREN (F. Von Erlach;
1749–67) is largest German
Rococo church.

Abbey church, Ottobeuren

Amalienburg Palace: *details of façade and Rococo decoration*

Neumann's supreme work is the church at VIERZEHNHEILIGEN (1743–72), showing a Rococo liquidity of light and space. Complex plan based on intersecting ovals and circles, gaily voluptuous interior.

The abbey church of DIE WIES (1745–54) is by Zimmermann; simple white exterior belies joyously colourful interior.

THE RESIDENZ, WURZBURG (begun 1722), has Neumann's Baroque GRAND STAIRCASE ◆; ceiling painted by Tiepolo.

Also in Bavaria: Theatine church of St Cajetan, Munich; abbey church, Banz (1710).

Vierzehnheiligen: *interior*

Spain and Portugal

Spanish 18th-c architecture, known as Churrigueresque after the Churriguera family of architects, features profuse and indiscriminate surface ornamentation, with a fondness for twisted columns (salomónicas) and pilasters shaped like inverted cones (estípites). Its chief exponents were Pedro de Ribera (*c.* 1683–1742) and Narciso Tomé (active 1715–42). It was partly influenced by Central and s American art. The opulent early 18th-c architecture of Portugal contrasts with the severer style of later work in Lisbon.

Iberian styles

The PALACE OF THE MARQUES DE DOS AGUAS, VALENCIA (1740–44), has elaborate carvings round doors and windows, and shows the Churrigueresque dissolution of form into decorative features, as does the SACRISTY OF THE CARTUJA, GRANADA (F. Manuel Vasquez; 1727–64), a Carthusian monastery.

Palace of the Marqués de Dos Aguas, Valencia: *doorway*

Cartuja, Granada: *detail of Sacristy interior*

The TRANSPARENTE, TOLEDO
CATHEDRAL (Tomé; 1721) is a
virtuoso example of Baroque
illusionism. By J. B.de Churriguera:
Plaza Mayor, Salamanca
(1731); churches at Orgaz
(1738) and Rueda (1738–47).

The pilgrimage church of
BOM JESUS (1723–44), near
BRAGA, Portugal, is
approached by typical zigzag
of steps between chapels.
Also in Portugal: Palace of
Queluz (1747–52), N of
Lisbon; S. Pedro dos Clérigos,
Oporto (1732–44).

Bom Jesus, *near* **Braga**

Britain

Sir John Vanbrugh, Nicholas Hawksmoor and James Gibbs
were the leaders of the English Baroque, which followed on
from the genius of Sir Christopher Wren (1632–1723). Their
sophisticated use of Classical elements in fluid designs has
only slight affinities with Continental Baroque. Then came a
return to Palladianism, combined with the deceptively
natural landscapes of William Kent and Lancelot
("Capability") Brown, evoking visions of antique paradise.

The mid 18th c saw two major movements evolve: Neo-
Gothic, an initially whimsical expression of literary
Romanticism; and Neo-Classicism, which reverberated into
the 19th c. The style of Robert Adam, greatest architect of
the later 18th c, treated Classical motifs in decoration of
almost Rococo gaiety. In the Regency years (1811–20) the
Georgian theme of Classicized elegance was further developed.
John Nash, leader of the Picturesque school, built in most of
the fashionable styles, from Neo-Classical to Chinoiserie.

A major Georgian building type was the terraced town
house, seen at its finest in London, Bath and Dublin.

Wren and his followers

One of Wren's most sophisticated early works is ST STEPHEN,
WALBROOK, LONDON (1672–9). Saucer-shaped dome resting on
8 arches is supported only by 12 slender columns, which also
carry right-angled entablatures. Highly complex use of space,
with varying ceiling levels.

 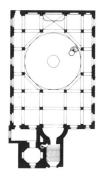

St Stephen, Walbrook, London: *interior detail and plan*

141

St Stephen, Walbrook, was part of Wren's rebuilding of the City of London after the Great Fire of 1666. As well as St Paul's Cathedral, he planned 51 City churches (many 1670–86), characterized by great variety of design and superbly inventive steeples, ranging from Neo-Gothic (ST DUNSTAN-IN-THE-EAST) to Italian Baroque (ST BRIDE, Fleet Street, and ST VEDAST, Foster Lane).

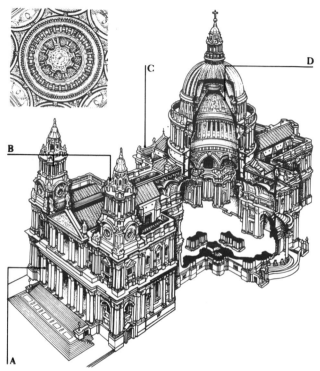

St Paul's Cathedral, London: *cutaway view and view into dome*
A *Portico*; **B** *Baroque towers*; **C** *Balustrade (added against Wren's will)*;
D *Inner dome*

ST PAUL'S (1675–1710) is England's only Classical cathedral. Superb majestic dome has a brick cone (supporting lantern) between inner round cupola and outer pointed shell. Screen walls over walls of aisles conceal flying buttresses. Curved porticoes on transepts recall S. Maria della Pace, Rome, and w towers (1705–8), with curves and countercurves, are Borrominesque. Two-storey portico with coupled columns.

The GREENWICH HOSPITAL, LONDON (from 1694), with fine painted hall ♦, is Wren's most Baroque building.

Other secular buildings: Pembroke College Chapel (1663) and Trinity College Chapel (1676–84), Cambridge; Sheldonian Theatre, Oxford (1663), modelled on Theatre of Marcellus, Rome; Chelsea Hospital, London (1682–92).

Associates of Wren included William Talman (1650–1719), whose CHATSWORTH HOUSE ♂, Derbyshire (1687–96), has lavish interior decoration, including England's best *trompe-l'œil*—a painted violin hung on a door ♦. Fine w façade.

The English Baroque

Sir John Vanbrugh (1664–1726) showed characteristic flamboyance in his first commission, CASTLE HOWARD, Yorkshire (1699–1712). Dome (reconstructed) rises above pedimented w front. Nicholas Hawksmoor was Vanbrugh's assistant here, as at monumental BLENHEIM PALACE ✚, Oxfordshire (1705–24), where kitchen wing and stable wing, each with own court, are linked to main wing by colonnades. Also by Vanbrugh: grimly austere Seaton Delaval, Northumberland (c. 1720–8); Kings Weston, Somerset.

Castle Howard　　　　　**Blenheim Palace:** *tower*

Hawksmoor's central block (1702) at EASTON NESTON, Northamptonshire, is indebted to Wren and Vanbrugh. As part of a church rebuilding programme, Hawksmoor produced ST MARY WOOLNOTH, LONDON (1716–27), which shows his respect for antiquity, and Thomas Archer (1668–1743) produced the Borrominesque ST JOHN, SMITH SQUARE, LONDON (1713–29).

Radcliffe Camera, Oxford:　　**St Martin-in-the-Fields:** *interior*
cutaway view

James Gibbs (1682–1754) built influential churches in a less Baroque style. ST MARY-LE-STRAND (1714–17) and ST MARTIN-IN-THE-FIELDS (1722–6), LONDON, both have tall steeples rising anomalously over Classical pediments.

Gibbs's brilliant geometrical RADCLIFFE CAMERA (1737–49), a library at OXFORD, has a dome recalling St Paul's.

Neo-Palladianism

The Palladian revival in England (*c.* 1715–*c.* 1750) was a Whig reaction against the Baroque, led by Colen Campbell (1673–1729) and Lord Burlington (1694–1753). Campbell based MEREWORTH CASTLE, Kent (1722–5) on Palladio's Villa Rotonda, but gave two sides decorative balconies instead of porticos. Same villa inspired Lord Burlington's CHISWICK HOUSE, LONDON (1726); only two side façades are identical.

Chiswick House   **Stourhead**

STOURHEAD ✿, Wiltshire (1720s), has well-proportioned temple-front façade, and superb landscaped garden. HOLKHAM HALL, Norfolk (Burlington and Kent; begun 1734) has magnificent apsed entrance hall ◆ and Palladian portico on S front. BATH shows Georgian town-planning at its best, with terraces unified by elegant palace-like façades.

The Neo-Classicists

The masters of early Neo-Classicism in England were William Chambers (1723–96) and Robert Adam (1728–92), both Scots. OSTERLEY PARK, Middlesex (1761–80), by Adam, contains his best decoration in Etruscan Room ◆. Greek-style portico added between existing wings. SYON HOUSE, ISLEWORTH, London (1762–9), also has sumptuous decoration, and typically varied room shapes.

Osterley Park: *detail*

KEDLESTON HALL, Derbyshire (1757–70), has S façade by Adam incorporating triumphal arch motif and free-standing columns behind curving stairs. Chambers' largest building is SOMERSET HOUSE, LONDON (begun 1776), with Neo-Palladian façades and French-inspired attic stories.

Kedleston Hall: *façade and detail of hall chimneypiece*

In later life Adam produced grandiose architecture in EDINBURGH, such as CHARLOTTE SQUARE and the UNIVERSITY.

By quirky Sir John Soane: his own house, London (rebuilt from 1812).

Neo-Gothic and the Regency

Irregularly planned STRAWBERRY HILL, TWICKENHAM (Horace Walpole; c. 1750–70), exemplifies the 18th-c "Gothick" taste. Rococo-like frivolity and novelty. Similar in spirit is Nash's Picturesque style, as shown in the ROYAL PAVILION, BRIGHTON (1815–21), an exotic fantasy of domes and minarets. Much cast iron. Nash's greatest work was layout of REGENT'S PARK AND REGENT STREET, LONDON (from 1811). Also by Nash: Luscombe Castle, Devon (1800); Carlton House Terrace and Cumberland Terrace, London (1820s).

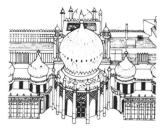

Brighton Pavilion: *detail*　　　　**Cumberland Terrace**

Russia

In 1703 Peter the Great founded the new city of St Petersburg (now Leningrad). Baroque architecture here reached a peak of achievement under the Empress Elizabeth, whose official architect, after 1741, was Bartolommeo Rastrelli.

Leningrad

Rastrelli's Leningrad architecture includes the magnificent turquoise-blue and white WINTER PALACE (1754–62), the STROGANOV PALACE (1752–4) and the SMOLNY CONVENT (1748–55). Palaces by Rastrelli outside the city: PETRODVORETS (Peterhof; 1747–52), with lavish Rococo décor, and PUSHKIN (Tsarskoe Selo; 1749–56), with exquisite small pavilions.

Leningrad: *Stroganof Palace (detail) and Cathedral of Smolny Convent*

145

Colonial America

Settlers' dwellings in the NE colonies developed from the one- or two-roomed wood cottages of the early 17th c into larger structures which, when a lean-to was added, were known as saltbox buildings. Regional variations were unified into the English-inspired Georgian style in the 18th c.

Early American architecture

Only at WILLIAMSBURG, Virginia, did early architecture reach a monumental scale, first exemplified at WILLIAM AND MARY COLLEGE (1695). Also there: Georgian Capitol (1701–5) and Governor's Palace (1706–20).

Early houses include BACON'S CASTLE, Virginia (1655), a Tudor brick dwelling with Flemish gables, WHIPPLE HOUSE, IPSWICH, Mass. (1639), is finest preserved saltbox building. Finest early Georgian house is WESTOVER, Virginia (1726).

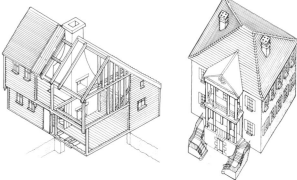

Typical houses of Colonial America: *mid 17th-*C *(cutaway) and mid 18th-*C *(Georgian)*

Early churches show an English influence, as at OLD NORTH CHURCH (Christ Church), BOSTON (1723). Puritans disliked Gothic-style churches and built meeting houses instead; the oldest is the OLD SHIP MEETING HOUSE, HINGHAM, Mass. (1681).

The earliest university buildings at HARVARD (1720) and YALE (1752) are Georgian. Other public buildings survive, such as the INDEPENDENCE HALL, PHILADELPHIA (1732). At MONTICELLO, near Charlottesville, Virginia (1780–1809) is Thomas Jefferson's country house, with Palladian influence. Also: Redwood Library, Newport, RI (P. Harrison; 1749–58).

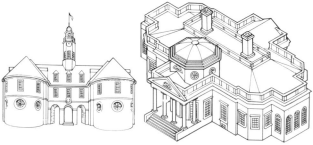

Colonial Virginia: *Governor's Palace, Williamsburg, and Jefferson's House, Monticello*

Iberian-American Baroque

Aleijadinho (1738–1814), a mulatto, was the main exponent of the architectural style of Portuguese Brazil, which resembled homeland Baroque. In Mexico the southern Spanish style, with much gold in churches, was heavily influenced by highly decorative native traditions.

Mexico

The CATHEDRAL, MEXICO CITY (1563–1667), has Roman Doric pillars and strict Classical detail combined with exuberant Churrigueresque decoration in wood in the CHAPEL OF THE THREE KINGS (1718–37) and in stone in the attached SAGRARIO. W front is Neo-Classical, dome and lantern 19th C. Also: Church of Octolán (1745).

Church of Ocotlán: *detail*

Sagrario, Mexico City Cathedral: *exterior detail*

Spanish Peru and Portuguese Brazil

The COMPAÑÍA, CUZCO, Peru (begun 1651), has unique façade, with turrets flanking cupola roofs of towers. Central panel ends in trefoil arch with heavy entablature over it.

The earliest Brazilian Baroque church is S. BENTO, RIO (1652). The white church of S. FRANCISCO, OURO PRETO (Aleijadinho; 1766–94) has striking round towers and gables with·spread wings. BOM JESUS, CONGONHAS DE CAMPO (1777), is on a podium; fine carved stairway.

Compañia, Cuzco, Peru

S. Francisco, Ouro Preto

THE NINETEENTH CENTURY

The 19th c was dominated by the momentous effects of the Industrial Revolution, which had begun in Britain in the last quarter of the previous century and now gradually spread across Europe and the New World. Architecture vividly reflected the changes that it brought. A new social order, as well as an explosive growth in population, resulted in a need for many new buildings, serving entirely new functions: department stores, hotels, offices, museums, factories, prisons, warehouses. With industrialization came a parallel boom in transport and a call for bridges, railway stations, viaducts, dockyards and factories. At the same time the technology, materials and services required to answer these demands were made available, and the systematized use of them literally changed the face of functional architecture. The structural potential of iron was demonstrated early on in the bridge at Coalbrookdale, England (1777–9). By the beginning of the 19th c, complete internal iron skeletons of vertical supports (stanchions) and beams were standard practice in British mills. The advantage of iron over masonry in terms of economy, and strength without bulk, enabled 19th-c engineers to cover great spaces and support heavy loads, resulting in wider spans, greater height and more flexible ground plans. Developments in plate-glass in the 1840s ensured its wide use. The combination of iron and glass featured notably in buildings put up for a number of exhibitions aimed at the glorification of progress. The first of these, the Great Exhibition of London (1851), was symbolized by Joseph Paxton's magnificent Crystal Palace, remarkable for its early use of standardized components. New York built its own Crystal Palace two years later, in 1853.

Architects and engineers moved wider apart as the latter became more progressive in their use of technology. Central heating, hot and cold water systems, sanitary plumbing, gas and, later, electric lighting, lifts and ventilation systems were gradually incorporated in municipal, commercial and residential buildings whose outer appearance seldom kept pace with the look of more purely utilitarian structures.

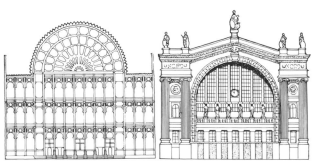

Crystal Palace, London   **Gare du Nord, Paris**

148

Style and decoration

One reason for this discrepancy was a shift in the emphasis of patronage from aristocracy to *nouveaux riches*, either individual or corporate. Middle-class patrons were unhampered by traditions of good taste and celebrated their wealth and civic pride in a multitude of styles. A new antiquarian interest led to the revival of past idioms (historicism), primarily Ancient Greek and Gothic. Neo-Classicism continued in a protean succession of forms and was most prominent in the USA, where Romanesque later came into favour for its robust simplicity. Gothic was the distinctive revival in Britain, ranging from the loosely associative Romantic Gothic to a more meticulous imitation which was treated as a religious imperative by A. W. N. Pugin and others. However, Gothic was used not only for churches but also for hotels, law courts and hospitals. Historical styles were sometimes chosen with unimaginative literalism—Roman for justice, Venetian for commerce, Oriental for leisure, Greek for government, etc.—but as the century progressed more eclectic borrowings became increasingly common.

A number of 19th-c developments paved the way for modern architecture (see pp 159–66).

Historicist themes

Italian Renaissance: *Reform Club, London*

Neo-Romanesque: *Trinity Church, Boston, Mass.*

Neo-Greek: *Schauspielhaus, Berlin*

Neo-Gothic: *Manchester Town Hall, England*

Britain

Neo-Gothic became a dominant force in English public architecture in the 1830s, with Charles Barry's Houses of Parliament. George Gilbert Scott (1811–78) built prolifically in this style. Modish alternatives included Italian and French Renaissance. High Victorian architects were notorious for rich decoration.

London

The finest late example of Neo-Classicism is the BRITISH MUSEUM (R. Smirke; 1824–47), with pedimented Ionic portico; central court later domed to form reading room. ST PANCRAS CHURCH (W. and H. Inwood; 1819–22) features replica of caryatids on porch of Erechtheion, Acropolis.

Influential façade of Barry's REFORM CLUB (1837–40) is 16th-c Italian, whereas his TRAVELLERS' CLUB (1829–31) looks back to 15th-c Italy. The HOUSES OF PARLIAMENT (plan Barry, detail A. W. N. Pugin; 1840–65) has a classically balanced plan decorated in Perpendicular style. The PALM HOUSE, KEW GARDENS (D. Burton and R. Turner; 1844–7) is an iron-and-glass, bubble-like greenhouse. The immense MIDLAND HOTEL, ST PANCRAS STATION (G. G. Scott; 1865–71) is a fine display of Gothic pointed arches, gables, chimneys and spires.

All Saints', Margaret St: *interior*

Midland Hotel, St Pancras Station

Westminster Cathedral: *detail of exterior*

Natural History Museum: *detail of exterior*

A bold design in yellow and blue terracotta, the NATURAL HISTORY MUSEUM (A. Waterhouse; 1873–81) is basically Romanesque; façade and towers crammed with decorative detail. NEW SCOTLAND YARD (Norman Shaw; 1887–8) is in Queen Anne style, all red brick and stone. The eclectic WESTMINSTER CATHEDRAL (J. F. Bentley; 1894–1903) is part Byzantine, part Early Renaissance, with domed tower and interior.

New Scotland Yard

The north of England

The vast ALBERT DOCKS, LIVERPOOL (J. Hartley; opened 1845) has frameworks of iron with brick façades carried on cast-iron Doric columns. Also in Liverpool, ORIEL CHAMBERS, WATER STREET (P. Ellis; 1864–5), is an important example of cast-iron frame construction with only decorative masonry; "oriels" are the bay windows on top storey. One of a bold series built by corporations of wealthy industrial cities, LEEDS TOWN HALL (C. Brodrick; 1855–9) has gigantic Corinthian colonnades and French-flavoured Baroque clock-tower. By same architect, GRAND HOTEL, SCARBOROUGH (1863–7) is first "château-hotel": a confection of brick and terracotta. Also: Town Hall, Manchester (see p 149); Cragside, Northumberland (Norman Shaw; begun 1870).

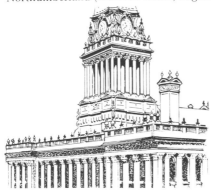

Leeds Town Hall: *detail*

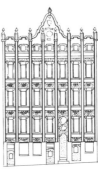

Oriel Chambers, Liverpool

Scotland

Queen Victoria's summer residence BALMORAL CASTLE, Aberdeenshire (W. Smith and Prince Albert; reconstructed 1853–5), is in castellated Scottish Baronial style. Contains a prefabricated iron ballroom. Also: Royal High School, Edinburgh (T. Hamilton; 1825–9).

Balmoral Castle: *detail*

France

Like Britain's, much of France's 19th-c architecture was Classical or Gothic. Italian and French Renaissance styles also made an appearance, followed by the Neo-Baroque "Second Empire" buildings of Napoleon III's Paris, which was laid out with wide, straight boulevards by George Haussmann. Appreciation of the architectural potential of iron was greater in France than in Britain.

The Paris Opera

The PARIS OPÉRA (1861–75), a triumph of sumptuous historicism by Charles Garnier, is a 19th-c masterpiece. Style is monumental Neo-Baroque based on an exquisitely ordered plan. Exterior and interior are extravagantly decorated with multicoloured marbles and statuary, over a steel framework. Central horseshoe auditorium decorated in Italian style. Also by Garnier: Casino, Monte Carlo (1878).

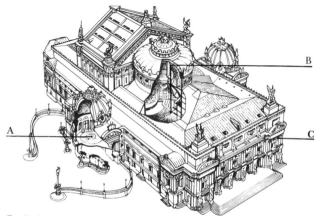

Paris Opera: *cutaway view*
A *Emperor's Wing;* **B** *Auditorium;* **C** *Main façade*

Other buildings in Paris

The BIBLIOTHEQUE STE GENEVIÈVE (1845–50) and the READING ROOM, BIBLIOTHEQUE NATIONALE (1862–8), both by H. Labrouste, one of the first architects to use iron conspicuously, have lofty interiors with slender iron columns. Earlier building (which inspired Boston Public Library, Mass.) has double-vaulted iron roofs; later has delicate domes. The NEW LOUVRE (L. T. J. Visconti and H. M. Lefuel; 1852–7) is a conglomeration of Renaissance and Baroque— a definitive example of the Second Empire style. Its mansard roofs, pavilions and richly sculptured surfaces were widely imitated.

Bibliotheque Ste Genevieve, Paris: *façade*

On the heights of Montmartre is SACRÉ-COEUR (P. Abadie; 1874–c. 1900), with a silhouette of clustered domes. Romanesque style imitates St Front, Périgueux. The EIFFEL TOWER (G. Eiffel; 1887–9), built for 1889 Exhibition, was then world's tallest structure. Prophetic in its metallic webbing and spatial complexities. Arches of base are purely decorative.

Sacré-Coeur, Paris

Germany and Austria

In Germany Karl Friedrich Schinkel produced some major buildings c. 1816–30, most notably in the Neo-Greek manner. The speciality of Friedrich von Gärtner was the *Rundbogenstil* ("round-arched style"), favoured by Ludwig I of Bavaria, but the greatest German architect of the age was Gottfried Semper (1803–79). An important centre of historicism after the mid-century was Vienna, where impressive buildings in a variety of period styles were built in the new green belt (Ringstrasse).

Vienna
The VOTIVKIRCHE (H. von Ferstel; 1856–79), in 14th-c style, is one of the largest Neo-Gothic churches: twin filigree towers and rich lacey detail. In contrast, the PARLIAMENT (T. von Hansen; 1873–83) is a distinguished essay in Corinthian Greek. The bold front of the BURGTHEATER (G. Semper and K. von Hasenauer; 1874–88) is a masterly performance in a Late Renaissance style.

Votivkirche, Vienna

West and East Germany
Schinkel's work in the Grecian style can be seen in BERLIN in the SCHAUSPIELHAUS (1819–21; see p 149) and the ALTES MUSEUM (1823–30), his masterpiece. A plan influential in later museums is that of High Renaissance ALTERE PINAKOTHEK, MUNICH (L. von Klenze; 1826–33). The Bavarian Rococo LINDERHOF near Oberammergau (G. von Dollman; 1870–6), was built for mad Ludwig II, as was NEUESCHWANSTEIN (E. Riedel; 1869–86), a medieval fairy castle.

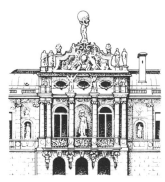

Schloss Linderhof, Oberammergau

153

Russia and eastern Europe

In Russia, as in Hungary and Poland, historicism was a main theme of the 19th C. One interesting variation was the Ancient Russian Revival that began in the 1830s and climaxed in Vladimir Sherwood's Historical Museum at Moscow (1878–83). Interior planning was often very successful, but exteriors were cluttered with towers and medieval motifs.

Moscow and Budapest

Typical of 19th-c urban exuberance is the GUM DEPARTMENT STORE, MOSCOW (A. N. Pomeranzer; 1888–93), a gargantuan glazed shopping arcade: one of first Moscow buildings with steel and glass in roof. Also in Moscow: Igumnov House (now French Embassy; 1896). In BUDAPEST one of the climaxes of historicism is the HOUSES OF PARLIAMENT 1884–1902)

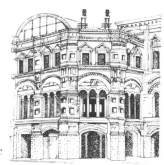

GUM Department Store, Moscow: *detail*

The Low Countries

Belgium and the Netherlands made no significant contributions to 19th-c architecture until the century's last three decades, when a burst of building, particularly secular, evolved styles that influenced many other parts of Europe.

Brussels

A powerhouse of exuberant Neo-Baroque, the PALAIS DE JUSTICE (J. Poelaert; 1868–83) with its high site and mountainous substructure has an effect like the monumental structures of the ancient East.

Palais de Justice, Brussels: *main staircase and façade*

Amsterdam

The premier architect of the late 19th C in the Netherlands was P. J. H. Cuijpers. His RIJKSMUSEUM (1877–85) is in a free Renaissance style with late Gothic flavouring. A good example of his superb architectonic skills, combining historicism with technical virtuosity in the vast internal courts of iron and glass. Cuijpers' AMSTEL (CENTRAL) STATION (1881–9) is in a somewhat stern early northern Renaissance style, which became popular for its adaptability and relative cheapness. Cuijpers' Gothic scholarship was joined with a formal and spatial verve when applied to his ecclesiastical buildings, as in the MARIA MAGDALENKERK (1887). The 20th c was anticipated by H. P. Berlage (1856–1934).

Rijksmuseum, Amsterdam: *cutaway view*

Italy

By the 19th c, Italy's pre-eminence in the arts was over. Successful buildings were produced in the idioms typical of the age but they were seldom innovatory.

Milan and Rome

Built with English money and technical advice, the GALLERIA VITTORIO EMANUELE, MILAN (G. Mengoni; 1865–77), a pedestrian street roofed in iron and glass, has a vast cruciform plan with a large, lofty domed octagon over the crossing. In ROME, two examples of overblown late Neo-Baroque are significant. The VICTOR EMMANUEL II MONUMENT (G. Sacconi; 1884–1922), on the slopes of the Capitol, is a typically 19th-c virtuoso performance. Also: the brashly self-confident Palazzo di Giustizia (1886–1910).

Victor Emmanuel II Monument, Rome

Denmark

Two notable buildings in COPENHAGEN are excellent examples of early and late European developments. The THORWALDSEN MUSEUM (M. G. B. Bindesbøll; 1839–48) is a very original Greek Revival structure that gives an almost Egyptian impression. The TOWN HALL (M. Nyrop; 1893–1902) is more advanced in its creative use of mixed motifs.

The United States and Canada

Greek Revival architecture in the USA, based on that in
England, was introduced by Benjamin Latrobe in 1798. It
appeared in both governmental and humbler wooden
buildings. Also English-influenced was, from *c.* 1830, the
picturesque Gothic Revival style, seen particularly in church
design. From *c.* 1870 H. H. Richardson built in an influential
Neo-Romanesque manner.

The United States: the East Coast

Greek Revival was of particular influence in the Middle
Atlantic states, though BALTIMORE CATHEDRAL (B. H. Latrobe;
1805–18), with French and ancient Roman borrowings, is
one of the finest monuments here. William Strickland created
a Greek Revival masterpiece in the PHILADELPHIA
MERCHANTS' EXCHANGE (1832–4) with its cupola and screen of
Corinthian columns. Classical modes were greatly exploited
in the government buildings and monuments of Washington
DC. The Classical elements of the US CAPITOL, completed by
Bulfinch *c.* 1827, later disappeared under the wings and the
great Neo-Baroque cast-iron dome of T. U. Walter (1851–65).
TRINITY CHURCH, NEW YORK (R. Upjohn; completed 1846),
designed in Decorated style, is one of the most famous
examples of the Gothic Revival in the USA. Patronage by the
newly wealthy led to an unrestrained eclecticism (from
c. 1870), best demonstrated by the ostentatious mansions of
Newport, RI, particularly THE BREAKERS (R. M. Hunt;
c. 1870), a Neo-Renaissance palazzo. H. H. Richardson's

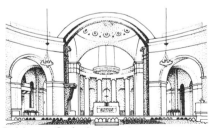

Baltimore Cathedral: *interior*

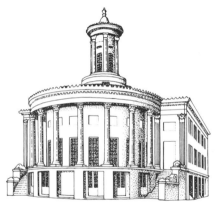

Philadelphia Merchants' Exchange

**Trinity Church,
New York**

The Breakers, Newport, RI
Neo-Renaissance

US Capitol, Washington DC
Greek Revival with Neo-Baroque dome

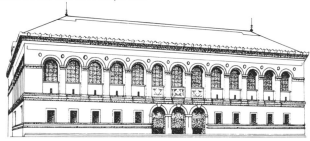

Boston Public Library

Neo-Romanesque TRINITY CHURCH, BOSTON (1874–7), is a rich
pyramidal mass of red granite. In contrast stands the BOSTON
PUBLIC LIBRARY (McKim, Mead and White; 1888–92), a
light Cinquecento essay of compelling elegance.

The United States: the Middle West

The Classical Revival is best demonstrated in the Middle
West in a series of state capitol buildings, finest example
being the Grecian STATE CAPITOL, COLUMBUS, Ohio (T. Cole
and others; 1839–61). Centre third of façade is columned.
Building is crowned by a flat-topped central lantern. With
steep, carved wooden gables, the large and pretentious
MACK-RYAN HOUSE, ANN ARBOR, Mich. (G. W. Lloyd; 1850–
67), admirably demonstrates a Midwestern type of Neo-
Gothic. But it is the work of Richardson that is most
significant in this region. His monumental ALLEGHENY

Allegheny County Buildings,
Pittsburgh

State Capitol, Columbus,
Ohio: *façade*

COUNTY BUILDINGS, PITTSBURGH (1884–7), with courthouse, tower and jail, are a superb example of granite masonry.

The Chicago fire of 1871 led to massive reconstruction by a number of impressively innovative architects. Richardson's masterpiece there was the Marshall Field's Wholesale Store (1885–7; now destroyed). It was, like Trinity Church, based on Romanesque styles of s France and Spain, with plain massive stone surfaces and mighty round arches. Its modern qualities, which were based on elementary forms, can be seen in the work of Louis Sullivan, especially the AUDITORIUM BUILDING, CHICAGO (Adler and Sullivan; 1887–9), now Roosevelt University. Exterior is largely derived from

Marshall Field's Wholesale Store, *Chicago (destroyed)*   **Auditorium Building, Chicago** *(now Roosevelt University)*

Richardson. A vast 10-storey complex of hotel, opera house and offices.

Canada
Throughout most of the 19th c, Canada followed England's stylistic lead. The muscular Gothic of the HOUSES OF PARLIAMENT, OTTAWA (Fuller and Jones; 1859–67), was, however, never seen on this scale in England. The central building was rebuilt after fire but the exceptional vitality of the original can be judged in the chapter-house structure containing the library. WINDSOR STATION, MONTREAL (B. Price; begun 1888), and TORONTO CITY HALL (E. J. Lennox; 1890–9) are both derived from H. H. Richardson's work and mark the beginning of American influence in Canada.

Houses of Parliament, Ottawa *(rebuilt after fire in 20th c)*

TURN OF THE CENTURY

The Industrial Revolution had brought new engineering discoveries and the mass-production of iron and steel. Viollet-le-Duc (1814–79) argued that such materials should be recognized for their intrinsic worth, a principle extended by A. W. N. Pugin, John Ruskin and William Morris.

Arts and Crafts and Art Nouveau

Inspired by medievalism, Morris pioneered the Arts and Crafts Movement in Britain, putting forward an alternative to the *impasse* of historicism, particularly in the establishment of a more logical relationship between design and materials. Other movements followed it. The German Werkbund promoted design in industry. It was founded in 1907 by the German Hermann Muthesius who had visited Britain to study low-cost housing. Architecture was an early beneficiary of these ideas, particularly in country houses. They are reflected in the work of H. H. Richardson in the USA, Ragnar Østberg in Sweden and C. F. A. Voysey in Britain.

House at Hog's Back, Surrey *(Voysey)*

Towards the end of the 19th c Art Nouveau developed as a romantic decorative movement which had no link with the past. Its flame-like lines were first seen in the Tassel House, Brussels (Victor Horta; 1892). Horta was followed by Hector Guimard in Paris and Antoni Gaudi in Catalonia, who worked in original and individualistic styles. A more rectilinear form which could contain the material and component requirements of industrialization appeared in the

Tassel House: *staircase*

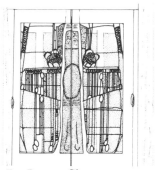

Tea Rooms, Glasgow
(Mackintosh) : door

work of Charles Rennie Mackintosh (1868–1928) in Scotland and Josef Hoffmann (1870–1956) in Austria. In Germany the movement was known as *Jugendstil*, in Vienna *Sezessionsstil*.

Structure and technology

The availability of the steel frame, reinforced concrete and environmental engineering challenged designers to combine them in an appropriate new form. A major breakthrough in the metal reinforcement of concrete came in the 1890s with the steel-reinforced systems of François Hennebique. New opportunities in the use of frame, cantilever and slab were grasped by Frank Lloyd Wright (1869–1959) and Auguste Perret (1874–1954). The traditional solidity of architecture could now be replaced by transparency, together with a visual release from gravity thanks to the thin column and cantilever. In Europe, certain designers modified or discarded decoration for form, such as Otto Wagner (1841–1918) and Adolf Loos (1870–1933).

In the USA the first steel-frame multi-storey building had been built in 1883. Richardson simplified the form, and Louis Sullivan (1856–1924) in Chicago perfected structures in glass and steel. The essential lines of 20th-c architecture had now been laid and the Europeans quickly refined the metal and glass system into envelopes of curtain walls. Wright, though largely ignored at home during this period, experimented with concrete and through his "prairie style" houses achieved a spatial flow by creating internal environments that were continuous and blended with the exterior. He revolutionized the private house and with his use of the cantilever and sparing original ornamentation was a seminal influence on European architects of the International Style after 1918.

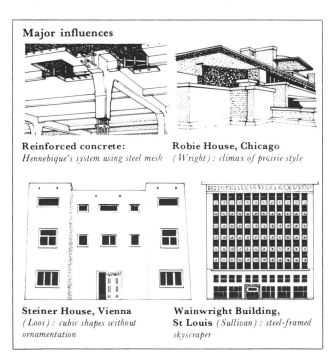

Major influences

Reinforced concrete:
Hennebique's system using steel mesh

Robie House, Chicago
(Wright): climax of prairie style

Steiner House, Vienna
(Loos): cubic shapes without ornamentation

Wainwright Building, St Louis *(Sullivan): steel-framed skyscraper*

Britain

A revival in the use of rustic materials through the influence of the Arts and Crafts Movement, combined with the foliate shapes of Art Nouveau derived from textile and book design, to create the "English house". The Domestic Revival influenced suburban housing and the garden city movement, inspired by Ebenezer Howard. Notable architects were C. F. A. Voysey and Edwin Lutyens, who built the last great country houses.

Domestic and public architecture

The RED HOUSE, BEXLEY HEATH, Kent (1859), was built for Morris by Philip Webb who created a simple vernacular exterior with the local red brick. R. N. Shaw combined motifs of different styles; SWAN HOUSE, 17 CHELSEA EMBANKMENT, LONDON (1875) is from his "Queen Anne" period. Shaw also contributed to the first garden suburb, BEDFORD PARK (1875).

Red House **Bedford Park**

The ORCHARD, CHORLEY WOOD, Herts (Voysey; 1899) has rough-cast walls and horizontal bands of windows. No period imitation. The early work of Lutyens, such as THE DEANERY, SONNING (1899), is in the Arts and Crafts style. He used much stylistic detail. His fine country houses include HEATHCOTE, ILKLEY, Yorkshire (1906).

The SCHOOL OF ART, GLASGOW (Mackintosh; 1896 and 1907–10) has functional plan and w wing with library, lit by oriel windows 8 m high. Climax of Art Nouveau in Britain. Influenced Sezessionists. Other buildings: Hill House, Glasgow (Mackintosh; 1903); Ritz Hotel, Piccadilly, London (C. Mewès and A. Davis; 1906); Whitechapel Art Gallery, London (C. Harrison Townsend; 1901); Cardiff City Hall and Law Courts (H. V. Lancaster and E. Richards; 1897).

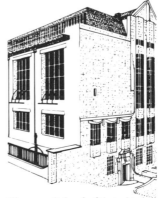

Glasgow School of Art: *detail*

The United States

The Chicago School pioneered the steel-frame skyscraper in commercial architecture. Frank Lloyd Wright, whose career began under Sullivan and spanned 70 years of versatility, expressed the desire for spatial living and communion with nature in his domestic buildings.

Frank Lloyd Wright

The ROBIE HOUSE, CHICAGO (1908) was the epitome of the "prairie style". Exquisitely laid brickwork, stone copings and leaded windows, as well as sophisticated light and heating systems. WILLITTS HOUSE, HIGHLAND PARK, Illinois (1902) was another example, again with low spreading profile. UNITY CHURCH, OAK PARK, CHICAGO (1906) consists of church, entrance, and parish hall. Composed of related cubic boxes. Early exploitation of reinforced concrete. (See also p 178.)

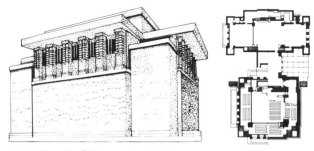

Unity Church, Chicago: *view and plan*
(Left side of plan shows upper level, right side lower level.)

The Chicago School

The CARSON, PIRIE AND SCOTT BUILDING (1899–1904) was the climax of Sullivan's career. Intricate cast-iron decoration. Other buildings: Tacoma Building, Chicago (Holabird and Roche; 1889); Reliance Building, Chicago (Burnham and Root; 1890–95); Guaranty Building, Buffalo, and Wainwright Building, St Louis (1890), both by Sullivan (see p 160).

Guaranty Building, Buffalo   **Carson, Pirie and Scott Building, Chicago**

France and Italy

Modern French architecture developed despite resistance
from the École des Beaux-Arts, the leading academy. There
were major architectural innovations in the use of iron and
steel (H. Guimard) and in the pioneer concrete structures of
Perret. Tony Garnier published designs for the new city
while, in Italy, Antonio Sant' Elia dreamed up a futuristic
metropolis.

France

CASTEL BÉRANGER, 16 RUE LA FONTAINE, PARIS (Guimard;
1894–8) has a façade developed from a multiplicity of
different natural materials. Guimard was also responsible for
the wrought-iron entrances to the Paris Métro. ST JEAN DE
MONTMARTRE (Anatole de Baudot; 1897–1905) was the first
major building with all the structural members made from
reinforced concrete. Also in Paris, APARTMENTS, 25B RUE
FRANKLIN (Perret; 1903), made concrete architecture
respectable. Concrete members faced with ceramic tiles.

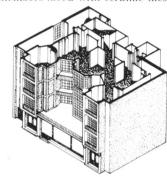

Castel Béranger: *door*   **Apartments, rue Franklin, Paris** *(Perret):* *cutaway view*

Other buildings: Theatre of the Champs Elysées, Paris
(Perret; 1911); Samaritaine Store, Paris (F. Jourdain; 1901).

Cité Industrielle (1904–17) was a series of drawings by
Garnier. He promoted new shapes which concrete made
possible: cantilevers, flat roofs, pilotis. Dom-ino House
project (1914–15) was a seminal architectural analysis by the
great architect Le Corbusier (1887–1966). Simple diagram
illustrates the essential features of the modern house.

Italy

The CENTRAL PAVILION OF THE
INTERNATIONAL EXPOSITION OF
DECORATIVE ARTS, TURIN
(Raimondo d'Aronco; 1902)
is a bizarre collection of styles.
Baroque-looking dome. CASA
CASTIGLIONI, CORSO VENEZIA,
MILAN (Giuseppe Sommaruga;
1901), has sinuous strands of
Art Nouveau wrought-iron
work. Also by Sommaruga:
Hotel Tre Croci, Campo dei
Fiori, near Varese.

Central Pavilion, Turin: *dome*

Spain

Antoni Gaudí (1852–1926) took Art Nouveau to a logical extreme, his imaginative work showing a highly personal exuberance.

Gaudí

SAGRADA FAMILIA, BARCELONA (begun 1884), was started as a Neo-Gothic church. Gaudí transformed it into a highly individualistic building. Reflects Art Nouveau, but bolder and original in structure and form. It owes something to the Spanish Gothic tradition, the Plateresque. CASA MILA (1910) and CASA BATTLÓ (1907) in Barcelona are equally idiosyncratic. Also S. COLOMA DA CERVELLO.

Sagrada Familia, Barcelona:
detail
Casa Milá, Barcelona

Belgium and the Netherlands

H. P. Berlage (1856–1934) led the Netherlands into the 20th c with his romantic architecture based on craft traditions. In Belgium, the Art Nouveau of Victor Horta (1861–1947) characterizes the period.

Brussels

TASSEL HOUSE, 6 RUE P-E JANSON, BRUSSELS (Horta; 1892), heralded Art Nouveau (see p 159). First private dwelling to use iron as structural material. SOLVAY HOUSE, 224 AVE LOUISE (Horta; 1895–1900), is a complete example of Art Nouveau of period. Furnishings, fittings and internal surfaces in a stylistic unity. Horta's MAISON DU PEUPLE (1896–9) had abundance of structural and decorative iron inside; destroyed. STOCLET PALACE (Hoffmann; 1905–11) is white marble arranged in series of flat rectangular planes with gilded friezes.

Maison du Peuple **Stoclet Palace**

The Netherlands

The EXCHANGE, AMSTERDAM (Berlage; 1898–1903) is steeped in traditionalism and stylistically derivative of Romanesque. Berlage considered the demands of logic and reason in his use of materials and the structure of the building. The VILLA at HUIS TER HEIDE (Robert van't Hoff; 1916) brought the flowing spaces of Wright's prairie style to Europe. Also: Shipping Palace, Amsterdam (J. M. van der Mey; 1912–16).

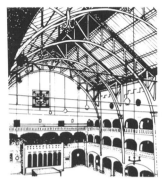

Villa at Huis *(Hoff)*

Exchange, Amsterdam: *brick was one of Berlage's favourite materials*

Germany and Austria

German and Austrian architects were responsible for a more ruthless reappraisal of the relation of form to function. In Vienna, the Sezessionist movement led the attack on historicism, and the German Werkbund's exhibition at Cologne (1914) showed revolutionary buildings in steel, glass and concrete.

Vienna

POSTAL SAVINGS BANK, VIENNA (Wagner; 1904), is a massive marble-faced building with scarcely any 19th-c stylistic features. Adolf Loos was more ruthless still in his STEINER HOUSE (1910). Reflects puritanical dogma of functionalism: Loos believed that beauty increased with the expression of utility. The MAJOLICA HOUSE (Wagner; 1898) showed how to place apartments over shops. Also in Vienna: Sezession House (Joseph Olbrich; 1896); Church of St Leopold, Am Steinhof (Wagner; 1906).

Postal Savings Bank, Vienna: *interior detail*

Majolica House, Vienna: *exterior detail*

165

Germany

The Grand Duke of Hessen invited the key Sezessionist, J. M. Olbrich, to DARMSTADT to design an artists' colony, the MATHILDENHÖHE. Major buildings (1907) here are EXHIBITION HALL and HOCHZEITSTURM, a curiously topped tower. Peter Behrens extended modern architecture into industry with his AEG TURBINE FACTORY, BERLIN (1909). FAGUS FACTORY, ALFELD (Walter Gropius and Adolf Meyer; 1911), was a step forward in steel and glass construction. The concept of a wall as smooth glass and steel membrane with corners free of visible supports was new. Other buildings: Model Factory, Cologne (Gropius and Meyer; 1914); Behrens' and Olbrich's houses at Darmstadt (1901).

AEG Turbine Factory, Berlin,   Fagus Factory, Alfeld

Scandinavia and Poland

Danish architecture attempted to escape from historicism via moderate traditional building. Ragnar Østberg (1866–1945) was a Swede interested in the rich textures and forms of traditional craftsmanship—a national romanticism.

Until he emigrated to the USA in the early 1920s, Eliel Saarinen was outstanding among forward-looking architects in Finland.

Scandinavia

TOWN HALL, STOCKHOLM (Østberg; 1909–23), is transitional, and an outstanding work of national romanticism. Sited by water; functional. Combines elements of Romanesque, Renaissance, Arts and Crafts, even Doge's Palace, Venice. COPENHAGEN TOWN HALL (Martin Nyrop; 1893) also used elements of the past. HVITTRÄSK, HELSINKI (E. Saarinen, A. Lindgren and H. Gesellius; 1902), was a group of houses and studios built for architects' use. Saarinen also built the HELSINKI RAILWAY STATION (1905–14), inspired by the Vienna Sezession. Also influenced by national romanticism, English Arts and Crafts Movement and local materials.

Poland

The CENTENNIAL HALL, WROCLAW (Max Berg; 1912), is a stupendous structure in massive reinforced concrete. Internal arches carry the stepped concentric rings of the roof. The largest span—65 m— of its constructional type. Other buildings: Water Tower, Poznan (Hans Poelzig; 1911); Church of St James, Warsaw (Oscar Sosnowski; 1909).

166

MODERN

Two essential issues common throughout the 20th c are functionalism and a concern for the social basis of architecture. Developments in other arts, including Futurism and Cubism in painting, also played a part. Expressionist architects, such as Erich Mendelsohn (1887–1953), attempted to reconcile the individual gesture with the demands of functionalism—the belief that a building must above all else fulfil its purpose. The alternative approach of the Bauhaus was to welcome anonymity as an inherent virtue of industrialization. In 1928, leading architects met at the Congrès Internationaux d'Architecture Moderne (CIAM). Though there was no concerted movement, there were certain consistencies; no ornamentation; flat roofs; rectangular outlines; white walls; large windows.

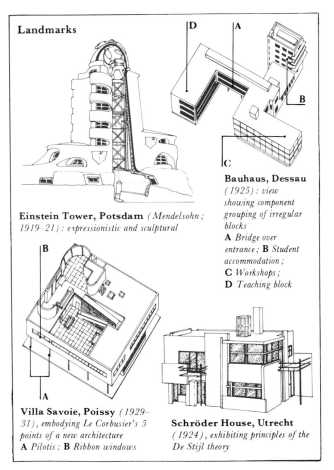

Landmarks

Einstein Tower, Potsdam *(Mendelsohn; 1919–21): expressionistic and sculptural*

Bauhaus, Dessau *(1925): view showing component grouping of irregular blocks* **A** *Bridge over entrance;* **B** *Student accommodation;* **C** *Workshops;* **D** *Teaching block*

Villa Savoie, Poissy *(1929–31), embodying Le Corbusier's 5 points of a new architecture* **A** *Pilotis;* **B** *Ribbon windows*

Schröder House, Utrecht *(1924), exhibiting principles of the De Stijl theory*

De Stijl and the Bauhaus

The artist Piet Mondrian derived from Cubism a type of design he called Neo-Plasticism, distinguished by interlocking geometrical forms, smooth, bare surfaces and primary colours. This was taken up by the De Stijl group, formed in Leiden (1917). Theo van Doesburg (1883–1931) and J. J. P. Oud (1890–1963) were notable members.

The Bauhaus school for architects and artists was founded by Walter Gropius in Weimar (1919). It emphasized industrial design and functionalism in architecture. It moved to Dessau in 1925, to Berlin in 1928, but was closed by the Nazis in 1933. The architects, including the last director Ludwig Mies van der Rohe (1886–1969), moved to the USA and spread the new architecture abroad. Le Corbusier expressed the new style clearly in his *Five Points of a New Architecture* (1925): free standing supports (pilotis); roof gardens; free plans; ribbon windows; freely composed façades —the house became "a machine for living in".

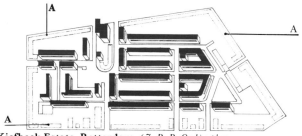

Kiefhoek Estate, Rotterdam *(J. P. P. Oud): plan*
A *Earlier houses on perimeter*

Structure and technology

Structural innovation was fundamental to the Modern Movement. The Italian Pier Luigi Nervi (1891–1979) invented a precast dense concrete reinforced with steel mesh to roof large public spaces. The space-frame, a three-dimensional system for evenly distributing loads, was extended into the geodesic dome, a lightweight structure of huge span. Reinforced concrete shells were pushed to the edge of the practical with the Sydney Opera House (see p 182).

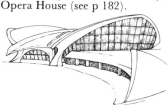

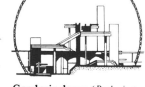

TWA Terminus, Kennedy Airport, New York *(Saarinen)*

Geodesic dome *(Buckminster Fuller): section*

Trends in modern architecture

Traditionalism, the conservative reworking of past styles, is still a potent impulse. Constructivism, dating from 1913 in Russia, gives an extreme emphasis to structure. Futurism continues in urban utopian schemes and functionalism pervades the whole period from 1850 to the present. New Brutalism (*c.* 1954) emphasized the function of every element.

The style was characterized by *béton brut* (naked concrete) and rough materials. In 1960, Metabolism was put forward in Japan using a biological analogy to describe structures which can grow or shrink by addition or subtraction of modules. The term Post-Modernism, since about 1976, has been applied to buildings which react against anonymity and communicate to architects and users alike through symbols.

Mass housing

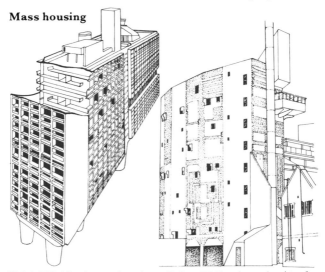

Unité d'Habitation: *a city unit perched on pilotis*

Byker Wall: *colour and variety of shapes give it human scale*

Since World War II, the concerns of architects have been with town planning and housing, as well as legislation to control building in the public interest. Le Corbusier's Unité d'Habitation, Marseilles (1952), led to new trends in the construction of housing on a high-rise basis. The Festival of Britain (1951) educated the British public in the new style. The clientèle was now both private and public, and architects grouped together to form partnerships with staffs of 100–1,000. Increasingly a concern for conservation and historical continuity runs through most of the modish issues, a tendency exemplified in Britain by Friars Quay Housing, Norwich (Feilden and Mawson; 1972–5). The Byker Wall, Newcastle (Ralph Erskine; 1974), uses a variety of materials, colours, graphics, gardens and walkways to give it a local identity. Massive redevelopment is now almost consistently opposed.

Although it is difficult to distinguish a coherent trend in all the vogue styles of the 20th c, for the moment, as Lewis Carroll's Dodo observed, "Everybody has won and all have prizes." However, one of the most prominent tendencies is the resurgence of the Neo-Vernacular, favouring the traditional look of low brick buildings with pitched roofs.

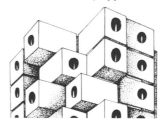

Nakagin Capsule Building, Tokyo *(Kurokowa)*: *Metabolism*

Britain

In 1930 Berthold Lubetkin (b. 1901) had formed a group of newly graduated architects into Tecton, an architectural team which aroused public interest in the International Style.

Britain's reputation after World War II rested on housing and pioneering school designs. The 1947 Town and Country Planning Act underpinned the social responsibility of architecture. The school building programme used mass-produced components and prefabrication techniques. New towns continued to be built in a garden-city type layout, also high-rise estates, despite growing unease.

Domestic housing

Tecton's triumph is HIGHPOINT I and II, HIGHGATE, LONDON (1936 and 1938), a pair of expensively furnished reinforced concrete blocks, 8-storied, designed on cruciform plan. SUNHOUSE, FROGNAL WAY, HAMPSTEAD (Maxwell Fry; 1936), was in probably the best home-grown pre-war English style. ALTON ESTATE, ROEHAMPTON (LCC Architect's Dept; 1952–9), housed nearly 10,000 people. A mixed development of slab, point, single and two- to four-storey blocks; an outstanding example of British response to Le Corbusier's urban theories. The BARBICAN HOUSING PROJECT, CITY OF LONDON (Chamberlin, Powell and Bon; begun 1955) is on a vast site almost cleared by wartime bombing. There is a theatre, concert hall and art gallery. Houses 6,500 people.

Other buildings: House in Old Church St, Chelsea (Gropius and Fry; 1935); "High and Over", Amersham (Amyas Council; 1930); Byker Wall Housing, Newcastle-upon-Tyne (Ralph Erskine; 1974; see p 169); "New Ways", 508 Wellingborough Rd, Northampton (Peter Behrens; 1925); Tower Block, Harlow New Town (F. Gibberd; 1951).

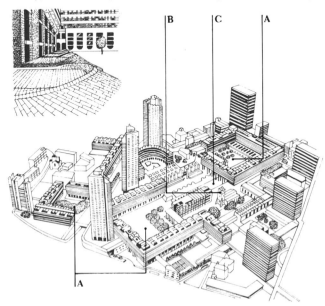

Barbican: *general view and detail*
A *Grass quadrangles :* **B** *Medieval church :* **C** *Lake*

Public and commercial buildings

In LONDON Owen Williams (b. 1890) built the black glass DAILY EXPRESS BUILDING, FLEET STREET (1933), in a flashy commercial style that works better than most doctrinaire examples of 1930s internationalism. ROYAL FESTIVAL HALL (R. H. Matthew, J. L. Martin and LCC Architect's Dept; 1949–51) has since had its front remodelled. Converted public opinion to the modern style. Magnificent sequence of flowing interior spaces. First building systematically to apply acoustical science. NATIONAL THEATRE, SOUTH BANK (Denys Lasdun; 1967–77), has superbly organized interior. The ECONOMIST BUILDINGS (Alison and Peter Smithson; 1962–4) are an example of the New Brutalism.

Also in London: Arnos Grove Underground Station (Adams, Holden and Pearson; 1932); Penguin Pool, Regent's Park Zoo (Tecton; 1934); Centre Point, Tottenham Court Rd (R. Seifert; 1962–6). Elsewhere: Willis Faber and Dumas Offices (Foster Associates; 1975); Boots Factory, Beeston, Nottinghamshire (Williams; 1932).

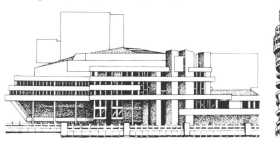

National Theatre: *riverside façade*   **Post Office Tower**

Religious and educational architecture

The SECONDARY SCHOOL, HUNSTANTON, Norfolk (Smithsons; 1954), exposes the brick, steel and service runs in severe framed blocks: first manifestation of the New Brutalism. The UNIVERSITY OF EAST ANGLIA, Norfolk (Lasdun; 1963) lies in parkland, but not campus-fashion. Buildings highly concentrated. On same site, the SAINSBURY CENTRE FOR THE VISUAL ARTS (Foster Assoc.; 1977) is a hangar-like space-frame with clear glass end-walls. COVENTRY CATHEDRAL (Basil Spence; 1951–62) combines the modern idiom with elements that recall Baroque and Gothic.

James Stirling has designed memorable university buildings at LEICESTER (Engineering; 1964) and CAMBRIDGE (History Faculty; 1964–9): ruthlessly logical appraisals of function and building economics. At Leicester, roof panels set at 45° to provide steady indirect light. Other buildings: Bousfield Primary School, The Boltons, London (Chamberlin, Powell and Bon; 1952–6); Imperial College, London (Sheppard, Robson, etc.; 1963).

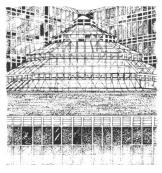

History Faculty Library, Cambridge: *detail*

171

Germany and Austria

The pioneering direction of the German Werkbund and the Bauhaus with its expressionistic (Mendelsohn and Scharoun) and rational (Gropius and Mies van der Rohe) phases was taken up again in post-war reconstruction. Frei Otto (b. 1925) took another direction with his "tent" roofs. Austria's significant architects went abroad, particularly to California. Roland Rainer (b. 1910), a town planner in Vienna, has introduced new techniques there.

Early efforts

EINSTEIN TOWER, POTSDAM (Mendelsohn; 1919–21), still serves purpose of housing the scientist's astrophysical equipment (see p 167). Mendelsohn also designed the prototype for later European stores in the SCHOCKEN STORE, STUTTGART (1927). FARM BUILDINGS, GUT GARKAU, LUBECK (Hugo Häring; 1924) was designed for the comfort of cows—a truly organic building. WESISSENHOF ESTATE, STUTTGART (Mies van der Rohe etc.; 1927), was an estate of model houses by the masters of the International Style, sponsored by the German Werkbund. Other buildings: Bauhaus Buildings, Dessau (Gropius; 1926); Bruchfeldstrasse Estate, Frankfurt (Ernst May; 1929).

 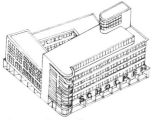

Weissenhof Estate, Stuttgart: *diagrammatic view*

Schocken Store, Stuttgart, *showing vertical stair-tower*

Post-war work

The PHILHARMONIC HALL, BERLIN (Scharoun; 1956–63), dramatically handles the function of a concert hall. Creative acoustical arrangement of seats in "vineyards". It owes much to Scharoun's organic functionalism. EVANGELICAL CHURCH OF ATONEMENT, DACHAU CONCENTRATION CAMP (H. Striffler; 1965–7), is a raw concrete *memento mori*. OLYMPIC STADIUM, MUNICH (Otto; 1968–72), is an enormous undulating weather shield made possible by advances in steel cable, high-strength fabrics and sophisticated calculation of stresses.

Other buildings: Candle Shop, Vienna (Hans Hollein; 1965); BMW Headquarters, Munich (K. Schwanzer; 1973).

 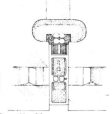

Philharmonic Hall, Berlin

Candle Shop, Vienna: *door*

The Netherlands and Belgium

The importance of De Stijl eventually overshadowed the evocative Amsterdam School influenced by Berlage and represented by Michael de Klerk (1884–1923). The historically based School of Delft dominated Dutch architecture until 1950, when post-war reconstruction in Rotterdam reintroduced functionalism.

The Netherlands

The SCHRODER HOUSE, UTRECHT (Gerrit Rietveld; 1924), is in brick with steel posts supporting projecting balconies (see p 167). EIGENHAARD HOUSING, AMSTERDAM (de Klerk; 1913–21) is a quirky interpretation of the romantic Dutch vernacular. KIEFHOEK ESTATE, ROTTERDAM (Oud; 1928), applies a fundamental modern solution to the ubiquitous problem of mass housing. The TOWN HALL, HILVERSUM (W. M. Dudok; 1930), demonstrates the deeply absorbed tradition of brick building. Deceptively simple cubic geometry. CHILDREN'S HOME, AMSTERDAM (Aldo van Eyck; 1961), is prefabricated from square precast concrete cupolas, wrapped around courtyards. Other buildings: Town Hall, Marl (1967), Reformed Church, Nagele (1960), Auditorium, University at Delft (1966), all by J. H. van den Broek and J. B. Bakema; Open-Air School, Amsterdam (J. Duiker; 1928); Van Nelle Factory, Rotterdam (1930).

Town Hall, Hilversum

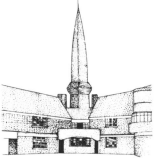

Eigenhaard Housing, Amsterdam

Open-Air School, Amsterdam

Van Nelle Factory, Rotterdam: *detail*

Belgium

The CITÉ MODERNE, BERCHEM-ST-AGATHE, Brussels (Victor Bourgeois; 1925) was one of the first concrete flat-roofed housing estates. Layout based on English garden city.

Finland

Alvar Aalto (1898–1976) has a reputation as an outstanding independent master with the ability to combine romance with technology in buildings that are pragmatic yet intensely personal. He experimented inventively with timber. A more impersonal school has developed since 1945, whose work can be seen in the satellite town of Tapiola, w of Helsinki.

Aalto and his successors

Aalto's achievements include the seminal PAIMIO SANATORIUM (1929–33), which uses reinforced concrete and plate glass to give height, openness, light and air. The CIVIC CENTRE, SÄYNÄTSALO (1950–2), is a collection of pitched-roofed, dark red-brick buildings. POLYTECHNIC INSTITUTE, OTANIEMI (1962–5), is organized round lecture theatre. Built in brick, timber, glass, asbestos.

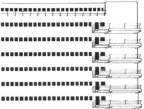

Paimio Sanatorium

Also by Aalto, VUOKSENNISKA CHURCH (1956–8) has a tall tower, identifying it among a mass of factory chimneys. Partitioned interior adaptable to different-sized congregations.

Civic Centre, Saynatsalo

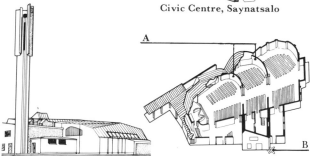

Church, Vuoksenniska: *exterior and cutaway view*

A *Partitions, giving flexibility;*
B *Base of tower*

UNIVERSITY CHAPEL, OTANIEMI (H. and K. Siren; 1957), unites with the surrounding landscape. Shows Finnish capacity to make evocative statements out of modest programmes. Also: Cemetery Chapel, Turku (1939).

Sweden and Denmark

The essence of Scandinavian architecture is progress rather than revolution. Sweden led Europe after 1918 in low-income housing, integrated with the landscape and with good community planning. The Stockholm Exhibition (1930), with Gunnar Asplund's light and free forms, made a huge impact on Europe. Vällingby (1953–9), a suburb of Stockholm, by Sven Markelius (1889–1972), was one of the first planned housing areas. Denmark too, after a flirtation with Classicism, applied modern techniques to housing and educational buildings with attention to simple structure and honest use of materials.

The Scandinavian achievement

FOREST CREMATORIUM, STOCKHOLM (Asplund; 1940), possesses order, clarity and formal repose. A most accomplished work, with great sensitivity to landscape. Also by Asplund: Stockholm City Library (1928). CARDBOARD FACTORY, FORS (R. Erskine; 1953), is in brick and reinforced concrete. Also in Sweden: Hälsingborg Concert Hall (Markelius; 1932).

In Denmark, the GRUNDTVIG CHURCH, COPENHAGEN (P. V. Jensen Klint; 1920–40), is a remarkable example of Nordic Expressionism. Self-confident, with enormous height and organ-shaped façade. Leading Danish architects include Kay Fisker and C. F. Møller, joint creators of ÅRHUS AND SØLLERØO TOWN HALLS (1937 and 1942) and SAS BUILDING, COPENHAGEN (1959).

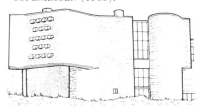

Cardboard Factory, Fors   **Grundtvig Church, Copenhagen**

Italy

Gruppo 7 formulated a revolt against historical styles in the 1930s, when the brilliant Pier Luigi Nervi began to reveal the aesthetic potential of concrete. There was a revival of Stile Liberty (a form of Art Nouveau) in the 1960s.

Nervi and other architects

CASA DEL FASCIO, COMO (Giuseppe Terragni; 1932–6) is by a member of Gruppo 7. Simply expressed concrete-framed half-cube. RAIL TERMINUS, ROME (E. Montuori etc.; 1950) uses reinforced concrete with panache, as does Nervi in his PALAZZO DE LAVORO, TURIN (1959–61). TORRE VELASCA, MILAN (BBPR; 1957), was built at the height of the Neo-Liberty movement. PIRELLI CENTRE, MILAN (Gio Ponti etc.; begun 1958), is a slim tower on a hexagon plan.

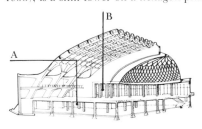

Exhibition Hall, Turin *(Nervi:* *1947): section* **A** *Basement:* **B** *Exhibition area*

Torre Velasca, Milan: *detail*

France and Switzerland

Le Corbusier dominates the scene. His innovatory ideas included grid town plans, traffic control, high blocks to free open spaces, and the creation of the "modulor" (1951)— a scale of building proportions based on the human body and the Golden Section. Jean Prouvé (b. 1901), a constructor in light metal, has mass-produced component parts and whole buildings, as in the estate at Meudon (1949). Switzerland is noted for progressive modern churches and schools and the bridge-builder Robert Maillart (1872–1940).

Le Corbusier

VILLA SAVOIE, POISSY (1929–31), is an elevated white concrete box (see p 167). The PAVILION SUISSE, CITÉ UNIVERSITAIRE, PARIS (1931), and the influential UNITÉ D'HABITATION, MARSEILLES (1952), are poised on the now familiar pilotis (see p 169). CHAPEL OF NOTRE DAME DU HAUT, RONCHAMP (1950–5), is a most personal building, abandoning rigid geometrical schemes. Irregular fenestration. Illustrates plastic capabilities of masonry. Light filters through the half-domed towers to fall on altars of chapels below. Also by Le Corbusier: Monastery, La Tourette, Évreux (1957); Maison Stein, Garches (1927); Maisons Jaoul, Neuilly (1956).

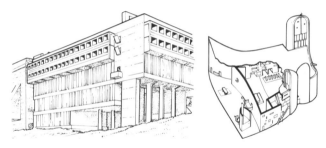

Monastery, La Tourette   Notre Dame, Ronchamp: *cutaway view*

Other buildings in France

NOTRE DAME, LE RAINCY (Perret; 1922–3), has columns, vaults and tracery in concrete, equivalent to Gothic design in stone. CENTRE POMPIDOU, PARIS (Piano and Rogers; 1972–7), is the *ne plus ultra* expression of a building's innermost workings. Also: School, Villejuif (André Lurçat; 1933); UNESCO, Paris (Breuer, Zehrfuss and Nervi; 1958).

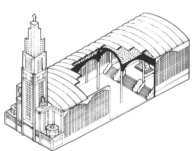

Notre Dame, Le Raincy

Pompidou Centre, Paris: *exterior detail*

Switzerland

GOETHEANUM II, DORNACH (R. Steiner; 1923–8), falls outside
the critical canons of modern architecture. Church of
ST ANTHONY, BASEL (Karl Moser; 1927), marked a rekindling
of interest in church building. Also: Halen Estate, near Berne
(Atelier 5; 1957–61), a modern village on wooded site;
Salginatobel Bridge (Maillart; 1930); Centre Le Corbusier,
Zurich (Le Corbusier etc; 1966–70).

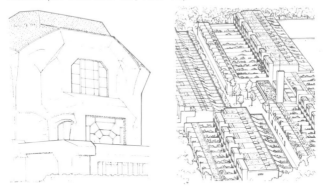

Goetheanum II,   **Halen Estate**
Dornach

Salginatobel Bridge: *traffic deck is integral part of structure*

Canada

The Montreal Expo exhibition (1967) gave a new impetus to
architecture previously dominated by the USA.

Expo 67, Montreal

HABITAT HOUSING (Moshe Safdie etc.) is 158 prefabricated
dwellings piled up in calculated disorder. Popularization of
Constructivist school. USA PAVILION (Buckminster Fuller) is a
geodesic structure of triangles and hexagonal elements
with a plastic skin (see p 168). Other buildings: Place
Bonaventure, Montreal (Affleck, Desbarats etc.; 1968);
Scarborough College, University of Toronto (John Andrews;
1966); Eaton Centre, Toronto (Bregman and Hamann;
1973–7).

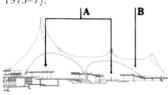

German Pavilion *(Frei Otto):*
A *Tubular steel masts;* **B** *Plastic skin*   **Habitat Housing**

The United States

Until 1945 the most noteworthy architecture was by Frank Lloyd Wright, apart from skyscrapers in the E and housing in California. Louis Kahn (1901–74) led the move away from the steel frame and curtain wall. Post-Modernism, with its anti-rational, neo-sculptural display, is particularly rich in the USA, where wealthy patronage abounds.

Frank Lloyd Wright and his influence

FALLINGWATER, BEAR RUN, Penn. (1936), integrates house and landscape, inner and outer space. Stone ledge on which house built forms some of walls. TALIESIN WEST, PHOENIX, Arizona (1938), was Wright's home and an atelier for his pupils. Personal statement of function using adaptable forms and natural materials (desert concrete etc.).

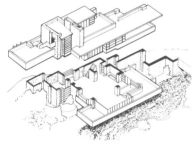

Taliesin West: *detail*   **Fallingwater:** *exploded view*

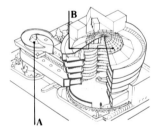

Johnson Wax Building: *detail*

Guggenheim Museum: *cutaway view* **A** *Administrative building;* **B** *Glass dome of main gallery*

The JOHNSON WAX BUILDING, RACINE, Wisconsin (1936–9) has square floors alternating with circular mezzanines. Walls are bands of brick and glass tubing. GUGGENHEIM MUSEUM, NY (1959), is a continuous spiral ramp surrounding an open well. Glass dome is main source of light. Also: Price Tower, Bartlesville, Oklahoma (1956). (See also pp 160, 162.)

Domestic buildings

LOVELL BEACH HOUSE, NEWPORT BEACH, Calif. (R. M. Schindler; 1926), brought to USA the influence of Wagner and Loos in Vienna. Strongly influenced by Cubism; reinforced white concrete frame. GROPIUS HOUSE, LINCOLN, Mass. (Gropius and Breuer; 1938) translated the International Style to suit timber building techniques.

JOHNSON HOUSE, NEW CANAAN, CONN. (Philip Johnson; 1949), is work of USA's most erudite architect. Exquisite group of buildings. Influenced by Mies van der Rohe. Echoes of Classicism, rationalism, Neo-Plasticism. BAVINGER HOUSE, NORMAN, Oklahoma (Bruce Goff; 1957), is a Post-Modern structure. A continuous spiral of space using materials which are natural, organic, often untreated. BURNS HOUSE, SANTA MONICA CANYON, LOS ANGELES (Charles Moore etc.; 1974), uses traditional elements in a surprising way. Robert Venturi in *Complexity and Contradiction in Architecture* (1966) sets out his case for an architecture of meaning and popular interest. He uses complex, unexpected and metaphorical architectural language. The TUCKER HOUSE, KATONAH, NY (with John Rauch; 1975), emphasizes images of American life. Other buildings: Westchester House, Armonk, NY (R. Stern and J. Hagmann; 1976); house, Chestnut Hill, Philadelphia (Venturi and Rauch; 1964); Kaufmann Desert House, Palm Springs (Richard Neutra; 1946–7).

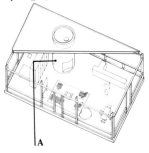

Burns House: *section, showing interlocking spaces*

Johnson House: *cutaway view*
A *Brick tower containing bathroom*

Public buildings

PHILADELPHIA SAVINGS FUND SOCIETY BUILDING, PHILADELPHIA (George Howe and William Lescaze; 1932) was one of the first architecturally pure skyscrapers. Repetition of windows and lack of shaping or ornamentation contrast with fanciful dome of CHRYSLER BUILDING, NY (W. van Alen; 1930), and Gothic style of CHICAGO TRIBUNE BUILDING (Hood and Howells; 1925).

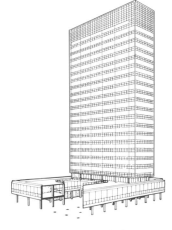

Chrysler Building, New York: *Art Deco spire*   **Lever House, New York:** *cutaway (see next page)*

MODERN

LAKE SHORE APARTMENTS, CHICAGO (Mies van der Rohe; 1951) are gracefully designed anonymous steel-frame boxes: highly influential. LEVER HOUSE, NY (Gordon Bunshaft at Skidmore, Owings and Merrill; 1952), and SEAGRAM BUILDING, NY (Mies van der Rohe and Johnson; 1958) are characterized by the curtain wall: the ultimate sophistication of the glass box principle. FORD FOUNDATION, NY (Roche and Dinkeloo; 1967) is a radical departure, with a greenhouse foyer soaring 12 stories: grand interpretation of 19th-C winter garden. AT & T BUILDING, NY (Johnson; 1978–82), a glass, steel and granite skyscraper, is a monument to Post-Modernism. CITY HALL, BOSTON, Mass. (Kallman, McKinnell and Knowles; 1967) is a belligerent pile of concrete. Sculptural roof hangs menacingly. PACIFIC DESIGN CENTER, LA (Cesar Pelli; 1976) uses a metaphor to describe its function. Unusual shape like a long moulding (it exhibits mouldings).

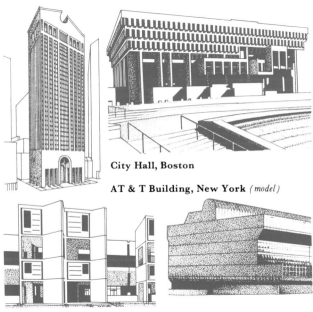

City Hall, Boston

AT & T Building, New York *(model)*

Salk Center Laboratories, La Jolla *(Kahn)*

Pacific Design Center, LA

RICHARDS MEDICAL RESEARCH BUILDING, UNIVERSITY OF PENNSYLVANIA (Kahn; 1960) has functional and formal spaces separate. Other buildings: Rockefeller Center, NY (Reinhard and Hofmeister; 1930–40); World Trade Center, NY (1961–73); Dulles International Airport, near Washington, DC (Eero Saarinen; 1962); Sears Tower, Chicago (Skidmore, Owings and Merril; 1974).

Latin America

Oscar Niemeyer (b. 1907) in Brazil was the first to turn away from international rationalism. Felix Candela (b. 1901) pioneered shell concrete structures in Mexico. Unprecedented opportunities arose with the building of Brasilia in central Brazil.

The New Architecture

Le Corbusier came to Brazil to help build the MINISTRY OF EDUCATION AND HEALTH, RIO DE JANIERO (1936–43). The ALVORADA PALACE, BRASILIA (Niemeyer; 1956–8), has a flamboyant monumentality and exaggerated refinement of concrete. Self-consciously styled pilotis. Also in Brasilia is Niemeyer's PALACE OF THE NATIONAL CONGRESS (1956–60).

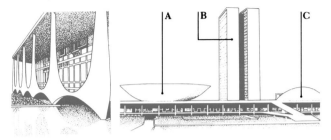

Brasilia: *Alvorada Palace and Palace of the National Congress*
A *Assembly hall;* **B** *Administrative office;* **C** *Senate building*

The CHURCH OF OUR LADY OF MIRACLES, MEXICO CITY (Candela; 1955), is reminiscent of the inspired structural explorations of Gaudí. Dramatic series of twisted columns; mid-century Expressionism. Other buildings: Church of St Francis, Pampulha, Brazil (Niemeyer; 1943); University Central Library, Mexico City (O'Gorman; 1953); Bank of London and s America, Buenos Aires (SEPRA; 1966); University City, Caracas (C. R. Villaneuva; begun 1952).

India, Japan and Australia

Le Corbusier was commissioned in 1950 to complete the design of Chandigarh, capital of the Punjab, where he fully realized his theories on zoning, traffic separation, etc. His influence was also felt in Japan, where a group of young architects has built up a nationalist and traditionalist Japanese school with a worldwide reputation. Beside the American-influenced commercial buildings in Sydney stands the famous Opera House.

India

At CHANDIGARH, the SECRETARIAT (1956) and the COURT OF JUSTICE (1956) are reinforced concrete with *brises-soleil* (i.e., sun-breaks) to combat the weather. Le Corbusier also designed the LEGISLATIVE ASSEMBLY (1956), with a hyperbolic concrete shell as the main hall. Also: Millowners' Association Building, Ahmedabad (1954).

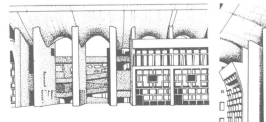

Chandigarh: *details of Court of Justice*

Japan

Kenzo Tange (b. 1913) built the OLYMPIC HALLS (1964) for the Tokyo Olympiad. He also built the YAMANASHI COMMUNICATIONS CENTRE, KOFU (1964–6), first megastructure to realize aims of Metabolists, expanding and contracting in response to circumstances. NAKAGIN CAPSULE TOWER (Kisho Kurokawa; 1972) is a Metabolist example of prefabricated housing (see p 167). Made up of 2.4 m-by-3.6 m living-units with all amenities save a stove. KAWARAMACHI NEW COMMUNITY, KAWASAKI (Sachio Otani; 1973), houses 15,000. Other buildings: Hajima City Hall (J. Sakakura; 1959); City Hall, Kurashiki (Tange; 1960); Municipal Hall, Tokyo (K. Maekawa; 1958–61); Aquapolis, Expo 75, Okinawa (Kiyonori Kikutake; 1975).

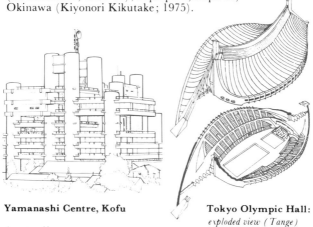

Yamanashi Centre, Kofu

Tokyo Olympic Hall:
exploded view (Tange)

Australia

The SYDNEY OPERA HOUSE ✪ (Utzon, completed by Hall, Todd and Littlemore; 1959–73) has massive, interlocking reinforced concrete shells. Sail-like roofs make a grand design gesture. A highly complex structure, difficult to build. Spectacular waterside site. Also in Sydney: Australia Square (H. Seidler; 1970).

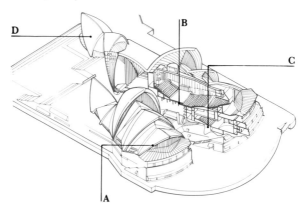

Sydney Opera House: *cutaway view*
A *Opera hall;* **B** *Concert hall;* **C** *Separate drama theatre;* **D** *Vault over restaurant*

POST-MODERN

Some time in the 1970s, any consensus about the meaning of modern architecture fell apart. The idiosyncratic, sometimes freakish and often outrageous forms of the work that took its place were described—by an American critic resident in England—as *Post-Modern* (PoMo). If the 19th-c architects had been searching for a style, and the 20th-c had rejected the idea of style altogether, architects now experimented with numerous styles, both ancient and modern. "Modern" architecture was now seen as just another of these styles, covering a period *c.* 1920-1970.

The turning point for this development was the publication in 1966 of Robert Venturi's *Complexity and Contradiction in Architecture* which recognized the essential ambiguity of good architecture, and its several layers of meaning. Opposing the architecture of *either-or*, and advocating the architecture of *both-and*, Venturi looked for a commonly understood imagery.

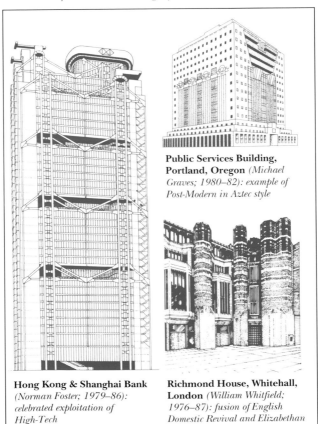

Public Services Building, Portland, Oregon *(Michael Graves; 1980–82): example of Post-Modern in Aztec style*

Hong Kong & Shanghai Bank *(Norman Foster; 1979–86): celebrated exploitation of High-Tech*

Richmond House, Whitehall, London *(William Whitfield; 1976–87): fusion of English Domestic Revival and Elizabethan*

Pluralism

An elaborate vocabulary of styles confused the new scene, with concepts like Personalism, New Rationalism, High-Tech Corporatism, Responsive Anarchism, Structural Dynamism and (most successful in Britain) Romantic Pragmatism. During the 1980s these terms gradually coalesced into a smaller group of main trends in design: Late Modern (the continuation of the modern style), High-Tech (the expression of sophisticated building technology), Post-Modern Classical (historical motifs usually reinterpreted) and Neo-Vernacular (a revival of ordinary day-to-day buildings now seen as itself a style). Parallel to all Post-Modern innovations was the conservation movement— not just preservation but the finding of new uses for old buildings.

The technical changes were not so much in the basic materials of modern architecture (steel and concrete) as in a greater use of plastics for components as well as structures, and more emphasis on spatial structures, for example using warped surfaces and sophisticated geometric forms. More significant was the unprecedented control of the physical environment—heat, light and ventilation. The new style was an architecture of space and light.

The United States

American enterprise of spirit, combined with a multiplicity of ethno-cultural traditions, has guaranteed a vigorous response to Post-Modernism. The early revolt from Modern led to the transformation of dull concrete blocks into three-dimensional coloured images. Examples include a precursor of Post-Modern, the ROOFLESS CHURCH, NEW HARMONY, Indiana (Philip Johnson; 1960), where timber parabolic arches on a plan of 6 interlocking circles give the impression of a cloth thrown over a figure bent double in mourning. Benjamin Franklin's house, now entirely destroyed, became a ghost in FRANKLIN COURT, PHILADELPHIA (Venturi and Rauch; 1972)— an open-frame outline of the house which can be walked through.

The WOMEN'S HOSPITAL & MATERNITY CENTER AND NORTH-WEST PSYCHIATRIC UNIT, CHICAGO, Ill. (Bertrand Goldberg Associates; 1975) features drum-shaped lobes on a striped glass box.

Women's Hospital & Maternity Center, Chicago

Piazza d'Italia, New Orleans:
aluminium columns round a map-of-Italy pool

The PIAZZA D'ITALIA, NEW ORLEANS (Charles Moore; 1979), built for the Italian community, incorporates classical colonnades. Aluminium columns splashed with colour are grouped round a pool shaped like the map of Italy.

Based on an excavated villa in Herculaneum, Italy, and on Roman writings, J PAUL GETTY MUSEUM, MALIBU, Calif. (Landon Wilson; 1974) is sited on a concrete raft. The rectangular pool with Tuscan colonnades on 3 sides and box edgings stretches away from the villa.

J Paul Getty Museum, Malibu: *rectangular pool, Tuscan colonnades*

The exteriors of the HYATT REGENCY HOTELS—PEACHTREE PLAZA, ATLANTA, Georgia, and the HYATT REGENCY, SAN FRANCISCO—(John Portman) present a smooth, high-rise exterior; inside an atrium is surrounded by balconies, galleries, hanging gardens, pools—and sometimes grand pianos. There are projecting podiums, transparent lift bubbles, spangled lighting. PIER 17, SOUTH STREET, SEAPORT, New York (Benjamin Thompson and Associates; 1985) marks the regeneration of the 19th-c waterfront in Lower Manhattan. The district has been transformed into a pleasure area of shopping arcades, restaurants and bars in buildings of glass and scarlet steel.

Britain

Post-Modern in Britain is less likely to be outrageous, more likely to draw on historical and vernacular traditions. A fine example is the PUMPING STATION, ISLE OF DOGS, London (John Outram; 1988). Instead of the usual glass box showing internal workings, this is a Greek temple form with thick columns, outsize details and vivid colours.

Pumping Station, Isle of Dogs: *Greek temple form*

The CLORE BUILDING, TATE GALLERY, London (James Stirling, Michael Wilford and Associates; 1987), which houses Turner's paintings, comprises a Classical stone facade, brick, glass and jazzily painted metal. THE ARK, HAMMERSMITH, London (Ralph Erskine; 1987) is a boat-like building wedged beneath an underpass.

The SAINSBURY WING, NATIONAL GALLERY, London (Robert Venturi and Denise Scott-Brown; 1991) is internally ingenious while, externally, Corinthian details continued from the main building fade to nothing round the corner. RICHMOND RIVERSIDE DEVELOPMENT, SURREY (Quinlan Terry; 1988) conceals offices with conventional interiors behind Georgian facades round green terraces falling to the river Thames. The colourful and classical ROYAL REGATTA HQ, HENLEY ON THAMES (Terry Farrell Partnership; 1985) plays around with classical elements and geometrical shapes. HORSLEYDOWN SQUARE, SOUTHWARK, London (Julyan Wickham; 1987) is a breezy complex with a nautical air off Tower Bridge. The LAW COURTS, TRURO, Devon (Evans and Shalev; 1989) have white geometrical forms, elegant and authoritative. The SAINSBURY BUILDING, WORCESTER COLLEGE, OXFORD (MacCormac Jamieson; 1983) has a cluster of gables over L-shaped rooms stepping down to a lake. This is an outstanding example of Romantic Pragmatism—a transformation of mundane social requirements into a romantic image.

The most popular modern building in Scotland is the BURRELL COLLECTION, POLLOCK PARK, Glasgow (Barry Gasson; 1983). The park is seen through glass walls; sunlight through glass roofs.

The DOCKLANDS enterprise zone in London petered out in the recession of the late 1980s. Most spectacular was CASCADES housing (Campbell Zogolovitch Wilkinson and Gough; 1988), where the steep rake on one side allows each flat to have a sunlit balcony. Also by the same architects: CHINA WHARF, BERMONDSEY, London (1988) is an office block apparently hung from a sculpted metal scarlet frame. CANARY WHARF DEVELOPMENT (Skidmore Owings and Merrill; 1980–) is famous for the 850-foot office tower with pyramid cap (Cesar Pelli; 1989), which is unfortunately out of scale.

HILLINGDON TOWN HALL, London (Robert Matthew Johnson Marshall & Partners; 1979) is an irregular "village" build-up of pitched roofs, to make local authority offices more welcoming.

LLOYD'S BUILDING, LONDON (Richard Rogers and Partners; 1986) is a 12-storey rectangular aluminium block with an enormous atrium at its core, and 6 service capsules clipped on round the outside.

MOUND STAND, LORDS CRICKET GROUND, London (Michael Hopkins; 1987) consists of a white steel and glass-crested wave of strung white tents. Also by Hopkins is the SCHLUMBERGER RESEARCH LABORATORIES, CAMBRIDGE (1985).

STANSTED AIRPORT, ESSEX (Norman Foster; 1991) has a great hangar. The unbroken space is a stunning exploitation of the latest technology.

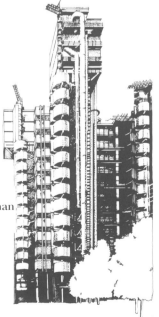

Lloyd's Building, London: *12-storey aluminium block with service capsules*

Mound Stand, Lord's Cricket Ground, London: *wave of strung white tents*

France

As in other European countries, International Modern is still the base for much French architecture, and concrete remains a favourite material. But there are backward glances to Art Nouveau, Bauhaus and Art Deco.

LOUVRE PYRAMIDS, PARIS (I M Pei; 1989) was one of the *grands projets* for the Bicentennial 1989. A steel mesh and reflective glass pyramid is sited in the courtyard between Classical buildings. A central pyramid, balanced by two smaller ones, provides entry and lighting to galleries.

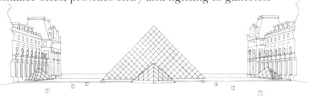

Louvre Pyramids, Paris

NEW OPERA HOUSE, PARIS (Carlos Ott; 1989), Place de la Bastille, is drum-shaped with smooth granite panels. PARC DE LA VILLETTE, PARIS (1989; idea by Bernard Schumi and Francois Barre) stands on the site of the Paris abbatoir, and has 42 *foies* (pavilions with inventive structures and forms). There is also museum space and a shiny spherical *géode*

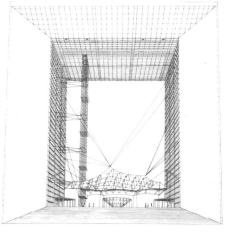

La Grande Arche, Bastille, Paris

that holds an "omnimax" cinema-in-the-round. LES ARCADES DU LAC and LE VIADUC, ST QUENTIN-EN-YVELINES, near Versailles (Ricardo Bofill and Taller d'Architectura; 1981) is a solid urban complex of flats, from which a 5-floor bridge of apartments juts into a lake. Concrete with mass-produced crude Post-Modern Classical details.

LA GRANDE ARCHE, PLACE DE LA BASTILLE, PARIS (Johann Otto von Spreckelsen; 1990) was the winning design from President Mitterand's competition of 1984. Sited beyond Les Halles, the *Arche* of white Carrara marble contains 35 storeys of office space. The colossal space (taller than a Gothic cathedral) is suggested by "cloud" canopy by Peter Rice stretched within the arch.

Germany

German architecture suggests free expression without any overall conformity to a "style". Three contrasting museums illustrate the variety.

ABTEIBURG MUSEUM, MUNCHEN-GLADBACH (Hans Hollein; 1982) has separate units functionally expressed and grouped on a piece of high ground within the town. VITRA FURNITURE DESIGN MUSEUM, WEIL-AM-RHEIN (Frank Gehry; 1988) is a heap of forms piled up higgledy-piggledy, the all-white stucco exterior somehow managing to retain a unity which is repeated in the cool, well-organized interior.

STRAATSGALERIE, STUTTGART (James Stirling; 1984) consists of a horizontally striped stone, circus shapes, bright colours and adventurous circulation patterns.

Straatsgalerie, Stuttgart:
horizontally striped stone

Austria

Viennese Art Nouveau informs many designs in Austria.

SAVINGS BANK, FAVORITEN, VIENNA (Gunter Dominig; 1980) has a street frontage that buckles and jerks upwards over the entry to the bank. Also by Dominig with Eilfried Huth is the MULTIPURPOSE HALL, GRAZ-EGGENBERG: a moulded brontosaurus of a building with a string of circular holes to emit light down the vertebrae.

The Netherlands

CENTRAL BEHEER INSURANCE COMPANY OFFICES, APELDOORN (Herman Hertzbarger; 1973) provides accommodation for a large workforce broken into identifiable human units; cube-shaped blocks of staggered heights. NMB BANK HEADQUARTERS, suburbs of AMSTERDAM (Ton Alberts and van Huut; 1988) uses prefabricated concrete panels and hand-made brick, but the building retains the thin vertical interest and skyline of pitched roofs associated with Dutch canal and windmill architecture.

Switzerland
SINGLE FAMILY ROUND HOUSE, STABIO TICINO (Mario Botta; 1982)
Solid geometric figures are cut through for doors and
windows, drum lit from top and by a window shaped like
an inverted Y from roof to ground.

Scandinavia
Vernacular sources are often used in Swedish Post-Modern.
CHURCH AT TAXVEJ, BAGSVAERD, DENMARK (Jorn Utzon; 1975),
near Copenhagen, surprises the visitors with a moulded
concrete interior that curves up to a crest above the
central space.
HOUSING, MALMO, SWEDEN (Ivo Waldhor; 1991) displays
infinite variety of window shape and size, colour of doors
and windows, details with Art Nouveau, Art Deco and
Modern memories, size of flats and position and orientation
of rooms, often to tenants' choice.

Finland
The strong tradition of Alvar Aalto is carried on by Pietila
and a thriving architectural profession.
LIBRARY TAMPERE (Reimä Pietila; 1988) has an elaborate
plan based on the native capercaillie bird (the tail is a fan
of feathers). Overlapping, interpenetrating forms make
extraordinary spaces, original and memorable.

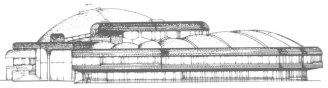

Library Tampere, Finland: *interpenetrating forms*

Japan
Economic success combined with population pressure has
ensured a spate of closely packed buildings. A flourishing
architectural community experiments with materials,
industrialized systems and advanced technology.
MUSEUM OF CONTEMPORARY ART, HIROSHIMA (1988) is sited on
a hill, wings spread north and south from a hollow circular
central building. Most of the exhibition space is below ground.
GYMNASIUM FUJISAIWA
(Fumihiko Maki;
1984) is a fine
example of High
Tech. FACE HOUSE,
KYOTO (Kazumasa
Yamishita; 1974)
has gnashing teeth
in the "jokey"
Post-Modern idiom.
AZUMA HOUSE, OSAKA
(Tadao Ando; 1976)
was designed
as a "bastion
of resistance"
against Western

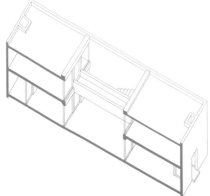

Azuma House, Osaka: *capturing nature*

189

consumerism. Entered through a slot in an otherwise blank concrete façade, the accommodation is arranged in two cubes framing an open courtyard, which links the occupants to nature.

Gulf States

Before the Gulf War, the oil-rich states spawned a burst of public, commercial and university buildings. Many of these buildings display interesting aspects of the Post-Modern movements.

MINISTRY OF FOREIGN AFFAIRS, RIYADH, Saudi Arabia (Henning Larsen; 1984) has a fortress-like exterior. The entry leads to a triangular full-height atrium at the centre of the building.

NATIONAL BANK HEADQUARTERS, JEDDAH, Saudi Arabia (Gordon Bunshaft and Son; 1983) has a triangular plan behind a tall flat-faced rectangular façade, cut into by two enormous square stretches of window.

The INTERCONTINENTAL HOTEL AND CONFERENCE CENTRE, MECCA, Saudi Arabia (Rolf Gutbrod Frei Otto; 1974) is a strung tent structure clad in insulated aluminium sheeting.

WATER TOWERS, KUWAIT (VBB, Sweden; 1981), shaped like mushrooms, received the Aga Khan award.

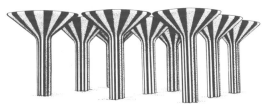

Water towers, Kuwait: *mushroom-shaped*

S-E Asia and Australasia

ASIAN (OLYMPIC) GAMES VILLAGE, NEW DELHI (Raj Rewell; 1982) has broad streets lined with massive barbaric blocks worthy of Babylon or Khorsabad.

BAHA'I TEMPLE, DELHI (Fariburz Sabha; 1987) is the central temple for the Baha'i faith; the main hall holds 1200. Water-lily concrete shells float on a pool.

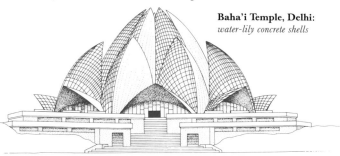

Baha'i Temple, Delhi: *water-lily concrete shells*

SCIENCE MUSEUM, BANGKOK (Sumet Jumsai Associates; 1978) is a technological exhibit in itself, consisting of a science park and 4-storey exhibition hall. Entry under slab cantilevered from three columns like golf pins.

MENARA MESINIAGA, SELANGOR, MALAYSIA (Ken Yeang; 1992) is a Modernist tower transformed by careful attention to energy conservation. Aluminium louvres, deep-set balconies and planting exclude the sun, and the tower culminates with a pool, gym and sun terraces beneath a giant solar shade.

Menara Mesiniaga, Selangor, Malaysia: *climatically responsive tower*

SYDNEY FOOTBALL STADIUM (Philip Cox, Richardson and Taylor; 1988. Engineers: Arup) holds 40,000. A continuous ribbon steel roof sweeps over the stands in a figure of eight, carried on steel trusses above concrete stanchions. It is known as the "Roller-Coaster".

Sydney Football Stadium: *the "Roller-Coaster"*

Also by the same firm is the DARLING HARBOUR REDEVELOPMENT, SYDNEY, part of New South Wales Bicentennial Project (1988). The double sail roof of the AQUARIUM leans back like a twin-mast schooner.

ROPOTA SHELTERED HOUSING AND MEDICAL CENTRE, LOWER HUTT, Wellington, New Zealand (Roger Walker; 1991) is a ship-like white assembly of Post-Modern and local timber details in the midst of suburban sprawl.

PRIVATE HOUSE, SOUTHERN HIGHLANDS, NEW SOUTH WALES (Glenn Murcutt; 1992) is a linear volume, with protective masonry to the (colder) south and a steel-framed box opening to the sun and views to the north. The delicate steel roof echoes the Aboriginal injunction to "touch this earth lightly".

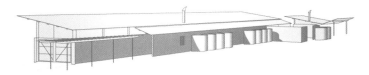

Private House, New South Wales: *sun-seeking linear volume*

CONTEMPORARY PLURALISM

The pluralism of the 1980s continued through the 1990s and into the new century, but beneath the bewildering variety of expression some broad trends were apparent. Most notable, perhaps, was the widespread rejection of the superficial use of historical styles that had characterized stylistic Post-Modernism, and a renewed interest in overtly Modernist forms of expression.

In tune with the global flow of capital and development of the World Wide Web, the 1990s saw the emergence of a worldwide market for architectural talent. Reinforced by unprecedented media interest in architecture, and by the conviction that an iconic "landmark" building could be a catalyst for urban renewal, this promoted an elite of architects to superstar status and encouraged them to deploy a trademark style almost regardless of location. In contrast, many fine buildings emerged in response to local conditions. This was most marked, perhaps, in Spain and Portugal, but true also of Norway and Switzerland and in less widely acclaimed centres such as the Republic of Ireland and Hungary.

A significant factor in the globalization of architecture was the advent of Computer Aided Design and Manufacturing (CADCAM) systems. These not only made it possible to conceive and build exceptionally complex forms, such as the Guggenheim Museum in Bilbao, but also promoted interest in biomorphic forms, described by the neologism "blobitecture".

Following the Earth Summit held by the United Nations in Rio de Janeiro in 1992, there was growing awareness of global environmental problems. These encouraged the elimination of air conditioning and promoted interest in manipulating a building's form to create "passive", low-energy systems of environmental control. However, to date the demand for environmentally responsive buildings has had only a modest impact on the visual language of architecture.

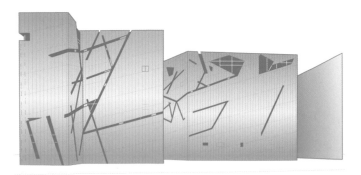

Jewish Museum, Berlin *(Daniel Libeskind; 1998): random slashes and a zigzag plan*

Spain and Portugal

With the re-establishment of democratic government following the death of General Franco, architecture flourished throughout Spain, receiving a level of political support rare elsewhere. The 1992 Barcelona Olympics acted as a catalyst for city-wide regeneration, as well as unique sporting venues. The ARCHERY FACILITIES, VALL D'HEBRON (Miralles and Pinós; 1991) epitomize the architects' exuberant style. The practice pavilion is roofed by floating planes of concrete: supported by tubular steel props and thin ties, they appear almost to flutter in the breeze.

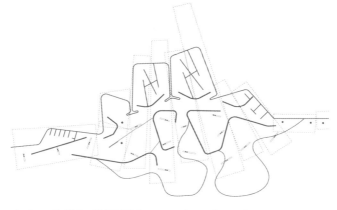

Archery Facilities, Vall D'Hebron: *complex, exuberant plan*

The all-white GASPAR HOUSE, ZAHORA (Alberto Campo Baeza; 1991) creates an introverted, minimalist vision of paradise. TOWN HALL, MURCIA (Rafael Moneo; 1998) is a beautifully integrated addition to an historic setting. Its stone piers, irregularly spaced like notes on a musical score, have been widely imitated.

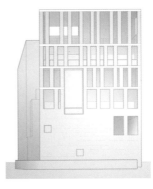

Town Hall, Murcia:
musical façade

The striking sculptural forms of the titanium-clad GUGGENHEIM MUSEUM, BILBAO (Frank Gehry; 1997) make this building the most successful of the new city icons. Culminating around the towering atrium, they open, petal-like, to flood light into the multi-level circulation space.

Guggenheim Museum, Bilbao: *sculptural forms*

193

KURSAAL AUDITORIUM AND CONGRESS CENTRE, SAN SEBASTIAN (Rafael Moneo; 1999) exhibits a similar disjunction between inside and outside, its slanted glass boxes revealing little of the volumes within.

In Portugal, the regional school centred on Oporto was dominant. The BOM JESUS HOUSE, BRAGA (Eduardo Souto de Moura; 1994) combines minimalist white planes and a wall of undressed granite. The FACULTY OF ARCHITECTURE, OPORTO (Alvaro Siza; 1996) was conceived as a miniature urban settlement, reminiscent of ancient Greece. Arranged around an elevated podium, the white-rendered buildings are Modernist in style, but given character by variations in fenestration and form.

Faculty of Architecture, Oporto:
miniature urban settlement

The PORTUGUESE PAVILION, HANOVER EXPO (Alvaro Siza and Eduardo Souto de Moura; 2000) uses a sweeping suspended roof to create a dramatic covered plaza.

Norway
In the 1990s Norway emerged as the most interesting of the Nordic countries, thanks largely to the work and teaching of Sverre Fehn. VILLA BUSK, BAMBLE (Sverre Fehn; 1990) seems to grow out of a rocky ridge, while the fissures between the elongated concrete volume, circular auditorium and triangular, glass-walled restaurant of the GLACIER MUSEUM, FJAERLAND (Sverre Fehn; 1991) echo the nearby Jostedal glacier.

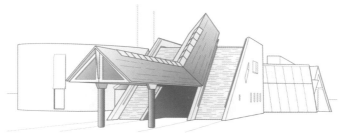

Glacier Museum, Fjaerland: *forms emulating landscape*

SUMMER HOUSE, RISØR (Carl-Viggo Hølmebakk; 1997) is threaded around the trees of its coastal site. FISHING MUSEUM, KARMOY (Snøhetta; 1998) connects the local and the universal. Alongside its concrete-framed end wall, addressing the horizon, are screens woven from a native coastal shrub.

194

Switzerland

In Switzerland, the continuity of the modern tradition was almost undisturbed by the Post-Modern stylistic interests that flourished elsewhere. SIGNAL BOX, BASLE (Herzog and de Meuron; 1995) and LINER MUSEUM, APPENZELL (Gigon Guyer; 1998) epitomize the so-called "Swiss Box" school, whose works are characterized by clear forms wrapped in a single material.

Thermal Baths, Vals: *labyrinthine interior*

The tiny SOGN BENEDETG CHAPEL, SUMVITG (Peter Zumthor; 1988) and imposing THERMAL BATHS, VALS (Peter Zumthor; 1996) exemplify Zumthor's craft-based approach. The former is made solely of wood, while the latter, clad entirely in locally sourced gneiss laid in narrow, striated bands, resembles a vast stone monolith externally and a labyrinthine constructed cave internally.

CULTURE AND CONGRESS CENTRE, LUCERNE (Jean Nouvel; 1998) occupies the site of a former shipyard on Lake Lucerne. In response, Nouvel conceived the performance spaces as three "vessels", ran water into the building, and arranged them beneath a boldly cantilevered roof that forms a covered plaza facing the Alps.

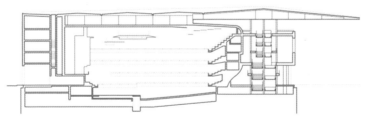

Culture and Congress Centre, Lucerne: *dramatically cantilevered roof*

BEYELER FOUNDATION MUSEUM, BASLE (Renzo Piano Building Workshop; 1997) offers a continuous sequence of rectangular rooms, framed by four parallel walls that reach out into the adjacent park. Above hovers an independent, multi-layered glass roof that can be adjusted to the needs of different media.

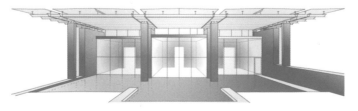

Beyeler Foundation Museum, Basle: *parallel walls link building and landscape*

195

Germany

A striking feature of recent German architecture is that many of the most admired buildings are by non-German architects. GOETZ GALLERY, MUNICH (Herzog and de Meuron; 1992) epitomizes the minimal, elegant forms and detailing of the "Swiss Box" school. FIRE STATION, WEIL-AM-RHEIN (Zaha Hadid; 1993) is one of several buildings by world-famous architects – including Tadao Ando, Frank Gehry and Alvaro Siza – built for the furniture-maker Vitra. Its shard-like geometry is shaped around the movements of the fire engines.

Fire Station, Weil-am-Rhein:
dynamic forms

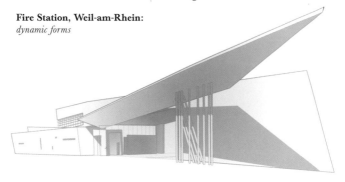

JEWISH MUSEUM, BERLIN (Daniel Libeskind; 1998) has a complex, zigzag plan through which runs a straight but discontinuous void intended to represent the victims of the Holocaust. The exterior, wrapped in zinc, is slashed by seemingly random cuts derived from what Libeskind described as the "memory" of the site. (*See* page 192 for illustration.)

The transformation of the REICHSTAG, BERLIN (Foster and Partners; 1999), the former German parliament, is symbolized by a publicly accessible glass cupola. A permanent roof made of giant timber umbrellas is a striking legacy of the HANOVER EXPO (Thomas Herzog; 2000), and the GSW BUILDING, BERLIN (Sauerbruch and Hutton; 2001) is made energy efficient by a playful façade of coloured sunblinds.

NORTH GERMAN REGIONAL CLEARING BANK, HANOVER (Behnisch, Behnisch & Partner; 2002) addresses both city and locality by wrapping a tower with 6 storeys of accommodation scaled to the street. Each floor of the tower has a different configuration, promoting a sense of identity and enabling the interiors to be naturally lit and ventilated.

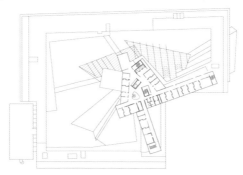

Regional Clearing Bank, Hanover: *urban complex*

The Netherlands

Architecture and design flourished in The Netherlands, with young practices springing off from, or developing in opposition to, Rem Koolhaas and his increasingly global Office for Metropolitan Architecture. VILLA VPRO, HILVERSUM (MVRDV; 1997) has a Koolhaas-inspired complexity of plan and section, while the rust-coloured concrete finish of the MINNAERT BUILDING, UTRECHT (Neutelings Riedijk; 1997) combines a fashionable interest in the skin with a Post-Modern jokiness – the building's name is spelled out as storey-high columns.

Britain

Across Britain, the establishment of the National Lottery to fund arts projects and Millennium celebrations proved the catalyst for many distinguished new buildings and transformations of old ones. EDEN PROJECT, ST AUSTELL, CORNWALL (Nicholas Grimshaw; 2000) boasts the world's biggest greenhouse, made from three intersecting geodesic domes. GREAT COURT, BRITISH MUSEUM, LONDON (Foster and Partners; 2000) is a major public space created by roofing a previously neglected courtyard.

TATE MODERN, LONDON (Herzog and de Meuron; 2000) features one of the world's most imposing foyers, courtesy of the former Turbine Hall at Bankside Power Station. NEW ART GALLERY, WALSALL (Caruso St John; 2000) is organized vertically into a small, tiled tower, punctuated by a scatter of windows.

Laban Dance Centre, London:
veiled interior

LABAN DANCE CENTRE, LONDON (Herzog and de Meuron; 2002), veiled by translucent polycarbonate sheeting and large sheets of reflective glass, contains an interior of spatial complexity.

SWISS RE HEADQUARTERS, LONDON (Foster and Partners; 2004) is a striking new addition to London's skyline. Nicknamed "The Gherkin", it has a complex, biomorphic form – made possible by computers – with floors linked by a spiral of "sky gardens".

Swiss Re Headquarters, London:
computer-generated biomorphic form

197

The United States

Although American cities continued to be dominated by corporate, Post-Modern towers, the best American architecture reflected the diversity typical of the period, and of the country's landscapes and cultures. The AMERICAN HERITAGE CENTER, WYOMING (Antoine Predock; 1993) takes the form of a giant concrete tepee. The exuberant forms of the INCE COMPLEX, CULVER CITY, LOS ANGELES (Eric Owen Moss; 1994) express the dynamism of the urban regeneration process.

CHAPEL OF ST IGNATIUS, SEATTLE (Steven Holl; 1997) has a complex interior animated by coloured light admitted through varied roof-lights. Spatial complexity is matched by tactile materials and crafted details, and at night the chapel becomes a beacon for the surrounding campus.

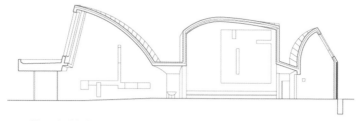

Chapel of St Ignatius, Seattle: *light-filled space*

DISNEY CONCERT HALL, LOS ANGELES (Frank Gehry; 2003) developed the sculptural language of the Bilbao Guggenheim Museum into a more integrated spatial whole. PUBLIC LIBRARY, SEATTLE (Rem Koolhaas/OMA; 2004) consists of a crystalline glass exterior framing a vast interior, through which a gentle ramp zigzags back and forth to link the multi-level book-stacks into a continuous "body of knowledge".

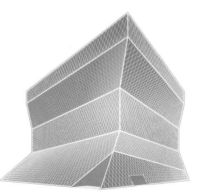

Public Library, Seattle: *crystalline exterior*

Japan

The experimentalism of Japanese architecture flourished despite a downturn in the national economy. SHONANDAI CULTURAL CENTRE, KANAGAWA (Itsuko Hasegawa; 1990), clad in perforated metal panels, was conceived as a miniature cosmos. NAOSHIMA CONTEMPORARY ART MUSEUM, KAGAWA (Tadao Ando; 1992) extends the calm, geometric clarity of Ando's houses to a group of buildings stretched along a headland. TAKATORI CHURCH, KOBE (Shigeru Ban; 1995) features an oval enclosure made of cardboard tubes.

MEDIATHEQUE, SENDAI (Toyo Ito; 2000) represents the flow of digital data in the modern city. Envisaged as a giant aquarium of "liquid space", it features columns formed from bundles of steel tubes: designed to house services, they undulate slowly through the interior like giant strands of seaweed.

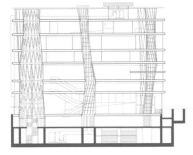

Mediatheque, Sendai:
liquid space

INTERNATIONAL PORT TERMINAL, YOKOHAMA (Foreign Office Architects; 2002) is a piece of computer-generated topography projecting from the coastline. Its timber-clad roof is an undulating public park, with depressions and cuts giving access to the terminal below.

International Port Terminal, Yokohama:
built topography

GLOSSARY

Numbers in brackets after a definition refer to pages on which the term is clarified by an illustration.

Abacus Flat slab on top of capital, beneath architrave. (22)

Acroterion Figure or ornament at apex or end of a pediment. (21)

Adyton Rear sanctuary of Greek temple. (23)

Agora Open space used by Ancient Greeks for assemblies and markets.

Aisle In a church, one of divisions parallel with nave, chancel or choir. (68)

Ambulatory Continuous aisle round a circular building; aisle round E end of Christian church. (80, 89)

Antae Pilasters terminating projecting walls of a portico, esp. in Greek temples. (23)

Antefixae Ornamental blocks concealing ends of roof-tiles. (24)

Apse Semicircular or polygonal recess, esp. at E end of church. (68)

Arcade Range of arches on piers or columns.

Architrave Lowest part of an entablature. (22)

Ashlar Squared, hewn stone laid in regular courses.

Atrium In Roman houses: inner courtyard. (41) In

Early Christian and medieval churches: colonnaded forecourt.

Bailey Open area of a castle. (95)

Baptistery Building containing font for baptismal rites.

Bar tracery Tracery using stone ribs in complicated patterns. (101)

Barrel vault Continuous vault of semicircular or pointed section. (92)

Basilica Ancient Roman hall of justice and commerce. (37) In Christian architecture: building

199

with nave, aisles and clerestory. (68)

Bay Compartment of a building. In churches: space between one column or pier and next, incl. vault or ceiling above it.

Bema In Early Christian churches, raised stage for clergy. (68)

Biomorphic Designed in imitation of natural forms. (197)

Blind arcade Arcade attached to wall. (90)

Boss Ornamental projection covering intersecting ribs of a vault. (100)

Buttress Mass of masonry or brickwork used to give support.

Campanile Italian term for bell-tower, generally free-standing. (72)

Cantilever Structural member which projects beyond line of support.

Capital Crowning feature of column or pilaster. (22, 69, 88)

Caryatid Carved female figure used as column. (28)

Cella Main body of Classical temple.

Chaitya hall Indian Buddhist prayer-hall. (46)

Chancel Part of church reserved for clergy and containing altar and choir.

Chapter house Ecclesiastical assembly building. (105)

Chevet French term for combination of an apse, surrounding ambulatory and radiating chapels. (89, 98)

Choir Part of church where services are sung, generally in W part of chancel but sometimes extending into nave. Also used as synonym for chancel. (89)

Clerestory Windowed upper walls of aisled building, above aisle roofs. (17, 99)

Cloisters Covered arcade around a quadrangle connecting a monastic church to the domestic parts of the monastery. (105)

Coffering Sunken ornamental panels in a ceiling or dome. (36)

Colonnade Row of columns supporting arches or an entablature.

Column Vertical cylindrical support, usually with base, shaft and capital. (22)

Composite Roman addition to the Classical Orders. (34)

Corbel Supportive bracket or block projecting from a wall.

Corbel vault Vault built on same principle as a corbelled arch.

Corbelled arch "False arch" bridging a gap by means of overlapping blocks of masonry.

Corinthian Third of Classical Orders. (22)

Cornice Projecting upper section of entablature. (22)

Crepidoma Stepped base of a Greek temple. (21)

Cross vault Another term for groin vault.

Crossing Space at intersection of nave, chancel and transepts in a cruciform church. (89)

Crypt Chamber beneath main floor of church, usually containing graves or relics. (93)

Cupola Dome, esp. a miniature dome surmounted by a lantern.

Curtain wall In castles: the surrounding fortified walls. In modern architecture: an outer, non-load-bearing wall.

Cusp Projecting point on inner side of an arch, window or roundel.

Donjon Castle keep inner stronghold.

Doric First and simplest of Classical Orders. (22)

Dormer window Small, gabled window projecting from a sloping roof.

Drum Circular or polygonal wall supporting a dome.

Dwarf gallery Small arcaded wall passage on outside of a building. (91)

Eaves Lower edge of an overhanging roof. (58)

Echinus Convex moulding beneath abacus of Doric capital; or corresponding part of Ionic capital. (22)

Embrasure Opening in a castle wall or parapet.

Engaged column Column attached to a wall of pier.

Entablature Upper part of a Classical Order, between capitals and pediment. (22)

Entasis Bulge sometimes given to a column shaft to counter optical illusion that it is thinner in the centre.

Exedra Large, semicircular or rectangular wall recess. (38)

Fan Vault Vault with ribs radiating from wall-shaft in fan-like patterns. (100)

Fillet Narrow band between mouldings, or separating the flutes in columns.

Finial Ornament crowning pinnacle, gable, etc. (102)

Fluting Vertical grooves on columns and pilasters.

Flying buttress Arch or half-arch springing from a detached pier and abutting against a wall to take thrust of a vault. (98, 99)

Forum In Roman architecture, a central open space surrounded by public buildings and colonnades. (35)

Frieze Part of entablature between architrave and cornice; or similar decorative band. (22)

Frontispiece Principal entrance bay of a building.

Gallery Upper floor, open on one side to

interior (e.g., in churches) or exterior of a building. In medieval or Renaissance houses: a long, narrow room.

Giant Order Order of columns or pilasters extending through two or more stories. (113)

Gopuram In s Indian temples, a huge, elaborate gateway.

Greek cross Cross with arms of equal length.

Groin vault Vault formed by intersection at right angles of two barrel vaults.

Half-hipped roof Roof with ends that have gabled upper parts, sloping lower parts. (54)

Hall-church Church with aisles same height as nave.

Hammer-beam roof Roof with beams projecting horizontally from top of wall but without meeting corresponding members on opposite side. (101)

Hipped roof Roof with sloped ends. (54)

Hypostyle Hall with flat roof supported by a forest of columns. (17)

Insula Ancient Roman tenement block. (41)

Ionic Second of Classical Orders. (22)

Iwan In Sassanian and Islamic architecture, vaulted hall with large arched opening. (78)

Jagamohan Assembly hall of N Indian Hindu temple. (47)

Joggled Applied to blocks joined by notches and corresponding projections. (79)

Keep Inner stronghold of a castle (62, 95)

Kōdō Lecture hall of Japanese temple.

Kondō Image hall of Japanese temple. (59)

Lancet Slim pointed window, characteristic of Early English building. (101)

Lantern Windowed

tower or turret crowning a cupola or dome. (73, 106, 115)

Lean-to-roof Roof with only one slope, against higher wall.

Lierne Tertiary rib in a Gothic vault. (100)

Loggia Gallery open on one or more sides, sometimes columned. (112)

Lombard strips Shallow pilasters on Romanesque exteriors, joined at top by small arches. (90)

Madrasa Islamic theological college or teaching mosque.

Mastaba Low oblong Egyptian tomb

Megaron Large oblong hall esp. Mycenean or Cretan.

Metope Space between two triglyphs in Doric frieze. (22)

Minaret Tower of mosque from which call to prayer is made. (82)

Modillion Small bracket beneath upper part of a cornice.

Motte Steep mound, a feature of 11th–12th C. castles. (95)

Mouldings Projecting or recessed bands used to ornament walls, arches, etc. (24)

Muqarnas Stalactite ornamentation in Islamic architecture. (79)

Naos Sanctuary of a Greek temple. (21)

Narthex Vestibule or portico stretching across main entrance of church. (70)

Nave Main body of a church W of crossing; more specifically, the central space bounded by aisles. (68, 71)

Oculus Round window or opening.

Opisthodomos Rear chamber of Greek temple. (23)

Order Design of a column and its entablature, corresponding to one of 5 Classical Orders used in Ancient Greece and Rome. (22, 34)

Palladian window Arch on twin columns flanked by flat-headed openings. (120)

Pediment Triangular gable above door, window or Classical entablature. (21)

Pendentives Inverted concave triangles springing from corners of a square or polygon and meeting at top to form circular base for dome. (68)

Peristyle Range of columns surrounding a building or courtyard. (41)

Piano nobile Raised main floor of an Italian Renaissance palace.

Piazza Open public space surrounded by buildings.

Pier Heavy masonry support, like a column only thicker; often square in section.

Pilaster Rectangular column projecting from wall.

Pillar Detached upright support that does not conform in shape or proportion with one of Orders.

Pilotis Pillars or stilts supporting a raised building. (167)

Pinnacle Pyramidal or conical ornament crowning a buttress, gable etc.

Plate tracery Tracery with simple openings "punched" in stone. (101)

Podium Continuous base on which a temple or other structure is built. (34)

Portico Colonnaded entrance to a building.

Pronaos Portico of Greek temple. (21, 23)

Propylaeum Monumental entrance to Greek sacred enclosure. (26)

Pteron Colonnade surrounding main body of Greek temple. (23)

Purlin Horizontal roof-beam resting on principal rafters and supporting subsidiary ones.

Pylon Tower-like Ancient Egyptian

gateway with sloping sides. (13)

Qibla In a mosque, wall facing Mecca.

Reinforced concrete Concrete strengthened by insertion of steel rods. (160)
Rib Projecting band separating cells of a groined vault. (100)
Rib vault Groin vault featuring arched ribs which cross diagonally. (100)
Rose window Circular window with radiating tracery. (103)
Rotunda Building or room that is circular in plan. (36)
Roundel Circular panel or medallion.
Rustication Masonry technique in which blocks have deeply recessed joints and often a roughened surface. (113)

Sexpartite vault Vault with bays divided into 6 parts by two diagonal ribs and one transverse rib.
Shikhara Cactus-shaped spire of an Indian Hindu temple. (47)
Shinden "Sleeping palace" style of Japanese domestic architecture.
Spandrel Triangular area between two arches or between an arch and a wall.

Springer Point at which an arch rises from its support. (100)
Squinch Small arch or series of concentric arches built across angle of a square or polygon usually to support a dome. (68)
Stilted arch Arch with vertical sides at bottom.
Stoa Detached colonnade in Greek architecture. (28)
Strapwork Interlaced bands of relief ornament on ceilings, walls, etc.
Stucco Plaster or cement used as low-relief decoration on ceilings or walls; also, plaster applied to entire façades to simulate stone.
Stupa In Buddhist architecture, a domical sacred mound. (43)
Stylobate In Classical architecture, top step of platform on which a colonnade is placed.

Thermae Roman public baths. (38)
Tholos Domed circular building.
Tierceron Secondary rib in a Gothic vault. (100)
Trabeated Built of upright post and horizontal beams.
Tracery Ornamental stone framework holding glass in a Gothic window. (101)
Transept Projecting

arms of a cruciform church. (89)
Triforium Arcaded wall-passage (or blind arcading) between nave arcade and clerestory in church interiors. (Also, sometimes used to refer to gallery). (99)
Triglyph Fluted block between two metopes in a Doric frieze. (22)
Tunnel vault Another term for barrel vault.
Tuscan Roman addition to Classical Orders; a plainer version of Doric.
Tympanum In medieval architecture, area between lintel of doorway and arch above.
Vault Arched ceiling or roof of stone or brick.
Venetian window Another term for Palladian window.
Volute Spiral scroll, e.g. on Ionic capital. (34, 135)
Voussoirs Wedge-shaped stone blocks forming an arch.

Westwork Tower-like structure in Carolingian and Romanesque churches. (91)

Ziggurat Stepped pyramid supporting temple or altar (8)
Ziyada Outer court of a mosque.

INDEX

Buildings are arranged by country, and then, where appropriate, by town. Modern national divisions are followed, although a separate entry is given for large islands. Names of architects are in italics.

The author has made a personal selection of buildings or sites that he considers to be of supreme artistic interest, marked by an asterisk.

Aalto, Alvar 174
Adam, Robert 141, 144
Alberti, Leon Battista 112, 113, 114, 115, 117
Algeria
Timgrad 43
Ando, Tadao 189, 196, 198
Archer, Thomas 143
Asam brothers 139
Asplund, Gunnar 174–5
Australia
private house, Southern

Highlands, New South Wales 191
Sydney Opera House* 168, 182
Austria
Linz: St Florian 138
Melk* 138
Salzburg 138
Vienna: Belvedere 138, Burgtheater 153, Karlskirche* 138, Majolica House 165,

Parliament 153, Postal Savings Bank 165, St Stephen's 108, Steiner House 160, 165, Votivkirche 153
Baeza, Alberto Campo 193
Ban, Shigeru 198
Barry, Charles 150
Behrens, Peter 166
Behnisch, Behnisch and Partner 196

Belgium
Antwerp: Cathedral 109, Town Hall 126
Bruges: Chancellery 126, Cloth Hall 109
Brussels: Grand-Place 126, Maison du Peuple 164, Palais de Justice 154, Solvay House 164, Stoclet Palace 164, Tassel House 159, 164
Louvain: Town Hall 102, 109
Tournai Cathedral 109
Ypres: Cloth Hall* 109
Berlage, H. P. 164–5, 173
Bernini, Gianlorenzo 118, 131, 133, 134
Boğazkale *see* Turkey, Hattushash
Bolivia
Tiahuanaco: Gate of the Sun 66
Borromini, Francesco 131, 132, 133, 135, 138
Boullée, Etienne-Louis 132
Bramante, Donato 112, 116, 117, 118, 121
Brazil
Brasilia: Alvorada Place 181, Palace of the National Congress 180
Congohas de Campo: Bom Jesus 147
Ouro Preto: S. Francisco 147
Rio de Janeiro: S. Bento 147, Ministry of Education and Health 181
Britain
Balmoral Castle, Scotland 151
Bath* 43, 144
Beaumaris Castle, Wales 102, 107
Bexley Heath: Red House 161
Blenheim Palace* 143
Blickling Hall 129
Bradford-on-Avon: St Laurence 94
Brighton: Royal Pavilion 145
Bristol Cathedral 106
Brixworth: All Saints' 94
Burghley House 128
Cambridge University*: History Faculty 171, King's College Chapel* 107
Canterbury Cathedral* 94, 106
Castle Howard* 143
Chatsworth House* 142
Chorley Wood: The Orchard 161
Coventry Cathedral 171
Durham Cathedral* 88, 94

Easton Neston 143
Eden Project, St Austell, Cornwall 197
Edinburgh: Charlotte Square 144, University 144
Eltham Lodge 130
Ely Cathedral 106
Exeter Cathedral 106
Fountains Abbey* 94
Glasgow: School of Art* 161, Willow Tea Rooms 159
Gloucester Cathedral 106
Hardwick Hall 128
Harlech Castle, Wales 107
Hatfield House 129
Holkham Hall 144
Hunstanton Secondary School 171
Ilkley: Heathcote 161
Kedleston Hall* 144
Kirby Hall 128
Leeds Town Hall* 151
Leicester University: Engineering Building 171
Lincoln Cathedral* 106
Little Moreton Hall 129
Liverpool: Albert Docks 151, Oriel Chambers 151
London: All Saints', Margaret St 150, Alton Estate, Roehampton 170, Banqueting House, Whitehall 130, Barbican 170, British Museum 150, British Museum Great Court 197, Chiswick House 144, Bedford Park 161, Cumberland Terrace 145, Daily Express Building 171, Economist Buildings 171, Greenwich Hospital (Palace) 130, 142, Hampton Court Palace 128, Highpoint I and II, Highgate 170, Houses of Parliament* 150, 154, Kew Gardens, Palm House 150, Laban Dance Centre 197, National Theatre* 171, Natural History Museum 151, New Scotland Yard 151, Osterley Park 144, Queen's House, Greenwich* 129, Reform Club 149–50, Regent St 145, Royal Festival Hall* 171, St Bride, Fleet St 142, St Dunstan-in-the-East 142, St John,

Smith Square 143, St Martin-in-the-Fields 143, St Mary-le-Strand 143, St Mary Woolnoth 143, St Pancras 150, St Pancras Station 150, St Paul's* 142, St Stephen, Walbrook 141, 142, St Vedast, Foster Lane 142, Somerset House 144, Sunhouse, Frognal Way, Hampstead 170, Swan House, 17 Chelsea Embankment 161, Swiss Re Headquarters 197, Syon House, Isleworth 144, Tate Modern 197, Tower of London 95, Travellers' Club 150, Westminster Abbey* 106, Westminster Cathedral* 150, 151, Westminster Hall 101, 106
Longleat House* 128
Manchester Town Hall 149
Mereworth Castle 144
Newcastle: Byker Wall 169
Norwich: Cathedral 94, Friar Quay Housing 169, University of E Anglia 171
Oxford* Radcliffe Camera* 143
Rievaulx Abbey 94
Salisbury Cathedral* 105
Scarborough: Grand Hotel 151
Sonning: The Deanery 161
Southwell Minster 94
Stourhead* 144
Twickenham: Strawberry Hill 145
The Vyne, Hampshire 130
Walsall: New Art Gallery 197
Wells Cathedral 99, 106
Wilton House 130
Windsor: St George's Chapel 107
Wollaton Hall 128
York Minster* 106
Brosse, Saloman de 124
Brown, Lancelot ("Capability") 141
Brunelleschi, Filippo 112, 115
Burlington, Lord 144
Burma
Pagan: Ananda Temple* 45, 52, Mingalazedi Stupa 51
Cambodia

Angkor Wat* 45, 52
Campen, Jacob van 126
Canada
Montreal: Expo 67 177,
    Windsor Station 158
Ottawa: Houses of
    Parliament 158,
Toronto City Hall 158
China
Jixian: Dule Temple 55
Mount Song: Shaolin
    Temple 55–6
Peking: Altar of Heaven
    57, Forbidden City*
    56, Palace of
    Purification 57,
    Summer Palace* 57,
    Temple of Heaven
    57, Zhihua Temple 56
Wutai Mountain:
    Foguang Temple
    55, 56, 60
Zhengdingxian:
    Longxing Temple 55
Churriguera family 140–1
Cortona, Pietro da 131, 134
Crete
Knossos: Palace
    of Minos* 25
Cuijpers, P. J. H. 154–5
Czechoslovakia
Prague: Cathedral
    109, Troja Palace 139,
    Vladislav Hall 109
Delorme, Philibert 122–4
Denmark
Arhus Town Hall 175
Copenhagen:
    Grundtvig Church
    175, SAS Building 175,
    Thorwaldsen Museum
    155, Town Hall 166
Frederiksborg Castle 130
Kronborg Castle 130
Roskilde Cathedral 95
Sollero Town Hall 175
Dientzenhofer family 138–9
Egypt
Abu Simbel* 18
Abydos: Temple
    of Seti I 18
Aswan: Tomb of
    Sarenput II 16
Cairo: mosques 80, 81
Dahshur:
    Bent Pyramid 12
Deir el-Bahri*:
    Mortuary Temple of
    Queen Hatshepsut
    16, Temple of
    Mentuhotep 16
Dendera: Temple of
    Hathor 14, 19
Edfu: Temple of
    Horus* 13
Giza*: pyramids 12, 15
Karnak 16, 17
Kom Ombo: Temple of
    Sebek and Haroeris 19
Luxor: Temple of
    Amon 17
Maidum: Pyramid 12

Medinet Ma'adi:
    Tomb Chapel of
    Amenemhet 16
Philae 19
Saqqara: Funerary
    Complex of Zoser15,
    Pyramid of Zoser 12
Thebes: Ramesseum 18,
    Temple of Medinet
    Habu 18, Valley
    of the Kings 18
*Erlach, Johann Bernhard
    Fischer von* 138
Fanzago, Cosimo 134
Finland
Helsinki: Railway
    Station 166,
    Hvitträsk 166
Otaniemi: Polytechnic
    Institute 174,
    University Chapel 174
Paimio Sanatorium 174
Säynätsalo: Civic
    Centre* 174
Vuoksenniska
    Church 174
Fischer, Johann Michael 139
Fontana, Carlo 134, 138
Foreign Office Architects 199
Foster and Partners 196–7
France
Albi 104
Alençon 104
Amiens Cathedral 99,
    104, 108
Anet, Château d' 124
Angoulême Cathedral 92
Autun Cathedral 93
Azay-le-Rideau
    Château d' 123
Beaune: Hôtel
    de Dieu 105
Beauvais Cathedral 104
Blois, Château
    de 123, 136
Bourges: Cathedral
    103, House of
    Jacques Cœur 105
Caen: St Étienne 92
Carcassonne 105
Chambord, Château
    de* 122
Chartres: Notre Dame
    Cathedral* 98–9, 103
Chenonceaux 123
Clermont-Ferrand:
    Notre-Dame-du-Port
    92
Conques: Ste Foy 93
Fontainebleau* 123
Laon Cathedral 103
Le Raincy: Notre
    Dame 176
Marseilles: Unité
    d'Habitation 169, 176
Moissac: St Pierre 93
Nimes: Maison Carrée
    42, Pont du Gard*
    33, 42, Temple of
    Diana 42
Noyon Cathedral 99, 103
Paris: Apartments 25b

rue Franklin 163,
    Bibliothèque
    Nationale 152,
    Bibliothèque Ste
    Geneviéve 152,
    Castel Béranger 163,
    Centre Pompidou*
    176, Cité Universitaire
    176, Eiffel Tower* 153,
    Invalides, Church of
    the 136, Louvre 124,
    Luxembourg, Palais
    de 124, Maisons-
    Lafitte 136, Notre
    Dame Cathedral* 103,
    137, Opéra* 152,
    Panthéon 137, Sacré-
    Cœur 153, St-Jean-
    de-Montmartre 163,
    Ste Chapelle 104,
    Soubise Hôtel de 137,
    Val-de-Grâce 136
Périgueux: St Front
    93, 153
Poissy: Villa Savoie
    167, 176
Poitiers: Notre-Dame-
    la-Grande 93
Rheims Cathedral* 104
Ronchamp: Chapel
    of Notre-Dame-
    du-Haut* 176
Rouen: Palais
    de Justice 105
St Denis: Abbey
    Church 97, 103
St-Savin-sur-Gartempe
    93
Strasbourg Cathedral 104
Toulouse: St Sernin 93
Tournus: St Philibert 93
Vaux-le-Vicomte 136
Versailles Palace* 137
Vézelay:
    Ste Madeleine 93
Gabriel, Jacques-Ange 137
Garnier, Charles 152
Gärtner, Friedrich von 153
Gaudi, Antoni 159,
    164, 181
Gehry, Frank 192, 193,
    196, 198
Germany, East
Berlin, E: Altes
    Museum 153,
    Brandenburg
    Gate 132, 139,
    Schauspielhaus
    149, 153
Dresden: Zwinger 139
Potsdam: Einstein
    Tower 167, 172
Germany, West
Aachen 91
Alfeld: Fagus Factory 166
Augsburg:
    Town Hall 127
Berlin W: AEG Turbine
    Factory 166,
    Philharmonic Hall 172
Bremen Town Hall 127
Cologne: Cathedral*

108, Church of the Apostles 91
Dachau: Church 172
Darmstadt 166
Dessau: Bauhaus 167
Fire Station, Weil-am-Rhein 196
Freiburg Cathedral 108
GSW Building, Berlin 196
Hanover: Hanover Expo 196, North German Regional Clearing Bank 196,
Heidelberg Castle 127
Hildesheim: St Michael's 89
Jewish Museum, Berlin 196
Lorsch: Abbey Gatehouse 91
Lübeck: Gut Garkau Farm Buildings 172
Marburg: St Elizabeth 108
Maris Laach: Abbey* 91
Munich: Altere Pinakothek 153, Amalienburg Palace 139, Goetz Gallery 196, Nymphenburg Palace* 139, Olympic Stadium 172, Residenz 127, St John Nepomuk* 139, St Michael 127
Neueschwanstein 153
Nuremburg: St Lawrence 108
Oberammergau: Schloss Linderhof 153
Ottobeuren: Abbey Church 139
Reichstag, Berlin 196
Rohr 139
Schwäbisch-Gmund: Church 108
Speier Cathedral 91
Stuttgart: Schocken Store 172, Wesissenhof Estate 172
Trier: Porta Nigra 42
Ulm Minster 108
Vierzehnheiligen* 140
Weltenburg 139
Wies, Die 140
Worms Cathedral* 91
Wurzburg: Residenz 140
Gibbs, James 141, 143

Greece
Aegina: Temple of Aphaia 21
Athens: Acropolis* 26–8, Erechtheion 24, 28, 150, Parthenon 23, 27, Propylaea 26, Temple of Athena Nike 27, Agora 28, Choragic Monument of Lysicrates 29, "Little Metropolitan"

Cathedral 75, Temple of Hephaestus (Theseion) 28, Temple of Olymoian Zeus 29, Theatre of Dionysos 29, Tower of the Winds 29
Bassae 30
Corinth: Temple of Apollo 23
Daphni 75
Delos 30
Delphi* 29–30
Epidauros: Theatre* 24, 30, Tholos 24
Kastoria 75
Mistra 76
Mount Athos 75
Mycenae*: Lion Gate 25, Treasury of Atreus 25
Olympia 30
Phocis: Hosios Lukas 75
Priene 31: Assembly Hall 24
Salonica: Church of the Holy Apostles 74
Samos: Heraeum 23
Sounion: Temple of Poseidon* 30
Tiryns 25
Grimshaw, Nicholas 197
Gropius, Walter 168, 172, 179
Guarini, Guarino 134–5
Guimard, Hector 159, 163
Guyer, Gigon 195
Hadid, Zafia 196
Hardouin-Mansart, Jules 136, 137
Hasegawa, Itsuko 198
Hawksmoor, Nicholas 141, 143
Herrera, Juan de 125
Herzog and de Meuron 195, 196, 197
Herzog, Thomas 196
Hildebrandt, Lukas von 138
Hoffmann, Josef 160, 164
Holl, Steven 198
Hølmebakk, Carl-Viggo 194
Horta, Victor 159, 164, 173
Hungary
Budapest: Houses of Parliament 154
India
Agra: Taj Mahal* 85
Aihole 47
Ajanta 47
Bhuvaneshvar* 47, 48
Chandigarh* 181
Delhi: Humayun's Tomb 85, Qutb Minar 85, Quwwat al-Islam Mosque 85, Tomb of Ghiyath ad-Din Tughluq 85
Ellura: Kailasanath Temple* 49
Fatehpur Sikri* 85

Gwalior 48
Karli: Chaitya Hall 46
Khajuraho* 48
Konarak 48
Lomas Rishi Cave 46
Madura 49
Mamallapuram: Shore Temple 49
Mount Abu 50
Sanchi: Great Stupa* 45–6
Sasaram: Tomb of Shir Shah Sur 85
Shrirangam 49
Somnathpur: Kesava Temple 49
Sudama Cave 46
Tanjore 49
Iran
Damghan: Tarik Khana Mosque 82
Isfahan: Friday Mosque 82, Masjid-i Shah* 78, 82
Kerman 82
Mashhad: Mosque of Gawhar Shad 82
Naqsh-i Rustam 10
Persepolis* 10
Iraq
Babylon 9
Baghdad: Abbasid Palace 80
Choga Zanbil 8
Ctesiphon* 10
Khafaje 8
Khorsabad: Palace of Sargon 9
Nimrud: NW Palace 9
Nineveh 7, 9
Samarra Great Mosque 80
Ur: Ziggurat* 8
Uruk: White Temple 8
Israel
Jerusalem: Aqsa Mosque 80, Dome of the Rock* 77, 80
Italy (see separate entry for Sicily)
Assisi: S. Francesco 111
Bari: S. Nicolo 90
Bergamo: Colleone Chapel 121
Caprarola: Villa Farnese 114, 121
Como: Casa del Fascio 175
Florence*: Biblioteca Laurenziana 116, Cathedral* 111, 115, Ospedale degli Innocenti 112, 115, Palazzo Gondi 116, Palazzo Medici-Riccardi 116, Palazzo Rucellai 115, Palazzo Strozzi 113, 116, Pazzi Chapel* 115, S. Lorenzo 115, S. Maria Novella 114–5, S. Miniato 90

Herculaneum 41
Mantua: Giulio
  Romano's House
  121, Palazzo del Tè
  121, S. Andrea 121
Mestre: Villa
  Malcontenta 114
Milan: Casa Castiglioni
  163, Cathedral 111,
  Galleria Vittorio
  Emanuelle 155,
  Pirelli Centre 175,
  S. Ambrogio 89, 121,
  S. Maria delle Grazie
  121, S. Marias presso
  S. Satiro 121, Torre
  Velasca 175
Naples:
  Palazzo Caserta 135
Orvieto 111
Ostia 41
Paestum: (Temple
  of Poseidon*) 31
Pavia: S. Michele 89
Pisa: Campo Santo*
  (Baptistery, Campanile,
  Cathedral) 90
Pompeii 37, 41
Ravenna*: Arian
  Baptistery 73,
  Orthodox Baptistery
  73, S. Apollinare
  in Classe 72, S.
  Apollinare Nuovo
  72, S. Vitale* 67,
  72, Tomb of Galla
  Placidia* 73, Tomb
  of Theodoric 73
Rome*: Arch of
  Constantine 40,
  Arch of Septimus
  Severus 40, Arch of
  Titus 40, Basilica of
  Maxentius 37, Baths
  of Caracalla 37, 38,
  Baths of Diocletian
  38, Capitol* 118,
  Circus of Maxentius
  39, Colosseum* 39,
  Column of Marcus
  Aurelius 40, Column
  of Trajan 40, Forum
  Romanum* 35, Gesù
  114, 118, 127,
  Mausoleum of
  Hadrian 39, Palazzo
  della Cancelleria 117,
  Palazzo Farnese 117,
  Palazzo Massimi 117,
  Palazzo Venezia 117,
  Pantheon* 36, 37,
  Rail Terminus 175, S.
  Agnese 132, 134, S.
  Agnese fuori le Muri
  71, S. Andrea al
  Quirinale* 133,
  S. Andrea in Via
  Flaminia 118, S.
  Carlo alle Quatro
  Fontane* 133, S.
  Clemmente 71, S.
  Costanza 71, S.

Lorenzo fuori le
  Mura 70, S. Maria
  della Pace 117, 134,
  Maria in Via Lata
  134, S. Maria
  Maggiore 71, S.
  Paolo fuori le Mura
  68, 71, St Peter's*
  118, 133, S. Sabina
  71, S. Stefano
  Rotonda 71,
  S. Susanna 133,
  Scala Regia* 133,
  Tabularium 35,
  Tempietto* 117,
  Temple of Antoninus
  and Faustina 36,
  Temple of Castor
  and Pollux 34, 36,
  Temple of Fortuna
  Virilis 36, Temple
  of Mars Ultor 36,
  Temple of Portunus
  36, Temple of Venus
  and Rome 36, Temple
  of Vesta 35–6, Theatre
  of Marcellus 33, 39,
  Tomb of Annia Regilla
  40, Tomb of Caecilia
  Metella 40, Vatican
  Scala Regia* 133,
  Victor Emmanuell II
  Monument 155,
  Villa Giulia 118,
  Villa Madama 117
Siena: Cathedral* 111,
  Palazzo Pubblico 111
Tivoli:
  Hadrian's Villa 42,
  Temple of Vesta 34, 42
Turin: Basilica di Superga
  134, Central Pavilion
  of the International
  Exhibition of
  Decorative Arts
  163, Chapel of SS
  Sindone 135, Palazzo
  Carignano 135,
  Palazzo de Lavoro
  175, S. Lorenzo 134
Urbino: Palazzo Ducale
  113, 121
Venice*: Doge's Palace*
  111, 119, 166,
  Library of St Mark's
  119, Palazzo Corner
  della Ca' Grande
  119, Redentore* 119,
  S. Giorgio Maggiore
  120, S. Maria della
  Salute 135, St
  Mark's* 73, Torcello
  Cathedral 73
Verona: Cathedral 89,
  S. Zeno Maggiore 89
Vicenza: Basilica 120,
  Palazzo Chiericati
  120, Palazzo Porto
  120, Teatro Olimpico
  120, Villa Capra*
  (Rotonda) 120

Ito, Toyo 198
Japan
Himeji Castle 62
Ise Shrine 59
Itsukushima Shrine 59
Izumo Shrine 59
Kawakasaki:
  Kawaramachi New
  Community 182
Kofu: Yamanashi
  Communications
  Centre 182
Kyōto: Daigo-ji 60,
  Katsura Palace* 61,
  62, Kinkaku-ji 61,
  Matsushita-an
  Teahouse 62, Nijō
  Castle 62
Maruoka Castle 62
Naoshima Contemporary
  Art Museum,
  Kagawa 198
Nara: Hōryu-ji* 59,
  Tōdai-ji 58, 69,
  Tōshōdai-ji 60,
  Yakushi-ji 60
Nikkō* 62
Osaka: Azuma House
  189–90
Shonandai Cultural
  Centre, Kanagawa
  198
Takatori Church, Kobe
  198
Tokyo: Nakagin
  Capsule Tower 169,
  182, Olympic Halls
  182
Uji: Byōdō-in, Hōō-do
  60
Yokohama:
  International Port
  Terminal 199
Java
Barabudur* 45, 52
Chandi Mendut 52
Jefferson, Thomas 146
Johnson, Philip 179, 180
Jones, Inigo 128–30
Jordon
Petra* 43
Kahn, Louis 178
Kent, William 141, 144
Key, Lieven de 127
Kayser, Henrik de 126
Klerk, Michael de 173
Koolhaas, Rem 197, 198
Labrouste, H. 152
Latrobe, Benjamin 156
Lebanon
Baalbek 43
Le Corbusier 163, 167–70,
  176–7, 181
Ledoux, Claude-Nicolas
  132, 137
Lepaultre, Pierre 137
Lescot, Pierre 122, 124
Le Vau, Louis 135–7
Libeskind, Daniel 196
Libya
Lepcis Magna 43
Sabratah: Theatre 43

Loos, Adolf 160, 166, 178
Lubetkin, Berthold 170
Lutyens, Sir Edwin 161
Mackintosh, Charles Rennie 159, 161
Maderna, Carlo 118, 133
Malaysia
Menara Mesiniaga, Selangor 190–1
Mansart, François 135–6
Markelius, Sven 175
Mendelsohn, Erich 167, 172
Mexico and **Guatemala**
Chicken Itzá 63, 66
Mexico City: Cathedral 147, Chapel of the Three Kings 147, Church of Our Lady of Miracles 180, Sagrario 147
Mitla 64
Monte Alban 64
Palenque 65
Tajin: Pyramid of the Niches 63, 64
Tenayuca 65
Tenochtitlan 63
Teotihuacán* 64
Tikal 65
Tula 64
Uxmal (Palace of the Governor*) 65
Xochicalco 64
Michelangelo 112, 113, 115, 116, 117, 118
Miralles and Pinós 193
Moller, C. F. 175
Moneo, Rafael 193, 194
Morocco
Fez: Bu-'Inaniyya Madrasa 86, Qarawiyyn Mosque 86
Marrakesh: Kutubiyya Mosque 86
Morris, William 150, 159, 161
Moss, Eric Owen 198
Murcutt, Glenn 191
MVRDV 197
Napoleon III 152
Nash, John 141, 145
Nepal
Katmandu* 51
Nervi, Pier Lugi 168, 175
Netherlands
Amsterdam*: Amstel (Central) Station 154–5, Children's Home 173, Eigenhaard Housing 173, Exchange 165, Maria Magadalenkerk 155, Rijksmuseum 154, Town Hall (Royal Palace) 126, Westerkerk 126, Zuiderkerk 126
Haarlem: Meat Hall 127
Heague, The:

Mauritshuis* 127
Hilversum: Town Hall 173, Villa Vpro 197
Leiden: Cloth Hall 127, Town Hall 127
Rotterdam: Kiefhoek Estate 173
's-Hertogenbosch: St Jan 109
Utrecht: Cathedral 109, Huis ter Heide, Villa 165, Schröder House 173, Minnaert Building 197
Neumann, Balthasar 139–40
Niemeyer, Oscar 180, 181
Norway
Fishing Museum, Karmoy 194
Glacier Museum, Fjaerland 194
Sogne, near Bergen: Borgund and Urnes Churches 95
Stavanger Cathedral 109
summer house, Risør 194
Trondheim Cathedral 109
Villa Busk, Bamble 194
Nouvel, Jean 195
Olbrich, J. M. 165, 166
Østberg, Ragnar 159, 166
Otto, Frei 172
Oud, J. J. P. 168, 173
Pakistan
Lahore 85
Palladio, Andrea 112, 114, 119–20, 129, 144
Parler, Peter 109
Paxton, Joseph 148
Perrault, Claude 124
Perret, Auguste 160, 163
Peru
Chan Chan 66
Cuzco: Compañia 147, Temple of the Sun 66
Machu Picchu* 66
Sacsahuamán 66
Poland
Wroclaw: Centennial Hall 166
Portugal
Alcobaça 96
Batalha Monastery* 110
Braga: Bom Jesus 141, 194
Oporto: Faculty of Architecture 194
Portuguese Pavilion, Hanover Expo 194
Tomar: Convent of Christ 110, 125
Post, Pieter 126
Prandtauer, Jakob 138
Predock, Antoine 198
Prouve, Jean 176
Pugin, A. W. N. 149, 150 159
Rainer, Roland 172
Raphael 116, 117

Rastrelli, Bartolomneo 145
Ribera, Pedro de 140
Richardson, H. H. 156, 157, 158, 159, 160
Riedjik, Neutelings 197
Rohe, Ludwig Mies van der 168, 172, 180
Romano, Giulio 113
Ruskin, John 159
Saarinen, Elial 166
Sanfelice, Ferdinando 134
Sansovino, Jacopo 119
Sant'Elia, Antonio 163
Sauerbruch and Hutton 196
Scharoun, Hans 172
Schinkel, Karl Friedrich 153
Scott, Sir George Gilbert 150
Semper, Gottfried 153
Shaw, Richard Norman 151, 161
Sherwood, Vladimir 154
Sicily
Agrigento: Temple of Olympian Zeus* 31
Cefalu Cathedral 90
Monreale Cathedral 90
Palermo: Martorana 73, Palatine Chapel 73, St John of the Hermits 73
Ragusa: S. Giorgio 135
Segesta: Temple 31
Selinus: Temple C 23
Siloé, Diego de 125
Sinan 81, 83
Siza, Alvaro 194, 196
Smythson, Robert 128
Snøhetta 194
Soufflot, Jacques Germain 135, 137
Souto de Moura, Eduardo 194
Spain
Archery Facilities, Vall d'Hebron 193
Barcelona: Casa Battló 164, Casa Mila 164, Sagrada Familia* 164
Burgos Cathedral 110, 125
Córdoba: Great Mosque* 86
Escorial* 125
Gaspar House, Zahora 193
Gerona Cathedral 110
Granada: Alhambra* 86, Cathedral 125, Palace of Charles V 125, Sacristy of the Cartuja 140
Guggenheim Museum, Bilbao 193, 198
Kursaal Auditorium and Congress Centre, San Sebastian 194
León Cathedral 110
Ripoll: S. Maria 96
Salamanca: Cathedral 96, 110, University 125

S. Domingo de Silos 96
Santiago de Compostela*
87, 89, 96
Seville Cathedral 110
Toledo: Cathedral 110,
Tavera Hospital 125,
Transparente 141
Town Hall, Murcia 193
Valencia: Palace
of the Marqués
de Dos Aquas 140
Vallodolid: Cathedral
125, S. Pablo 110
Zamora Cathedral 96
Sri Lanka
Anuradhapura 45, 50
Polonnaruwa 50
St John, Caruso 197
Stirling, James 171
Sullivan, Louis H.
158, 160, 162
Sweden
Drottningholm
Castle 130
Fors: Cardboard
Factory 175
Lund Cathedral 95
Skaraborg: Husaby
Church 95
Stockholm: Forest
Crematorium 175,
Town Hall 166,
Vällingby 175
Uppsala Cathedral 109
Switzerland
Basel: St Anthony 177
Beyeler Foundation
Museum, Basle 195
Culture and Congress
Centre, Lucerne 195
Dornach:
Goetheanum II 177
Liner Museum,
Appenzell 195
Renzo Piano Building 195
signal box, Basle 195
Sogn Benedetg Chapel,
Sumvitg 195
Thermal Baths, Vals 195
Syria
Damascus:
Great Mosque 81
Krak des Chevaliers* 96
Mari (Tell Harriri) 8
Palmyra 53
Tange, Kenzo 182
Tibet
Lhasa: Potala "Palace" 51
Toledo, Juan Bautista de
125
Tomé, Narciso 140, 141
Tunisia
Qairouan: Great
Mosque 86
Turkey
Didyma: Temple
of Apollo 23, 31
Edirne 84
Ephesus: Temple
of Artemis 31,
Hattushash

(Boğazkale) 8
Istanbul: Santa Sophia*
67, 70, SS Sergius
and Bacchus 74,
Shehzade Mosque
83, Sokollu Mehmet
Pasha Complex 84,
Süleymaniye
Complex 84,
Topkapi Palace 84
Konya 83
United Kingdom
see Britain
USSR
Bukhara: Tomb
of the Samanids 84
Kiev: St Sophia 76
Leningrad* 145
Moscow: "Faceted
Palace", Kremlin 30,
GUM Department
Store 154, Historical
Museum 154,
St Michael the
Archangel, Kremlin
130, St Basil's* 130
Novgorod: St Sophia 76
Samarkand 84
USA
American Heritage
Centre, Wyoming 198
Ann Arbor, Mich:
Mack-Ryan House 157
Bacon's Castle Va 146
Baltimore Cathedral 156
Bear Run, Penn.:
Fallingwater* 178
Boston Mass.: City
Hall 180, Old North
Church 146, Public
Library 156, Trinity
Church* 156
Chicago: Auditorium
Building 158, Carson,
Price and Scott
Building* 162,
Chicago Tribune
Building 180, Lake
Shore Apartments
180, Marshall Field's
Wholesale Store
157-8, Robie House
162, Unity Church,
Oak Park* 162
Columbus Ohio:
State Capitol 157
Harvard University 146
Highland Park Ill.:
Willitts House 162
Hingham, Mass:
Old Ship Meeting
House 146
Ipswich Mass.:
Whipple House 146
Katonah, NY: Tucker
House 179
Lincoln, Mass.:
Gropius House 179
Los Angeles: Burns
House, Santa Monica
Canyon 179, Disney

Concert Hall 198,
Ince Complex, Culver
City 198, Pacific
Design Centre 180
Monticello Va* 146
New Canaan, Conn.:
Johnson House 179
New York: AT & T
Building 180, Chrysler
Building 179, Ford
Foundation 180,
Guggenheim Museum
178, Kennedy Airport
168, Lever House* 180,
Seagram Building 180,
Trinity Church 156
Newport, RI:
The Breakers 156
Newport Beach,
Calif.: Lovell Beach
House 178
Norman, Okla.:
Bavinger House 179
Philadelphia:
Independence Hall 146,
Merchants' Exchange
156, Savings Fund
Society Building 179,
Richards Medical
Research Building,
University of
Pennsylvania* 180
Phoenix, Arizona:
Taliesin West* 178
Pittsburgh, Ohio:
Allegheny County
Buildings 157
Racine, Wis.: Johnson
Wax Building 178
St Louis, Miss.:
Wainwright Building
160
Seattle: Chapel
of St Ignatius 198
Washington, DC:
US Capitol 156
Westover, Va 146
Williamsburg, Va*:
William and Mary
College 146
Yale University, New
Haven Conn. 146
Vanbrugh, Sir John 141, 143
Vignola, Giacomo 114,
116, 118
Voysey, C. F. A. 159, 161
Wagner, Otto 160, 165, 178
Workshop 195
Wren, Sir Christopher 128,
141, 142
Wright, Frank Lloyd 160,
162, 178
Yeang, Ken 190
Yugoslavia
Gračanica 75
Lake Ohrid 75
Split: Palace of
Diocletian* 42
Zimmermann, Dominikus
139-40
Zumthor, Peter 195